A CRITIQUE OF PROPORTIONALITY
AND BALANCING

The principle of proportionality, which has become the standard test for adjudicating human and constitutional rights disputes in jurisdictions worldwide, has had few critics. Proportionality is generally taken for granted or enthusiastically promoted or accepted with minor qualifications. *A Critique of Proportionality and Balancing* presents a frontal challenge to this orthodoxy. It provides a comprehensive critique of the proportionality principle, and particularly of its most characteristic component, balancing. Divided into three parts, the book presents arguments against the proportionality test, critiques the view of rights entailed by it, and proposes an alternative understanding of fundamental rights and their limits.

FRANCISCO J. URBINA is Assistant Professor of Law at the Pontificia Universidad Católica, Chile. His research focuses on human rights, legal reasoning, and public law.

A CRITIQUE OF PROPORTIONALITY AND BALANCING

FRANCISCO J. URBINA

CAMBRIDGE
UNIVERSITY PRESS

CAMBRIDGE
UNIVERSITY PRESS

University Printing House, Cambridge CB2 8BS, United Kingdom

One Liberty Plaza, 20th Floor, New York, NY 10006, USA

477 Williamstown Road, Port Melbourne, VIC 3207, Australia

4843/24, 2nd Floor, Ansari Road, Daryaganj, Delhi – 110002, India

79 Anson Road, #06-04/06, Singapore 079906

Cambridge University Press is part of the University of Cambridge.

It furthers the University's mission by disseminating knowledge in the pursuit of education, learning, and research at the highest international levels of excellence.

www.cambridge.org
Information on this title: www.cambridge.org/9781107175068
© Francisco Urbina 2017

First published 2017

A catalogue record for this publication is available from the British Library.

Library of Congress Cataloging-in-Publication Data
Names: Urbina Molfino, Francisco Javier, author.
Title: A critique of proportionality and balancing / Francisco Urbina.
Description: Cambridge [UK] ; New York : Cambridge University Press, 2017 |
    Includes bibliographical references and index.
Identifiers: LCCN 2016032817 | ISBN 9781107175068 (hardback)
Subjects: LCSH: Proportionality in law. | Human rights. | BISAC: LAW /
    Jurisprudence.
Classification: LCC K247 .U73 2017 | DDC 342.08/501—DC23 LC record
available at https://lccn.loc.gov/2016032817

ISBN 978-1-107-17506-8 Hardback

CONTENTS

ACKNOWLEDGEMENTS

Thanks are due to Angela Wu, Thana Campos, Marcelo Barrientos, Nick Barber, Gonzalo Candia, Richard Ekins, Benjamín Gutiérrez, Luis Carlos Valdés, Clemente Recabarren, Ricardo Cruzat, Julie Maher, Fernando Contreras, Andrés Peñaloza, Pavlos Eleftheriadis, Jon Kirwan, Olivia Kirwan, Joseph Suttie, Madeleine Suttie, Bradford Wilson, José Manuel Díaz de Valdés, Isabel Zuluaga, Arturo Ibañez, Alberto Pino, Hna Ana Luisa, Daniel Wang, Marisol Peña, Arturo Fermandois, Sebastian Lewis, Tarek Yusari, Germán Vera, Andrés Biehl, Pierina and Antonia Orchard, Cristobal Orrego, Michael Sadler, Rama Ganguli, Sherif Girgis, Santiago Legarre, Roberto Durrieu, James Stoner, Felipe Mono Álvarez, G Allan Tarr, and Julian Nowag. I am also grateful to the anonymous reviewers contacted by Cambridge University Press for taking the time to assess my proposal and offering extremely helpful comments and suggestions, and to Finola O'Sullivan, Fiona Allison, Rebecca J Roberts, Helen Francis, Sarah Starkey, Geetha Williams, and their team at the Press for their professionalism and support from the beginning.

This book originated as a doctoral thesis at the University of Oxford. I am especially grateful to my supervisor, John Finnis, for his generosity and indispensable guidance. I was fortunate to have Timothy Endicott and Jeff King as examiners, and I am grateful for their insightful and meticulous comments, as well as for their valuable advice. Paul Yowell and Grégoire Webber deserve very special thanks for their constant encouragement and support.

I gratefully acknowledge the support of the Beca Chile scholarship and of the CONICYT FONDECYT Iniciacion N° 11150872 grant, awarded by the Chilean Ministry of Education, and of the James Madison Program at Princeton University, which allowed me to spend a year as a postdoctoral fellow at Princeton.

Chapter 3 is a revised version of a paper published as 'Incommensurability and Balancing' (2015) 35 OJLS 575. Parts of Chapters 6–8 were previously published in 'Is It Really That Easy? A Critique of Proportionality and "Balancing as Reasoning"' (2014) 27 Can JL & Jurisp 167. Parts of 'A Critique of Proportionality' (2012) 57 American Journal of Jurisprudence 49 are scattered throughout this book. I am grateful to all the editors and reviewers of these journals.

Most importantly, I owe a debt of gratitude to my family. My mother, my father, and my brother have been unwavering in their support. Francisco Javier has provided me with a deeper sense of purpose for everything that I do, including this book. Above all, I am grateful to my wonderful wife, Marguerite, for her wisdom, patience, and joy. This book is dedicated to her.

ABBREVIATIONS

Balancing and Subsumption	Alexy R, 'On Balancing and Subsumption. A Structural Comparison' (2003) 16 4 Ratio Juris 433
Challenging Critics	Möller K, 'Proportionality: Challenging the Critics' (2012) 10 3 Int'l J Const L 709
CR	Kumm M, 'Constitutional Rights as Principles: On the Structure and Domain of Constitutional Justice' (2004) 2 Int'l J Const L 574
ECHR	European Convention on Human Rights
ECtHR	European Court of Human Rights
Global Model	Möller K, *The Global Model of Constitutional Rights* (Oxford University Press 2012)
LE	Dworkin R, *Law's Empire* (Harvard University Press 1986)
Negotiable Constitution	Webber G, *The Negotiable Constitution: On the Limitation of Rights* (Cambridge University Press 2009)
NLNR	Finnis J, *Natural Law and Natural Rights* (2nd edn, Oxford University Press 2011)
PCC	Cohen-Eliya M and Porat I, *Proportionality and Constitutional Culture* (Cambridge University Press 2013)
PCJ	Cohen-Eliya M and Porat I, 'Proportionality and the Culture of Justification' (2011) 59 2 American Journal of Comparative Law 463
PL	Kumm M, 'Political Liberalism and the Structure of Rights: On the Place and Limits of the Proportionality Requirement' in Pavlakos G (ed), *Law, Rights and Discourse: The Legal Philosophy of Robert Alexy* (Hart 2007)

Proportionality   Barak A, *Proportionality: Constitutional Rights and Their Limitations* (Cambridge University Press 2012)

Socratic   Kumm M, 'The Idea of Socratic Contestation and the Right to Justification: The Point of Rights-Based Proportionality Review' (2010) 4 2 Law & Ethics of Human Rights 142

Theory   Alexy R, *A Theory of Constitutional Rights* (Julian Rivers tr, Oxford University Press 2002)

1

Introduction

1.1 The Aim of This Book

The proportionality test has become the dominant legal tool for addressing cases regarding the limitation of human rights.[1] It is the default test for adjudicating human rights disputes in jurisdictions from all five continents, both national and international, and in civil and common law legal traditions.[2] Proportionality is referred to as 'the received approach to human rights law' (Webber), '*the* central concept in contemporary constitutional rights law' (Möller), a 'near universal' legal test (Gardbaum), a 'staple of adjudication on fundamental rights in international and domestic courts' (Verdirame), 'the main engine of human rights law and constitutional rights adjudication' (Finnis), and 'unquestionably the dominant mode of resolving public law disputes in the world today' (Schneiderman).[3]

---

[1] In what follows I generally speak of 'human rights' to refer to both constitutional rights and human rights, as is the usage in the United Kingdom and elsewhere. I am aware that both these terms ('human rights' and 'constitutional rights') often, but not always, refer to different legal regimes. Nevertheless, these differences are of little relevance in the analysis and critique of proportionality I offer in this book. My argument bears on the use of the proportionality test in both constitutional and human rights law.

[2] On the spectacular spread of proportionality on a global scale, see Aharon Barak's comprehensive study in his *Proportionality: Constitutional Rights and Their Limitations* (Cambridge University Press 2012) [hereinafter *Proportionality*], Chapter 7 B)–L).

[3] This is noted by Webber in Grégoire Webber, 'On the Loss of Rights' in Grant Huscroft, Bradley Miller, and Grégoire Webber (eds), *Proportionality and the Rule of Law: Rights, Justification, Reasoning* (Cambridge University Press 2014) 123. See Grégoire Webber, *The Negotiable Constitution: On the Limitation of Rights* (Cambridge 2009) 55 [hereinafter *Negotiable Constitution*]; Kai Möller, *The Global Model of Constitutional Rights* (Oxford University Press 2012) 13 [hereinafter *Global Model*]; Stephen Gardbaum, 'Proportionality and Democratic Constitutionalism' in Grant Huscroft, Bradley Miller, and Grégoire Webber (eds), *Proportionality and the Rule of Law: Rights, Justification, Reasoning* (Cambridge University Press 2014) 260, 261, cited in Webber (n 3) 'On the Loss of Rights' 123; Guglielmo Verdirame, 'Rescuing Human Rights from Proportionality' in Rowan Cruft, S Matthew Liao, and Massimo Renzo (eds), *Philosophical Foundations of Human Rights* (Oxford University Press 2015) 341; John Finnis, 'Judicial Power: Past, Present, and Future' (a lecture in Gray's Inn Hall, 20 October 2015), available at

It can be said with no exaggeration that we live in an 'age of proportionality'[4]

Proportionality is the new orthodoxy in human rights law. It is also,
I believe, a deeply flawed test for deciding human rights cases. Human
rights adjudication can do better. There is a need for a general critique
of the proportionality test. To provide this critique is the main aim of
this book. The study of proportionality in this book is normative, rather
than descriptive or doctrinal. The book focuses on proportionality, and
addresses the question of balancing as the final and most characteristic
part of the proportionality test.

There are different ways of understanding the proportionality test. The
main conceptions of the proportionality test fall into two groups: one
adopts what I call a 'maximisation account of proportionality', and the
other an account of 'proportionality as unconstrained moral reasoning'.
I argue that as interpreted by any of these accounts, the proportionality
test is unsuited for human rights adjudication. I will argue that the proportionality test is *either* insensitive to important moral considerations
related to human rights and their limitations; *or* it can accommodate the
relevant moral considerations, but at the price of leaving the judge undirected, unaided by the law. I will further argue that lack of legal direction is a deficiency in legal adjudication, which has important negative
effects. These arguments ground a more ambitious claim: that there can
be no understanding of proportionality that escapes objections of the kind
offered here, and that there can be no single method for deciding whether
an interference with a human right (or even with a set of human rights) is
substantively justified. In the last chapter, I outline an alternative understanding of human rights and their limitation. As a whole the book offers
a comprehensive critique of the proportionality test that I believe has been
absent from the literature so far. Given the current dominance of proportionality reasoning in human rights law, this mostly critical enterprise
seems to me justified.

Though the main aim of this book is critical, in developing my argument against proportionality I sustain a number of positive claims. In the
first part of this book I revisit some commonly discussed issues in the proportionality debate: whether proportionality captures the special force

---

http://judicialpowerproject.org.uk/john-finnis-judicial-power-past-present-and-future/
accessed 20 January 2016; David Schneiderman, 'Proportionality and Constitutional
Culture (book review)' (2015) 13 Int'l J Const L 769, 769.
[4] To borrow from the title of an important recent article on the topic: Vicky C Jackson,
'Constitutional Law in an Age of Proportionality' (2015) 124 Yale LJ 3094.

rights are taken to have, and whether balancing requires commensurating the incommensurable. These are established questions, yet I have found that there was need in both cases to clarify what is the precise scope and force of the objections. To do this, it was necessary to develop my own account of incommensurability, and to offer a positive characterisation of rights reasoning for the purposes of the proportionality debate. A more recent account of the proportionality test, reviewed in the second part of the book, provides me with the opportunity to address new arguments and develop new objections. The account of rights reasoning that I offer in Chapter 5 and particularly the account of legally directed adjudication I present in Chapter 7 are the basis for the alternative to proportionality reasoning that I sketch in the last part of this book.

An important part of this book is dialectical: it engages closely with ideas of other scholars. This follows from the overall aim of the book, which is to offer a general critique of proportionality as applied in human rights adjudication. The most fruitful and fair way to criticise an idea is to engage with it *as it is presented by its most sophisticated proponents*, as opposed to a version of the same idea that a critic could construe only to then demolish it. The same applies to the proportionality test, particularly if one considers the sophistication and influence of some of the more prominent scholarly accounts of proportionality. Courts, by contrast, do not typically argue openly in favour of proportionality.

A further reason for the dialectical nature of this work is that my aim is not proportionality as applied in a particular case or in a particular jurisdiction, but proportionality in general, as a way of thinking about limitations of human rights. Defenders of proportionality often claim that some purported deficiency in the use of proportionality in human rights is not a deficiency of proportionality as such, but of a certain case or line of cases, and thus that the critic has misinterpreted the proportionality test.[5] Here my aim is to establish that proportionality as such is flawed, and not only that it has been on occasions misapplied. Thus I level my critique at general accounts of proportionality, rather than at specific cases where proportionality is applied. And, to avoid the charge of misinterpretation, I have attempted to present the arguments in favour of proportionality as closely as possible to the writings where those arguments are made. I allude to specific legal cases as a way of illustrating more general claims.

---

[5] See Madhav Khosla, 'Proportionality: An Assault on Human Rights?: A Reply' (2010) 8 Int'l J Const L 298, 302; and Kai Möller, 'Proportionality: Challenging the Critics' (2012) 10 3 Int'l J Const L 709, 710–11 [hereinafter *Challenging Critics*].

I do believe (see Chapters 2 and 6) that the main accounts of proportionality provide an insightful general articulation of the legal practice of proportionality, such that the most illuminating way of evaluating the practice in general is to engage with those academic accounts that undertake the task of displaying its underlying logic and making the case for it. This book criticises a way of thinking about human rights and their limitations that is entailed in a specific legal test – the proportionality test – and which can be seen at work in judicial decisions around the world. It will be thus useful to start by fixing ideas on what is meant here by the proportionality test.

1.2   The Proportionality Test in Human Rights Adjudication

Proportionality features in some way or another in several areas of law.[6] What concerns us here is a specific legal test used for evaluating so-called interferences with human rights. On proportionality analysis, human rights interferences are addressed through a two-step inquiry. First, it is established whether a particular measure affects a human right. At this stage the right is commonly defined generously, and thus it is often found or at least assumed that there has been an interference with a human right.[7] The second step is concerned with whether this 'interference' with a

---

[6] For example, in intellectual property law (see Robert P Merges, *Justifying Intellectual Property* (Harvard University Press 2011); Justine Pila, 'Pluralism, Principles and Proportionality in Intellectual Property' (2014) 34 OJLS 181); criminal law (see Morris J Fish, 'An Eye for an Eye: Proportionality as a Moral Principle of Punishment' (2008) 28 OJLS 57); land law (see Christopher J St Jeanos, 'Dolan v. Tigard and the Rough Proportionality Test: Roughly Speaking, Why Isn't a Nexus Enough?' (1995) 63 Fordham LR 1883); investor-state arbitration (see Gebhard Bücheler, *Proportionality in Investor-State Arbitration* (Oxford University Press 2015) and Caroline Henckels, *Proportionality and Deference in Investor-State Arbitration: Balancing Investment Protection and Regulatory Autonomy* (Cambridge University Press 2015)); labour law (see Pnina Alon-Shenker and Guy Davidov, 'Applying the Principle of Proportionality in Employment and Labour Law Contexts' (2013) 59 McGill LJ 375); procedural law (Jonah B Gelbach and Bruce H Kobayashi, 'The Law and Economics of Proportionality in Discovery' Georgia LR (forthcoming, available in http://papers.ssrn.com/sol3/papers.cfm?abstract_id=2551520## accessed 28 January 2016); law of war (Jens David Ohlin, 'The Doctrine of Legitimate Defense' (2015) 91 Int'l L Stud 119; Robert D Sloane, 'Puzzles of Proportion and the "Reasonable Military Commander": Reflections on the Law, Ethics, and Geopolitics of Proportionality' (2015) 6 Harvard National Security Journal 299); and tax law (Joao Dacio Rolim, 'Proportionality and Fair Taxation' (2015) 43 Intertax 405).

[7] Tsakirakis speaks of 'definitional generosity' in this regard, particularly with respect to the European Court of Human Rights (ECtHR). Stavros Tsakyrakis, 'Proportionality: An Assault on Human Rights?' (2009) 7 Int'l J Const L 468, 481. It has been noted that 'in Canada the court typically adopts a generous view of the scope of what is protected by the

human right is justified. The proportionality test is said to provide a framework for analysing this second question. It works as a test composed of the following four parts:

a.   Legitimate aim: the measure interfering with the right has to have an objective of sufficient importance;
b.   Suitability: the measure interfering with the right has to be rationally connected to the legitimate aim;
c.   Necessity: the measure should impair as little as possible the right in question;
d.   Proportionality *stricto sensu*: there must be a proportionality between the *effects* of the measures which are responsible for limiting the right, and the objective which has been identified as of sufficient importance.

This formulation of the proportionality test is that of the well-known Canadian *Oakes* test,[8] which influenced the adoption of a similar version of the test by UK courts.[9] In some jurisdictions the first prong requires that the measure pursue a 'legitimate aim' (rather than an objective of 'sufficient importance'), and sometimes this aim needs to be one of those mentioned in a (usually broadly formulated) limitation clause.[10] Even in Canada this part of the test commonly requires no more than that the aim be legitimate.[11] In some formulations of the proportionality test, the first

---

right'. Jackson (n 4) 3111. Sometimes courts entertain doubts as to whether the interests or actions of the applicants are protected by a human right, and nevertheless decide on the assumption that they do. See for example *R (S) v Chief Constable of South Yorkshire Police* [2004] UKHL 39, [2004] 1 WLR 2196 [31]–[32]; *Laskey v United Kingdom* (App nos 21627/93, 21826/93, 21974/93) (1997) 24 EHRR 39 [36].

[8]   See *R v Oakes* [1986] 1 SCR 103 [69]–[70].
[9]   See *Bank Mellat v HM Treasury* [2013] UKSC 39, [73]–[74] (Lord Reed), referring to Oakes as 'the clearest and most influential judicial analysis of proportionality within the common law tradition of legal reasoning'; and Timothy Endicott, Administrative Law (3rd edn, Oxford University Press 2015) 96–7.
[10]   This is how the Inter-American Court of Human Rights and its European counterpart formulate the first subtest. See, for example, *Kimel v Argentina* C No 177 (2008) (IACtHR) [58], [68]–[71]; *Mémoli v Argentina* C No 265 (2013) (IACtHR) [126], [130], [138]; *Handyside v United Kingdom* (1979–80) 1 EHRR 737 [43], [45]–[46]; *Smith and Grady v United Kingdom* (App nos 33985/96 and 33986/96) (2000) 29 EHRR 49 [74]; *S and Marper v United Kingdom* (App nos 30562/04 and 30566/04) (2009) 48 EHRR 1169 [100].
[11]   See Jackson (n 4) 3112 n 81; Sujit Choudhry, 'So What Is the Real Legacy of Oakes? Two Decades of Proportionality Analysis Under the Canadian Charter's Section 1' (2006) 34 Sup Ct LR 501, 509–10; PW Hogg, *Constitutional Law of Canada* (5th edn, Thomson Carswell 2007) 132, quoted in *Proportionality* 283.

two subtests are consolidated into one requiring that 'the means used [are] appropriate [. . .] to the achievement of a legitimate end'.[12]

The necessity subtest in its strictest form is understood to require that the measure be compared with alternative potential measures that would have realised the same aim to the same extent.[13] It has been noted that often the available alternatives that would be less burdensome on the human rights at stake are also less effective in achieving the legitimate aim sought by the measure under review, or they can involve greater costs for other rights or public goods.[14] In choosing a less restrictive alternative, some degree of realisation of the legitimate aim or of some other right or public good would be lost. The question then is whether achieving that additional degree of realisation of the legitimate aim or of some other right or public good justifies the increased burden on the human rights affected by the measure under review. Thus, the necessity subtest sometimes collapses into the last subtest of proportionality, the balancing requirement.[15]

Balancing or 'proportionality stricto sensu' is the last part of the proportionality test. It is often seen as the most important and characteristic part of the test.[16] As formulated above, the test is notoriously vague. It requires that the effects of the limitation of a human right are 'proportional' to the achievement of a legitimate aim.[17] In a number of cases the European Court of Human Rights (ECtHR) requires that the state 'strikes a fair

---

[12] Donald P Kommers and Russel A Miller, *The Constitutional Jurisprudence of the Federal Republic of Germany* (3rd edn, Duke University Press 2012) 67, attributing this formulation to German jurisprudence.

[13] The most common illustration of this test is provided by the Israeli *Beit Sourik* case. *Beit Surik Village Council v Government of Israel*, HCJ 2056/04 [2004] IsrSC 58(5) 807. The case concerned the building of a fence for the purposes of protecting the population from attacks in the context of the Israeli–Palestinian conflict. With regard to the necessity subtest, the question was 'whether among the various routes which would achieve the objective of the separation fence, is the chosen one least injurious'. Ibid [44], translation from the official Israeli Judicial Authority website http://elyon1.court.gov.il/files_eng/04/560/020/a28/04020560.a28 .pdf accessed 12 January 2016. In assessing less injurious alternatives, the court sought to determine whether such alternatives would have satisfied 'the security objective of the security fence to the same extent as the route set out by the military commander'. Ibid [58].

[14] *Global Model* 194–5; *Bank Mellat* [20].

[15] *Global Model* 195.

[16] See *Proportionality* 340; Matthias Klatt and Moritz Meister, *The Constitutional Structure of Proportionality* (Oxford University Press 2012) 6; Finnis (n 3); Richard Ekins, 'Legislating Proportionately' in Grant Huscroft, Bradley Miller, and Grégoire Webber (eds), *Proportionality and the Rule of Law: Rights, Justification, Reasoning* (Cambridge University Press 2014) 343.

[17] See *Oakes* [71]. The same formulation is found in other jurisdictions. See, for example, *Schmidberger Internationale Transporte und Planzüge v Austria* (C-112/00) [2003] ECR I-5659 [81] and [90].

balance between the competing interests' protected by the human right of the applicant, and those of 'the community as a whole'.[18] These formulations are notoriously formal, and provide no guidance as to how to determine when a concrete measure fails to strike the right balance, or to achieve a proportionality between the measure's effects on the affected right and the realisation of the legitimate aim of the measure. It is not, however, uncommon that the balancing subtest is further specified. Thus, in *Oakes*, after formulating the four parts of the test, the court states that the last subtest requires that 'the more severe the deleterious effects of a measure, the more important the objective must be'.[19] Along the same lines, the last part of the test has been formulated thus: 'the benefits of infringing the protected interest must be greater than the loss incurred with regard to the protected interest'.[20] Each of these ways of formulating the balancing test (the first highly abstract; the second more specific, requiring that gains match loses) correspond to and support one of the two main interpretations of proportionality that I explain below: proportionality as unconstrained moral reasoning, and the maximisation account of proportionality.

There is another version of the test that does without the balancing stage, consisting only in the first three parts. Such a version of the test was used in early proportionality cases in the UK.[21] This incomplete version of proportionality needs to be distinguished from versions of proportionality that do not explicitly formulate the balancing stage, but nevertheless apply it. This was the case with some Canadian jurisprudence, in which balancing considerations were assessed in applying the previous subtests.[22] Also, on some versions of the proportionality test the different subtests are not seen as separate and distinct stages in the application of proportionality analysis, but rather as factors to be taken into consideration in a less structured form of balancing reasoning.[23]

---

[18] See *Hatton v United Kingdom* (2003) 37 EHRR 611 [119], [122]; *S and Marper v United Kingdom* [118]; *Von Hannover v Germany* (2004) 40 EHRR 1 [57].

[19] *Oakes* [71].

[20] Mattias Kumm, 'Who Is Afraid of the Total Constitution?: Constitutional Rights as Principles and the Constitutionalization of Private Law' (2006) 7 German LJ 341, 348. Similarly Julian Rivers, 'Proportionality and Variable Intensity of Review' (2006) 65 Cambridge LJ 174, 181; and Steven Greer, '"Balancing" and the European Court of Human Rights: A Contribution to the Habermas–Alexy Debate' (2004) 63 Cambridge LJ, 412, 434; and *Kimel* [83].

[21] Endicott (n 9) 97.

[22] See Dieter Grimm, 'Proportionality in Canadian and German Constitutional Jurisprudence' (2007) 57 2 University of Toronto LJ, 383, 394–5.

[23] See Jonas Christoffersen, *Fair Balance: A Study of Proportionality, Subsidiarity and Primarity in the European Convention on Human Rights* (Martinus Nijhof 2009) 69–73.

The four-parts formulation of the proportionality test is the most clear in articulating the considerations that the test is generally taken to assess – regardless of whether those considerations are understood as separate stages or as factors in a balancing assessment. Such a version of proportionality, as opposed to those that lack the last balancing part, is also the most defensible one. This is because the force of the affected human right is only assessed at the balancing stage. Before that, the proportionality assessment is only about means–ends rationality.[24] It is clear that some measures can be necessary for the achievement of a legitimate aim, yet still unacceptable in the violation of human rights. Dieter Grimm provides one such example, among many that could be provided: imagine 'a law that allows the police to shoot a person to death if this is the only means of preventing a perpetrator from destroying property'.[25] According to Grimm, this law could satisfy the first three subtests of proportionality, yet still fail the fourth test.[26] The law affects the right to life, and if this right is to be considered at all in assessing this particular measure, the balancing part of the test is needed. Because the four-part version is the most complete, explicit, and defensible formulation of the test, it is best to focus on this formulation for the purposes of a general normative analysis of the proportionality test.

Given the diversity of the jurisdictions where the proportionality test is applied, it is natural that there will be differences in how the test is applied and understood in each jurisdiction. Nevertheless, scholars and practitioners are right in treating the proportionality test as a single legal method that is essentially the same in different jurisdictions. The issues presented to the court are framed in essentially the same way according to the different formulations of the proportionality test. The type of reasoning required of judges and others who use the test is the same: means–ends rationality and balancing reasoning to weigh the interests, values, or

---

[24] Such a test, though less defensible as a method for assessing human rights limitations, could still serve a valuable and more modest role. For example, in societies where one thinks it is likely that government officials may be ill motivated against a part of the population, judicial review of those measures may be an effective way of controlling the government. Because measures adopted on the basis of animus against a group are likely to impose excessive burdens on them, beyond what would be necessary to achieve a worthwhile aim, or be disconnected to such an aim (which is held only for the purposes of justifying the measure), or have no plausible legitimate aim, a three-stage proportionality test could help filter out these measures without having to go through the difficult process of establishing that the measures were ill motivated.

[25] Grimm (n 22) 396.

[26] Ibid.

principles at stake. And the test performs the same function across different jurisdictions: to determine whether the negative effects of a government measure on human rights interests are acceptable, or whether they
are somehow excessive and therefore a violation of human rights.

1.3   Whose Proportionality? Which Balancing?

A first difficulty in analysing the proportionality test is to establish its content. Much discussion about proportionality depends on the language of
'balancing' and 'weighing',[27] but what do these metaphors convey? What
makes a measure 'disproportionate'? These questions are not answered
explicitly by doctrinal analyses of the proportionality test or by the case
law that applies the test. The task of articulating the methodology implied
by the proportionality test – its essential characteristics, its justification,
and its relation to other legal ideas – has been undertaken by theoretical
accounts of proportionality.

In engaging with these accounts, a second difficulty arises. '[A]ny number of different "theories" about how to resolve any existing normative
conflict can be operating under the rubric of a proportionality-based test
of justified rights limitation.'[28] The doctrinal formulation of the proportionality test (the four-pronged test) is vague enough to allow for different
accounts of proportionality – different proposals as to what proportionality is. I identify two main accounts of proportionality.[29] One sees proportionality as a doctrinal tool aimed at maximising the interests, values,
or principles at stake in the case. For this account some of the characteristic advantages of proportionality relate to it being largely a technical,
structured, and manageable test, and, on some versions, also neutral and
fact-dependent. This is the 'maximisation account of proportionality'. The
other account sees proportionality as a doctrinal tool that allows judges to
engage in open-ended moral reasoning, unconstrained by legal sources.
For this account, proportionality has the advantage of allowing for appropriate deliberation on justice and rights. I call this account 'proportionality

---

[27] See Matthias Jestaedt, 'The Doctrine of Balancing – Its Strengths and Weaknesses' in
Matthias Klatt (ed), *Institutionalized Reason: The Jurisprudence of Robert Alexy* (Oxford
University Press 2012) 165.

[28] Denise Réaume, 'Limitations on Constitutional Rights: The Logic of Proportionality'
(2009) 2009 Oxford Legal Research Paper Series 1, 3.

[29] The distinction between these two accounts is hinted at, though not explicitly articulated,
in Charles-Maxime Panaccio, 'In Defence of Two-Step Balancing and Proportionality in
Rights Adjudication' (2011) 24 Can JL & Jur 109, 119, 128 n 62.

as unconstrained moral reasoning'. Each account has its own characteristic understanding of the balancing test. For one account, balancing consists in a commensuration of rights, interest, values or principles; for the other, it means assessing the reasons in favour and against a particular measure. I explain these two accounts of proportionality in Chapters 2 and 6.

These two accounts of proportionality are very different, though they are sometimes confused and treated under the same label. Thus, proportionality can seem at times to be a moving target.[30] But when both accounts are clearly defined, it becomes obvious that they are incompatible. Proportionality cannot be narrow and technical, and at the same time allow for every consideration to be assessed through unconstrained moral reasoning.[31]

There is a need for a general framework for understanding the proportionality debate, and assessing the arguments and counterarguments made against and in favour of proportionality. This general framework has been lacking, and as a consequence, it is not always clear whether defenders and critics of proportionality are discussing the same thing, and properly engaging each other's arguments. This book provides such a framework, and this framework is put to use at the service of my general critique of proportionality. The framework is based on two basic distinctions. The first is the distinction between the two main accounts of proportionality outlined above, which allows us to understand which account of proportionality is at stake when a particular objection to proportionality is discussed.

The second basic distinction is between two different kinds of flaws that can be imputed to proportionality. This is relevant because the two different accounts of proportionality have flaws of different kinds. Generally speaking, legal categories can be analysed from two perspectives. One I call 'moral', and the other 'technical'. The moral perspective is aimed at

---

[30] 'The criticism that the doctrine of proportionality is too technical, too reductive, or stultifying is met with the reply that in truth it is open to all possible considerations, whereas the criticism that it is too open or empty, unfit for judges, is met with the reply that it disciplines reasoning and is hence suitable for judicial consideration and application.' Ekins (n 16) 345.

[31] Because I engage with proportionality as stated by the theories that defend it, I engage with the two accounts of proportionality addressed in this book (the maximisation account of proportionality and proportionality as unconstrained moral reasoning), and not other potential accounts that might be offered. For example, there is what Julian Rivers calls the 'state-limiting' account of proportionality. See Rivers (n 20) 176–80. But defenders of proportionality do not promote or elaborate on this account. Rivers himself favours a different account (see Chapter 2). I believe that engaging with the two main accounts of proportionality will provide us with the resources for evaluating other potential accounts of the test – but I cannot assess all potential interpretations of the test here.

discovering the relevant moral considerations that should bear on a particular question. When considering adjudication, this perspective tries to establish what would be a correct or reasonable solution to a case and the right reasons for justifying such a conclusion. It focuses on what kinds of reasons should bear upon the different types of cases.

The technical perspective is aimed at analysing the enterprise, familiar to lawyers, of designing technical legal categories that would be successful at expressing and enforcing the demands of morality through law, considering the circumstances in which cases will take place in the real world, so that the application of those technical categories increases as much as possible the likelihood of a reasonable decision of legal cases (I explain this further in Chapter 7). The technical perspective also evaluates existing legal categories from the perspective of how successful they are in achieving the aim of expressing and enforcing through the law the relevant demands of morality. In this sense, the technical perspective is always subordinated to the moral, as a tool for the fulfilment of its demands.[32]

A legal category can be morally defective, or technically defective, or both. In designing a legal category, sometimes the moral issue is the harder one to settle. For example, we can argue about whether it is right for the state to impose a duty to vote in general elections. There can be a vexed moral debate on this question. But once that debate is settled, it may be relatively simple to design legal institutions that can enforce and express that moral requirement (for example, by establishing the duty to vote in the electoral law and a punishment for breach of that duty).

Sometimes the technical issue can be the more complex one. For example, morality can tell us that the rich should pay tax at a higher rate than the poor, and that there is some need for arbitrary lines in any tax system between the different categories of salaries that one is going to tax progressively, as well as other considerations that are relevant for designing a tax system. But when crafting legislation, we need to be aware that many lawyers and accountants may seek loopholes so that their customers pay as little as possible. Even if one had all the relevant moral information, crafting

---

[32] The distinction between the moral and the technical perspective is different from Dworkin's famous distinction between the dimensions of fit and justification in interpretation. See Ronald Dworkin, *Law's Empire* (Harvard University Press 1986) Chapter 7, especially 255 ff. The distinction between moral and technical perspective offers two distinct criteria for evaluating institutions and technical doctrinal categories. It is aimed at improving our understanding and evaluation of the legal materials that Dworkinian interpretation must 'fit'.

the legal categories necessary to express and enforce these demands of morality can be extremely challenging.

It is important to distinguish these two perspectives, because they point to different ways in which the law can succeed or fail in achieving its tasks. The most important defects of the maximisation account of proportionality relate to the moral perspective. The idea of proportionality as allowing for unconstrained moral reasoning, on the other hand, has flaws that relate to the technical perspective.

1.4   The Plan of This Book

This book is divided in three parts. Part I engages with the maximisation account of proportionality. I first explain this account and the different theories of proportionality that fall under it (Chapter 2). In the subsequent chapters (3–5), I offer a critique of this account. In Chapter 3, I revisit the question of incommensurability. Incommensurability is the most underestimated objection to proportionality. I present a general account of incommensurability and explain why and to what extent incommensurability is a problem for the maximisation account of proportionality. I also engage with recent arguments levelled against the incommensurability objection. My main critique to the maximisation account is in Chapters 4 and 5. Chapter 4 builds up from the previous chapter and poses the question at the heart of the moral perspective: why apply proportionality? It argues that there is no reason for applying the proportionality test in human rights cases, because there is no reason to think that the test is able to capture what is morally relevant in those cases. Chapter 5 pushes the argument further, defending the claim that proportionality does not reflect the special force that rights are taken to have. It also argues against recent defences of proportionality that address this objection. Part I concludes that the maximisation account of proportionality does not provide an adequate method for deciding cases regarding human rights infringements.

Part II criticises the second main conception of the proportionality test, proportionality as unconstrained moral reasoning. Its first chapter (Chapter 6) explains this account of proportionality and the theories that fall under it, and how it avoids the objections made against the maximisation account of proportionality. It also introduces the objections to this account. The following chapter (Chapter 7), on the need for legal direction in adjudication, provides a general explanation for why legal reasoning generally does not consist in open-ended moral reasoning unconstrained by the law. This chapter explains the importance for legal adjudication of having relatively precise legal categories able to express the relevant moral considerations that bear on the different issues to which the legal categories are applied. Thus, Chapter 7 sets a standard for doctrinal tools to meet. Chapter 8 shows how proportionality as unconstrained moral reasoning fails to meet this standard, and how as a consequence, proportionality adjudication is likely to have all the deficiencies that adjudication that is not aided by legal categories is likely to have. This suggests that some deficiencies that in principle might seem peculiar to a court or to a judicial decision are best understood as the likely manifestation of some underlying defect of the proportionality test.

The two first parts contain the main, critical, argument of the book. Part II concludes with a general summary of the argument of the book and its results. It claims that none of the main accounts of proportionality represent an adequate test for deciding human rights cases. It also claims that, if the argument presented here is correct, we should not attempt to replace these accounts of proportionality with a somehow 'better' or 'correct' account of proportionality. There are reasons why attempts to provide such an account have failed so far. Also, we should not try to replace proportionality with some other similarly far-reaching test. What is the alternative, then? In the last chapter, I offer an outline of a general understanding of human rights as legal categories. This account builds on the positive contributions of previous chapters. I argue that what is required is a body of legal categories of human rights, and explain the general characteristics of such a body of legal categories, as well as its use in legal adjudication as an alternative to proportionality and other similar tests.

PART I

2

The Maximisation Account of Proportionality

In this chapter I analyse one of the most prominent and widespread theoretical accounts of the proportionality test: what I call 'the maximisation account of proportionality'. The analysis here is mostly descriptive, leaving the criticism of this account for the next chapters. In what follows, I begin by providing a general characterisation of this understanding of the proportionality test as found in doctrinal literature and case-law. This account has enjoyed a great influence in many jurisdictions, and it can be justly referred to as the 'orthodox' account.[1] One of the reasons for its influence is that some of the most important theories of proportionality have adopted it. Here I explain these theories and analyse them from the two perspectives explained in the Introduction: the moral perspective and the technical perspective. The moral perspective is the most interesting one for analysing this account of proportionality. Legal categories (such as a legal test) are not arbitrary: they attempt to capture something that is perceived as morally relevant in the situations where they are to be applied. They presuppose a view about what is of moral relevance in those situations. There are two relevant questions for assessing the maximisation account of proportionality from the moral perspective: what view of what morally matters in the human rights cases to which proportionality is applied is presupposed by the maximisation account of proportionality? And: is this view correct? In this chapter I address the first question. Though the main theorists of proportionality do not engage with this question explicitly, I argue that all the theories that adopt a maximisation account of proportionality entail a similar answer to it. From the technical perspective, we can see how the doctrinal articulation of the proportionality test is apt to express what (for the maximisation account) is morally relevant in the cases to which this test is applied.

---

[1] See George Letsas, 'Rescuing Proportionality' in Rowan Cruft, S Matthew Liao, and Massimo Renzo (eds), *Philosophical Foundations of Human Rights* (Oxford University Press 2015) 322–8.

Here I will not describe some of the complex details of the different theories, but their essential traits. In the following chapters I will criticise the general features of the maximisation account of proportionality explained in this chapter.

2.1   Proportionality and Maximisation

Proportionality and balancing are often seen as aiming to determine whether the loss for a right is somehow compensated by gains for another right or the public good. The proportionality test 'requires the seriousness of any rights-infringement to be matched by the importance of a competing right or public interest'.[2] On this view, the question that proportionality poses to decision-makers and review courts is the following:

> given the importance of this right and the extent to which enjoyment of it
> will be limited by the act in question, and given the importance of the pub-
> lic interest pursued, and the degree to which it is going to be realised, *does*
> *the act realise the public interest to such an extent that, all things considered,*
> *the gain to the public interest at least balances out the cost to the right?*[3]

The four subtests of proportionality can be seen as posing this question in a structured way. When proportionality is understood as oriented towards establishing whether the infringement of a right is somehow compensated by the gains derived from the measure that infringes it, then the fourfold structure of the test makes much sense: the fourth prong, the balancing test, addresses this question squarely. The first three subtests set the stage for the fourth: the former are oriented towards establishing what are the colliding values, principles, or interests at stake – the gains and losses that need to be compared in the fourth subtest.[4] This view of proportionality entails that conflicts concerning human rights are conflicts the solution of which requires relating the right at stake with the public good or some other competing right, and determining whether the loss on the side of the engaged right is somehow compensated by the benefit achieved on the side of the competing right or public good. This is what is distinctive about it: that limitations on human rights must be *justified by reference to* gains on some other interest, principle, or value. The question is whether the gains

---

[2] Julian Rivers, 'Proportionality and Variable Intensity of Review' (2006) 65 Cambridge LJ 174, 177.
[3] Ibid 181, characterising 'the optimisation conception' of proportionality.
[4] See Denise Réaume, 'Limitations on Constitutional Rights: The Logic of Proportionality' (2009) 26 Oxford Legal Research Paper Series 9 and 11.

are enough to compensate for the loss on the side of the right engaged by the measure.[5] If they are, then the measure is proportional. If they are not, then it is disproportionate. Thus, the last test of the prong can be more precisely formulated as inquiring whether the measure 'represent[s] a net gain, when the reduction in enjoyment of rights is weighed against the level of realisation of the aim'.[6] This involves a quantitative comparison: a comparison in terms of more, less, or equal (or other similar terms) of the losses for the engaged right and the gains for the public interest or some other right.

This understanding of proportionality is referred to as the 'optimising' or 'maximising' conception of proportionality.[7] What these labels highlight is that the point of the quantitative comparison in which proportionality ultimately consists is to achieve or secure the maximum level of realisation of the interests, values, or principles at stake. When proportionality determines whether the measure produces a 'net-gain' (or at least no net-loss), it determines whether the maximum level of realisation is achieved. As we will see below in analysing the different theories of the maximisation account of proportionality, such a method must be premised on the idea that what morally matters in the cases where the method should be applied is precisely to maximise the realisation of the relevant values, interests, or principles at stake. On this understanding of proportionality, the whole test is aimed at maximising some property or properties, and it is aptly structured through technical legal categories designed to shape the reasoning of the judge in doing so.

An illustration of the judicial use of proportionality as presented here is the United Kingdom Supreme Court's judgement in *R (Aguilar Quila) v Secretary of State for the Home Department*.[8] The case concerned an amendment in immigration rules that raised the age from 18 to 21 that both spouses need to meet for permission to leave, enter, or remain in the UK to be granted as a spouse of a person lawfully present and settled in the UK. The aim of the amendment was to deter forced marriages. The court addressed the proportionality of the measure in relation to article 8 of the European Convention on Human Rights (right to respect for private and

---

[5] And thus the characterisation of proportionality *strictu sensu* offered in *R v Oakes* [1986] 1 SCR 103 [71]: 'the more severe the deleterious effects of a measure, the more important the objective must be'.

[6] Rivers (n 2) 181.

[7] See ibid 176; Letsas (n 1).

[8] [2011] UKSC 45, [2012] 1 AC 621.

family life). It held that the measure was disproportionate, and as such an impermissible interference with the right of article 8. The court considered the issue as falling on two sides: 'One side asks whether, and if so to what extent, the amendment is likely to have deterred, and to continue to deter, forced marriages. The other side asks how many parties to unforced marriages are likely to be condemned by the amendment to suffer the interference with their rights exemplified in the two cases before the court.'[9]

Considering the (limited) available evidence on the impact of the measure, the majority of the court concluded that 'the number of unforced marriages which [the measure] obstructs from their intended development for up to three years vastly exceeds the number of forced marriages which it deters', and that the Secretary of State had not addressed this imbalance.[10] She had thus failed to address the third and fourth prongs of the proportionality analysis: to establish that the measure was necessary, and that 'it strikes a fair balance between the rights of the parties to unforced marriages and the interests of the community in preventing forced marriages'.[11]

The maximisation logic is displayed more clearly in the standard set by the court for the measure to have been proportionate. This standard is entailed by the court's framing of the issue as involving a comparison between the detrimental effect of the measure on unforced marriages, and the deterrent effect on forced marriage: had the deterrent effect been big enough, it would have justified the interference with the right of article 8.[12] The harm done to a right is justified by reference to the amount of good achieved for some relevant public interest or right. This is most clearly expressed by Lady Hale, in remarking how the Secretary of State has failed to address the relevant proportionality question: 'No one has said: "We know that many innocent young people will be caught by this rule but we think that the impact upon them will not be so great while the protection given to victims of forced marriage will be *so much greater*."'[13]

---

[9] *Quila* [47].
[10] *Quila* [58]. See also [74].
[11] *Quila* [58].
[12] This way of framing the issue is shared by the dissenting judge. Thus, Lord Brown's dissent emphasises that the duty of the court is to assess the proportionality of the measure (not the sufficiency of the government's research or reasoning) and that this case concerns matters of policy not suitable for judicial settling. But he agrees with the majority in presenting the substantive question as one regarding 'the proportionality [. . .] between the impact of the rule change on such innocent young couples as are adversely affected by it and the overall benefit of the rule in terms of combating forced marriage'. *Quila* [89] (Lord Brown).
[13] *Quila* [74] (Lady Hale, emphasis added).

Of the evidence presented by the Secretary of State, it is said that: 'None of it amounts to a sufficient case to conclude that the good done to the few can justify the harm done to the many.'[14] It is implied in this way of addressing the issue that the harm done to the right (of the many, in this case) is to be justified by the realisation of some other relevant public good, value, or interest (in this case, the rights of the few).

2.2 Theories of the Maximisation Account of Proportionality

2.2.1 Robert Alexy's Theory of Constitutional Rights and Proportionality

This understanding of the proportionality test is reflected in some of the most prominent theories of proportionality. In his *A Theory of Constitutional Rights* Robert Alexy has provided the most influential and sophisticated theory of proportionality and of the conception of rights implied by it. For this reason, and because in later chapters I engage with different aspects of Alexy's theory that are at the centre of debates on proportionality, I explain it here at greater length than other theories of the maximisation account of proportionality.

2.2.1.1 The Theory Described

In *A Theory of Constitutional Rights*, Alexy's 'central thesis' is that 'constitutional rights are principles and that principles are optimisation requirements.'[15] The underlying crucial distinction is between rules and principles. Rules are *definitive requirements*, while principles are *prima facie requirements*. This means that rules 'are norms which are either fulfilled or not. If a rule validly applies, then the requirement is to do exactly what it says.' Principles, by contrast, are *optimisation requirements*. They are 'norms which require that something be realised to the greatest extent possible given the legal and factual possibilities', and thus, they 'can be satisfied to varying degrees.'[16] On this account, 'the nature of principles implies the principle of proportionality.'[17] The different stages of the proportionality

---

[14] *Quila* [77] (Lady Hale).
[15] *Theory* 388. Note the shift from a rule-principle structure in the original book, to a purely principle structure in the later postscript (though in the earlier account the principle character was in the end the predominant feature and the one that was at work in Alexy's account of the justification of potential limitations of rights through the proportionality test). See ibid 80–110.
[16] Ibid 47–8, and 57.
[17] Ibid 66.

test follow from the requirement to optimise relative to what is legally and factually possible. The necessity and suitability prongs of the proportionality test concern what is factually possible. The balancing stage concerns optimising within what is legally possible, by weighing the particular principle with other legally recognised principles that bear on the case.[18]

This weighing is done according to a rule that 'expresses a law for balancing all types of principles', which Alexy calls the *Law of Balancing* (later 'the first Law of Balancing' or the 'substantive Law of Balancing'[19]), according to which 'the permissible level of non-satisfaction of, or detriment to, one principle *depends* on the importance of satisfying the other'. The law is formulated thus: 'The greater the degree of non-satisfaction of, or detriment to, one principle, the greater must be the importance of satisfying the other.'[20] Alexy claims that the idea behind his Law of Balancing could be 'illustrated by the use of indifference curves', which he defines as 'a means of representing a relation of substitution between interests'. The curves would illustrate that the law of marginal utilities applies to principles, as is expressed by the Law of Balancing requiring increasing levels of satisfaction of one principle for justifying greater interferences with the other.[21]

Later on Alexy further developed his theory of principles and its application to balancing. The substantive Law of Balancing remains the same. We must not be distracted by Alexy presenting the balancing exercise as assessing the weight of, on the one hand, the 'intensity of interference' that the measure produces to one principle, and the 'degree of importance' of satisfying the principle that the measure promotes. Alexy uses different terms to refer to the same thing, since he equates 'degree of importance' with 'degree of interference'. Thus, Alexy says that 'the concrete importance of P_j is the same as the intensity with which the non-interference with P_i interferes with P_j'.[22] By interference Alexy means 'the degree of non-satisfaction, or detriment to one principle'.[23] Hence, the comparison that the Law of Balancing commands is between degrees of satisfaction and non-satisfaction of the two principles at stake.[24]

---

[18] Ibid 67–8.
[19] Ibid 418.
[20] Ibid 102 (emphasis added).
[21] Ibid 103.
[22] Ibid 407.
[23] Ibid 405. See also Robert Alexy, 'The Weight Formula' in Jerzy Stelmach and Wojciech Załuski (eds), *Game Theory and the Law* (Copernicus Center Press 2011) 15–17.
[24] Alexy acknowledges this, but believes that his terminology (using different terms in relation to the satisfaction and non-satisfaction of the different principles at stake, talking

Alexy proposes that the relevant aspects that the Law of Balancing captures – a comparison between the degree of satisfaction of the principle promoted by the measure under review, and the degree of non-satisfaction of the principle interfered with by the measure[25] – can be rationally assessed. To do so, the Law of Balancing 'breaks the balancing process down into three steps', the first two consisting in establishing the intensity of interference with each principle at stake.[26] To undertake these two initial steps, he proposes a scale of light, moderate, and serious, in relation to which to assess the degree of non-satisfaction or satisfaction with each opposing principle, 'which are identified with the letters *l*, *m*, and *s*, respectively'.[27] Thus, according to the balancing formula the first step is to categorise the level of non-satisfaction of the principle interfered with by the measure as *l*, *m*, or *s*. Then the second step is to categorise the level of satisfaction of the principle promoted by the measure as *l*, *m*, or *s* (the level of non-satisfaction of that principle if it were not promoted by the measure).

After performing these two steps, Alexy says, 'the question is now how the third step can be carried out, in which the evaluations are to be set in relationship with each other'.[28] Alexy does not give an argument as to how this relationship is established, but rather asserts, in his characteristically technical nomenclature, right after posing the question on 'how the third step can be carried out', that:

> There are three circumstances in which P_i takes precedence [over P_j]:
>
> $IP_iC: s / SP_jC: l$
> $IP_iC: s / SP_jC: m$
> $IP_iC: m / SP_jC: l$[29]

---

in relation to one about 'interference' and in relation to the other about 'importance') is clearer for the non-specialist. See *Theory* 406–7. I think it is misleading, since it suggests that what is compared are different considerations in relation to the conflicting principles. I will follow Da Silva in talking about 'degrees of satisfaction and non-satisfaction' in relation to the considerations that are assessed by the Law of Balancing. See Virgilio Alfonso Da Silva, 'Comparing the Incommensurable: Constitutional Principles, Balancing and Rational Decision' (2011) 31 OJLS 273. Similarly, Klatt and Meister refer to 'intensities of interference' for both principles. See Matthias Klatt and Moritz Meister, *The Constitutional Structure of Proportionality* (Oxford University Press 2012) 11.

[25] For ease of exposition I assume that only two principles are at stake. More principles could be promoted or infringed by the measure.

[26] *Theory* 407.

[27] Ibid 405. For Alexy, 'the letter *l* stands not only for the common term "light", but also for other expressions such as "minor" or "weak", and *s* includes "high" and "strong" as well as "serious"'. Ibid.

[28] Ibid 407.

[29] Ibid.

where IP_iC means 'intensity of interference with principle i (P_i) under circumstances C', and SP_jC means 'degree of importance of satisfying [which
is the same as "degree of satisfaction" of] principle j (P_j) under circumstances C'.[30] This solution implies, in non-technical parlance, that a principle takes precedence over another *when that principle would be satisfied to
a greater degree by a favourable decision (or non-satisfied to a greater degree
by an unfavourable one) than the other.*

There are two further considerations that Alexy mentions as bearing
on the comparison between the different principles at stake. The first is
the 'abstract weight of a principle'. For Alexy, 'abstract weights only have
an influence on the outcome of balancing if they are different. If they are
equal, which in the case of competing constitutional rights is often the
case, the only relevant factor is their concrete importance.'[31] The second
consideration is what Alexy calls the 'second Law of Balancing' or the
'epistemic Law of Balancing', which states: 'The more heavily an interference in a constitutional right weighs, the greater must be the certainty of
its underlying premises.'[32]

These considerations can also be assessed by reference to a triadic
scale. A principle's abstract weight or importance can be categorised as l,
m, or s in the same way as the degrees of satisfaction or non-satisfaction.
And the reliability of the empirical premises as to the satisfaction or
non-satisfaction of a principle can be categorised as 'reliable', 'plausible',
and 'not evidently false', which are expressed with the letters r, p, and e,
respectively.[33]

Alexy does not provide an argument as to how these different considerations should be related to each other to establish which principle
has greater concrete weight in a particular conflict. Below (Sections 3.2
and 3.4) I show some of the difficulties that his theory faces in this respect.
What Alexy provides is a 'Weight Formula', 'which expresses the weight of
a principle under the circumstances of the case to be decided'.[34] That is, it
expresses whether a principle is 'weightier' than (i.e., should prevail over)
the rival principle at stake in that concrete case. This formula attempts to
give numerical expression to the different considerations and principles
that are balanced, thus expressing the concrete weight of a principle as a

[30] Ibid 405–7.
[31] Ibid 406.
[32] Ibid 418.
[33] Ibid.
[34] *Balancing and Subsumption* 444.

quotient of the considerations (abstract weight, degree of satisfaction or non-satisfaction, and reliability of premises) that apply to each principle at stake. For Alexy this formula 'illustrates the structure of balancing. In legal argumentation, it is only analogous to a quotient. But the analogy is an instructive one.'[35]

When one wants to express all the considerations that affect the weight of a principle, the Weight Formula looks like this:

$$W_{i,j} = \frac{I_i \bullet W_i \bullet R_i}{I_j \bullet W_j \bullet R_j}$$

where '$W_{i,j}$' means 'concrete weight of principle of principle 'i' in relation to principle 'j'; 'I' stands for 'interference', or satisfaction or non-satisfaction of a principle, 'W' for abstract weight, and 'R' for reliability of empirical premises as to the satisfaction or non-satisfaction of the principles. Letters 'i' or 'j' as subscript indicate the principle to which the variables I, W, and R apply.

For the first consideration (degrees of satisfaction or non-satisfaction), Alexy proposes to ascribe numbers to the different points in the scale following a 'geometric sequence 2^0, 2^1 and 2^2, that is 1, 2, and 4. On this basis l has the value 1, m has the value 2, and s the value 4.'[36] Regarding the second consideration, if the values are of equal abstract weight, then they cancel each other. If they are not, 'one can express the values of W_i and W_j by the same triadic scale as in the case of I_i and I_j.'[37] For the third consideration (reliability of premises) the value of r is 2^0, the value of p is 2^{-1}, and the value of e is 2^{-2}.[38]

For a given case, the different numbers are to be introduced into the formula, which consists in a division. If the quotient of the division is greater than 1, then it means that principle 'i' is of greater weight than principle 'j', and thus should prevail over it in that case. If the quotient is less than one, it means that the latter principle should prevail over the former. If the result is 1, it means that there is a stalemate: both principles are of the same weight and thus the court should be deferent and grant discretion to the primary decision-maker.[39]

---

[35] *Theory* 409.
[36] *Balancing and Subsumption* 444.
[37] Ibid 446.
[38] Ibid 447.
[39] Ibid 444–5, *Theory* 401–14. These central features of Alexy's theory have remained largely unchanged during the last decade or so. See Robert Alexy, 'The Construction of Constitutional Rights' (2010) 4 Law & Ethics of Human Rights 1.

2.2.1.2   Analysis from the Moral Perspective

Alexy does not deal directly with the question of what are the relevant moral considerations that ought to bear on the kinds of cases he is analysing, and which his model for proportionality analysis should therefore capture. But he does say what are the considerations that his theory captures, as when he talks of 'what is significant in balancing exercises, namely the degree of intensity of non-satisfaction of, or detriment to, one principle versus the importance of satisfying the other'.[40] These considerations are about maximisation of principle realisation.

Alexy talks about 'optimisation requirements' to highlight that, according to his theory, conflicting principles should be realised to the greatest extent possible: one should attempt to optimise realisation of each principle, and therefore, sub-optimal decisions should be avoided. This is the case when a measure fails the necessity or adequacy subtests of the proportionality test. But Alexy also acknowledges that any principle seen in isolation is a 'maximisation requirement', since it requires maximising the realisation of something.[41]

Furthermore, Alexy's theory of balancing is not simply about achieving Pareto-optimality in the realisation of each principle (i.e., achieving a situation where none of the principles could be realised more without negatively affecting the realisation of the other), since this is achieved by the previous adequacy and necessity subtest. In Alexy's model, when applying the balancing test one is to attempt to choose the alternative that realises principles to a greater degree. One does so by choosing to satisfy one principle at the expense of the other if this brings overall greater principle realisation. In the standard case,[42] for Alexy, satisfying a principle will bring overall greater principle realisation if this principle has more at stake in the decision. This occurs when the degree to which the principle would be satisfied by a favourable decision is higher than the degree to which the opposing principle would be satisfied by a decision favourable to this opposing principle.

---

[40]   *Theory* 105.

[41]   Ibid 51 (n 37).

[42]   It could be that one principle is more important in the abstract than the other. Nevertheless, as said in the previous subsection, Alexy believes this is not common with constitutional rights. Also, it could be that some of the premises put forward for establishing the degree of satisfaction or non-satisfaction of the principles are more reliable than others, which also affects the result. Nevertheless, this last consideration is at the service of establishing well degrees of satisfaction or non-satisfaction, so that it can be said that it is the latter that matters intrinsically in conflicts of principles.

This method for solving conflicts of principles must be premised on the idea that what morally matters in the cases to which it is applied is to maximise principle realisation. This is so because if the criterion proposed for choosing between A and B consists in establishing whether A or B realises more *P*, then this criterion can only be justified if what is relevant for this choice is to realise *P* as much as possible, that is, to maximise *P*. Theories that promote the maximisation account of proportionality all have this structure, and thus all are premised on the idea that what morally matters in the cases to which proportionality is applied is to maximise something specified (perhaps vaguely) by the relevant theory. Alexy's theory is no exception to this.

Alexy does not deal directly with a prior question: what are the considerations that are of moral importance in the kinds of cases that he is interested in (human or 'constitutional' rights cases)? Perhaps for that reason he never explains why the considerations that his theory captures are what morally matters in those cases and accordingly should be the decisive considerations in those cases. This will be assessed in the following chapters.

2.2.2   David Beatty's Theory of Proportionality

In the Anglo-American context, Canadian scholar David Beatty introduced an account of proportionality that is also based on the idea of maximisation. Beatty does not articulate his proposal for proportionality analysis as clearly and explicitly as Alexy. This is partly a consequence of his method, since Beatty proposes to focus 'on how the practice of judicial review actually works', using the methods of the common law. This method is characterised by 'its pursuit of theory and overarching principles from the bottom up. [. . .] Instead of starting with a preconceived theory of law and democracy [. . .] to which jurisprudence is made to conform, the order is reversed and theory emerges out of the cases.'[43]

In his analysis of different human rights cases, Beatty mentions a number of different considerations that apply to the circumstances of those cases. But there is one major principle on which Beatty insists all along: that the challenged measure should be assessed 'from the perspective of those who reap its greatest benefits and those who stand to lose the most.'[44] Beatty's method (though he does not articulate it explicitly) consists in asking which party stands to win or lose the most in a human

---

[43]   David Beatty, *The Ultimate Rule of Law* (Oxford University Press 2004) 34.
[44]   Ibid 160. See also 47, 53, 59, 60, 74, 93, 94, 98, 114.

rights case: this party should be the one favoured by the decision. For example, Beatty sees the judgement by Aharon Barak, former judge of the Israeli Supreme Court, in *Lior Horev v Minister of Communication/ Transportation* case as

> an especially powerful image of the great jurist [. . .] reasoning pragmati-
> cally to resolve a highly charged, politically volatile issue of church/state
> relations in a way that is equally sensitive to both. At issue was a govern-
> ment regulation that would have closed a major artery running through
> the heart of Jerusalem – Bar Ilan Street – during the hours of prayer on
> the Jewish sabbath. The street cut across a number of orthodox neigh-
> bourhoods and the Government's hope was that a partial closing would be
> accepted as a compromise between the orthodox community who argued
> for a complete ban on all traffic for the duration of the sabbath and secu-
> lar Israelis who insisted their mobility rights guaranteed them unimpeded
> access to the street seven days a week, twenty-four hours a day.[45]

Beatty approves of Barak's analysis, which Beatty reports as focusing on first establishing the harm that the orthodox community 'would suffer from an unrestricted flow of traffic' during the period of the day when prayers were being said, which Barak considers to be 'harsh and bitter'. This is contrasted with the 'inconvenience most Israelis would suffer from being denied access to the street during such times', which Barak characterises as 'trivial', since it would consist in no more than in them having to take an alternative route and add two minutes to their trip. According to Beatty's assessment, 'At least during the times when prayers were being said, *the proportionalities – in the significance of the closing for the two communities* – were clear.'[46]

What for Beatty needs to be compared in the proportionality test ('the proportionalities') is the significance of the measure for the parties, which, as in the *Bar Ilan* case, refers to how it impacts on the parties' interests. The party for whom the case is more significant, that is, the one that has the stronger interest in the decision, is the one that should be favoured. A measure would be disproportionate when, in a conflict of interests, it sacrifices those of the party that has a greater interest in the issue, the party for which the issue is of greater significance.

Like Alexy's, this way of understanding human rights cases is about maximisation – in Beatty's account, maximisation of interest or preference satisfaction of the parties. Recall: if the criterion proposed for choosing

---

[45] Ibid 58.
[46] Ibid 59 (emphasis added).

between A and B consists in establishing whether A or B realise more P, then this criterion can only be justified if what is relevant for this choice is to realise P as much as possible, that is, to maximise P. If the criterion for deciding a case is whether the interests of A or B would be more heavily impacted by an adverse decision, then the decision is about which course of action would satisfy more or stronger interests or preferences. And if this is so, then this method is about maximising interests, and can only be justified if what morally matters for the cases to which it is applied is the maximisation of interests.

It is a necessary premise for Beatty's theory that what morally matters in proportionality cases is to maximise interest or preference satisfaction: Beatty's account needs it to have moral appeal. This premise renders the more characteristic and pervasive aspects of Beatty's account intelligible. It explains (a) Beatty's insistence on the need for assessing the parties' interests as the parties themselves see them[47] (since what matters is maximising their preferences or subjective interests); (b) his intriguing statement that proportionality 'transforms questions that in moral philosophy are questions of value into questions of fact'[48] (since the question the judge is facing is about facts: which outcome would maximise preference satisfaction for the parties? If it is impossible to satisfy the preferences of both parties, the question is: who has a stronger interests in the decision?); (c) his claim that proportionality 'makes the concept of rights almost irrelevant',[49] and that 'rights lose the special force they are taken to have'[50] (since the method of maximising preference satisfaction filters out considerations of rights [see Chapter 5]); and (d) his claim that proportionality is more neutral and objective than alternatives[51] (since it requires comparing preferences and the intensity by which they are desired by the parties, which is in principle a technical undertaking).

2.2.3 Aharon Barak's Theory of Proportionality

Aharon Barak has also proposed a general account of the proportionality test. The most characteristic aspect of Barak's account is his understanding

---

[47] For example, see Beatty (n 43) 47, 53, 70, 72, 74, 93, 116, 160
[48] Ibid 170. See also 171.
[49] Ibid 160.
[50] Ibid 171.
[51] See especially ibid 166–8. See also 64, 73.

of the balancing stage of the proportionality test. For Barak, balancing is 'the most important of proportionality's tests'.[52] It demands that

> a proper relation ('proportional' in the narrow sense of the term) should exist between the benefits gained by fulfilling the purpose and the harm caused to the constitutional right from obtaining that purpose.[53]

By 'purpose' here Barak refers to the legitimate aim sought by a measure that interferes with a right. This 'proper relation' that the balancing test attempts to establish implies a comparison between 'the positive effect of realising the law's proper purpose' and 'the negative effect it has on the constitutional right'.[54]

But what constitutes a 'proper relation'? How is it established? Barak resorts to metaphors: 'We should establish a normative rule which determines the relative weight of each side of the scale. Based on this weight we could determine which end of the scale is heavier.'[55]

But what does 'weight' consist of and how is it assigned? For Barak the crucial concept is that of social importance. He says:

> The relevant rule according to which the weight of each of the scales should be determined is that of the social importance of the benefit gained by the limiting law and the social importance of preventing harm to the limited constitutional right at the point of conflict.[56]

Social importance generally

> is derived, inter alia, from different political and economic ideologies, from the unique history of each country, from the structure of the political system, and from the different social values. The legal system at issue should be observed as a whole. The assessment of the social importance of each of the conflicting principles should be conducted against the background of the normative structure of each legal system. This kind of balancing should be affected by the entire value structure of the particular legal system. We should consider the constitutional status of the conflicting principles. Principles found in the constitution are *prima facie* of greater social importance than those external to the constitution. That is insufficient. The importance of principles – and the importance of the prevention of their harm – is not determined solely by their normative status. Principles at the same normative level can be considered to be of different social importance. These kinds of values may be influenced by both

---

[52] *Proportionality* 340.
[53] Ibid.
[54] Ibid 342.
[55] Ibid (citations omitted).
[56] Ibid 349.

intrinsic and extrinsic factors. The extrinsic factors are of a social nature. They reflect a society's history and culture. The intrinsic factors are of a normative nature. They reflect the internal relations of the different principles. Thus, for example, a right that constitutes a precondition to another right may be considered more important.[57]

These are extremely vague sources, which furthermore can be contradictory. It is doubtful whether Barak's enumeration of many considerations that affect the social importance of a right or public interest amount to a method at all, let alone a sound one.[58] In specifying what social importance is, Barak does no more than enumerate the sources for the different considerations ('society's fundamental perceptions', 'political and economic ideologies', 'the legal system as a whole') together with a type of internal consideration that *may* be relevant ('a right that constitutes a precondition to another right may be considered more important'). He does so without providing a method specifying how these different considerations relate so as to actually establish the social importance of realising a principle for a concrete case.[59]

Barak clarifies that what is balanced is not the social importance of the right and the public interest, but 'the marginal effects – on both the benefits and the harms – caused by the law',[60] that is, the 'marginal social importance' of realising one principle or the other in the particular case under review. Also, what needs to be compared is not necessarily 'the state of affairs before the law was enacted' to a state of affairs where the law is enacted and implemented, yielding benefits for one principle and harm for another (a right). When there are alternatives to the government's measure (when these alternatives 'do not fulfil fully the purpose of the limiting law', and thus the measure under review passes the necessity test) the comparison of marginal social importance has to be between the state of affairs that the measure under review would bring about, and that which the viable alternatives would bring about.[61] Therefore, the balance is one 'between the marginal social importance of the benefits gained by one principle (beyond the proportional alternative) and the marginal social

---

[57] Ibid 349 (citations omitted). See also 361.
[58] See Grégoire Webber, 'Proportionality: Constitutional Rights and Their Limitation' (review article) (2013) Public Law 433, 436, where he argues that 'Barak provides too little an account of social importance for it to convince his reader'.
[59] Thus, he concedes that: 'We must assume that, with time, it will be possible to establish more specific criteria on this matter.' *Proportionality* 361.
[60] Ibid 350 ff.
[61] Ibid 353.

importance of preventing the harm to the constitutional right (beyond the proportional alternative).[62] Also, the probability of the realisation of the benefits for one principle, and the harms for the opposing principle should also be considered in establishing the weight of each scale.[63]

Taking all these elements into consideration, Barak believes it is possible to formulate a 'balancing rule' for establishing whether there is a proper relation between the benefits of a measure and its impact on a right:

> The higher the social importance of preventing the marginal harm to the constitutional right at issue and the higher the probability of such an additional marginal harm occurring, then the marginal benefits created by the limiting law – either to the public interest or to other constitutional rights – should be of a higher social importance and more urgent and the probability of its realisation should be higher. Therefore, we cannot justify a serious and certain limitation of a socially important constitutional right in the fulfilment of a minimal social benefit, to the public interest or to the protection of other less important constitutional rights, whose probability is low.[64]

When the weight of the benefits achieved by the measure is greater than the weight of the cost to the right engaged by the measure (as specified by the idea of marginal social importance and the probability of the benefits and harms occurring), the measure is proportional. When the weight of the benefits is less than the weight of the cost to the right, then the measure is disproportionate. What happens when there is a stalemate? Here Barak's solution is slightly different from the one proposed by Alexy, for whom in a case of stalemate the court should be deferent to the decision of the primary decision-maker. We must distinguish between two types of cases. The first are cases were 'both scales carry constitutional human rights'. Here 'there is no reason not to leave the limiting law intact, since its limitation of one constitutional right is equal to its protection of another. [. . .] The role of the courts as defenders of human rights is fulfilled.' The second are cases where 'one scale carries the marginal social importance of the benefit gained to the public interest, while the other carries the marginal social importance of preventing harm caused to the constitutional right'. Here 'the issue of the balanced scales should be resolved in favour of the constitutional rights'.[65]

As with Alexy and Beatty's account, one can understand Barak's account as being also premised on the idea that what morally matters in human

---

[62] Ibid 357.
[63] Ibid 358 and 362.
[64] Ibid 363. It is unclear to me what the words 'more urgent' add to the formula.
[65] Ibid 367.

rights cases is the maximisation of something. In this case, it is of 'social importance'. The assessment required by Barak's method is structurally quantitative and oriented towards establishing which alternative would realise more social importance. This presupposes that what matters morally in the cases to which the method is applied is to realise social importance as much as possible, that is, to maximise social importance.

There is an ambiguity, though, in Barak's theory of proportionality, and it is worth spelling it out. On the one hand, Barak presents what has the form of a relatively precise method for deciding cases involving limitations of human rights for the sake of the public interest or other rights. He claims that '[p]roportionality is a framework based on a structured method of thought. It determines the information which should be considered.'[66] He attributes to proportionality certain benefits that it could only yield if it were in fact a relatively precise method. Barak says, for example, that proportionality 'establishes a uniform analytical framework for any state action that may affect constitutional rights', and that it 'ensures constitutional uniformity in the search for a justification'.[67] He claims that the 'structured nature of the discretion involved in proportionality has many advantages', particularly that 'it allows the person conducting proportionality to think analytically, not to skip over things which should be considered, and to consider them in their time and place'.[68] All this would only be possible if proportionality were in fact a relatively precise method, establishing with enough precision which considerations should be taken into account, and how to relate them, and also weeding out considerations that are deemed irrelevant. Only thus could proportionality guide legal adjudication so as to yield the benefits Barak attributes to it (I expand on the idea of legally directed adjudication, and particularly on the epistemic benefit mentioned by Barak, in Section 7.4.1). The maximisation accounts of proportionality attempt to provide such a method.

Nevertheless, on other occasions Barak seems to suggest a different view of proportionality, one closer to what I have called 'proportionality as unconstrained moral reasoning' (see Chapter 6). This view conceives of proportionality as a legal doctrinal tool that simply allows judges to demand justification for certain actions, and to assess those actions through open-ended moral reasoning. Thus, Barak also says that

---

[66] Ibid 457–8.
[67] Ibid 457.
[68] Ibid 461.

proportionality 'is a legal framework that must be filled with content',[69] that it is 'led by extrinsic data', and that one can 'incorporate most current human rights theories into the concept of proportionality'.[70] He claims that 'proportionality *strictu sensu* may well incorporate the notions of "rights as trumps" or "rights as firewalls"' (though he had earlier suggested the contrary[71]).[72] It is particularly noteworthy that in attempting to accommodate within proportionality some features that rights are taken to have in the liberal tradition, Barak adopts an argument proposed by Mattias Kumm.[73] I will address Kumm's argument in detail in the second part of this book (Sections 6.1–2). For now it is necessary only to say that for Kumm, proportionality can accommodate the priority of rights over collectivists goals, because the balancing stage can be interpreted as requiring 'the decision-maker to engage in theoretically informed practical reasoning'.[74] If the idea of rights having some pre-emptive force is the most reasonable one, then this should inform the balancing stage. But this understanding of proportionality deprives it of any content (Section 6.2), and thus, if proportionality is to be understood in that way, it cannot be the relatively precise method aimed at maximisation that Barak assumes it is. It is also in tension with the idea that proportionality cannot accommodate absolute requirements because it is committed to a form of reasoning that presupposes the possibility of trade-offs.[75] This idea is defended by Barak, and indeed by Kumm in his paper quoted by Barak. Nevertheless, if the balancing stage requires open-ended moral reasoning, it can accommodate any relevant moral requirement, including absolute ones, as Kumm later came to accept.[76] Furthermore, it cannot be said to yield any of the benefits that a structured and more precise test would yield, since the

---

[69] Ibid 489.

[70] Ibid 467.

[71] 'Dworkin's notion of "rights as trumps" is not based on the concept of balancing: in fact, it is meant to prevent it.' Ibid 365. Nevertheless, Barak thinks that his conception could 'lead to the same results'. Ibid.

[72] Ibid 490.

[73] Ibid 470.

[74] Mattias Kumm, 'Political Liberalism and the Structure of Rights: On the Structure and Limit of the Proportionality Requirement' in George Pavlakos (ed), *Law, Rights and Discourse: The Legal Philosophy of Robert Alexy* (Hart 2007) 148.

[75] *Proportionality* 471.

[76] See Mattias Kumm and Alec D Walen, 'Human Dignity and Proportionality: Deontic Pluralism in Balancing' in Grant Huscroft, Bradley Miller, and Grégoire Webber (eds), *Proportionality and the Rule of Law: Rights, Justification, Reasoning* (Cambridge University Press 2014) 67.

freedom to engage in open-ended practical reasoning comes at the price of lack of guidance and external structure. I expand on these ideas in Chapter 6. For now it is relevant only to notice these tensions in Barak's theory.[77] I will regard it generally as aimed at maximisation, since this seems to be the pretension at the core of his proposal; but I will acknowledge the tension in his work when necessary. The structure of this book, which argues against both understandings of proportionality, is well suited to address this type of ambiguity.

2.3   The Proportionality Test and the Maximisation Account of Proportionality

For the theories explained above, proportionality is oriented towards establishing which alternative (whether to allow the measure that engages a right or not) would realise more of some property, be it interest or preference satisfaction, value or principle realisation, or social importance.

This account of proportionality is premised on the view that conflicts concerning human rights are conflicts the solution of which requires relating the right at stake with the public good or some other competing right, and determining whether the loss on the side of the engaged right is somehow compensated by the benefit on the side of the competing right or public good. This is what is distinctive about this account of proportionality, and, because of how prevalent it is, it could be said that it is what is distinctive about proportionality itself: that limitations on human rights must be *justified by reference to* gains on some other interest, principle, or value. The question is whether the gains are enough to compensate for the loss on the side of the right engaged by the measure. If they are, then the measure is proportional. If they are not, then it is disproportionate. As seen above, this account is adopted in doctrinal writings on proportionality and in judicial decisions.

---

[77] Some of these tensions can be seen, in lesser degree, in Robert Alexy's remarks on the ability of proportionality to reflect absolute rights. Alexy claims: 'Proportionality analysis is, as the weight formula shows, a formal structure that essentially depends on premises provided from the outside.' Robert Alexy, 'Thirteen Replies' in George Pavlakos (ed), *Law, Rights and Discourse: The Legal Philosophy of Robert Alexy* (Hart 2007) 344. As I show below, this underestimates the level of substantive guidance (and thus constraint) provided by Alexy's model (see Section 5.5.3). A similar statement can be seen in Klatt and Meister (n 24) 54–5, also quoting from Kumm. Nevertheless, Alexy and Klatt and Meister remain committed to Alexy's method, and these remarks are to be seen as attempts to express that Alexy's method does require some independent moral and prudential reasoning as input, in, for example, establishing whether an infringement with a principle is 'serious' or 'light'.

Whether the gains are enough is established through a quantitative comparison of the losses for the engaged right and the gains for the public interest or some other right. If the gains are more (and on some accounts, equal) than the losses, the measure is proportionate. If the gains are less (or equal, on Barak's account, when the measure does not promote a right but only a public good), then the measure is disproportionate. This type of quantitative comparison presupposes that there is a common property that captures what is relevant in the elements compared, according to which the elements can be compared in terms of realising more, or less, or equally the said property. I will say more about this in the next chapter.

As said above, this method for deciding cases involving human rights is premised on the idea that what morally matters in those cases is to maximise something. If the criterion proposed for choosing between A and B consists in establishing whether A or B realise more P, then this criterion can only be justified if what is relevant for this choice is to realise P as much as possible, that is, to maximise P. The different theories of proportionality analysed in this chapter specify differently what it is that should be maximised. But they all follow the maximisation logic, and are premised on the idea that what morally matters in the cases in which proportionality is applied is to maximise a relevant property.

From the technical perspective we ask what technical legal categories can aptly express the considerations that are morally relevant in the kinds of cases to which proportionality is applied. If one considers that what is morally relevant in those cases is to maximise something, then the technical doctrinal formulations of the different prongs of the proportionality test make much sense. The proportionality test can be seen as a doctrinal tool aimed precisely at establishing whether an 'interference' with a human right is justified by reference to the gain in the fulfilment of some other interest, principle, or value, thus maximising interest satisfaction or principle or value realisation. The different prongs of the test can be understood as a structured way of analysing this: first asking whether there is a relevant interest, value, or principle that is fulfilled by the measure that engages the human right at stake; second, whether the measure is apt to realise that interest, value, or principle; third, whether there are other less restrictive means for realising the interest, value, or principle (and thus, whether there is a way of realising all the interests, values, or principles at stake, including the engaged human right, to a greater degree than under the proposed measure); and fourth, whether the measure in question produces more or the same interest satisfaction or value or principle realisation than what would be lost by limiting the right (or, on Barak's account, whether the marginal social importance of realising the principle promoted by the measure is greater than the marginal social importance of realising the principle infringed by the measure).

On this understanding of proportionality, the whole test is aimed at maximising some property, and it is aptly structured through technical legal categories designed to shape the reasoning of the judge in doing so.

The idea of maximisation can explain not only the general doctrinal structure of the proportionality test, but also two peculiar features of the test.

First, it can explain the pre-eminence of the final prong of the proportionality test, the 'balancing test'. The balancing prong is the most characteristic part of the proportionality test, which is suggested by the fact that it is referred to as 'proportionality *stricto sensu*'. Barak considers it to be 'the most important of proportionality's tests',[78] and Klatt and Meister, who have proposed a defence of Alexy's version of the proportionality test and added further refinements to it, have said that 'balancing [is] the most important prong of the proportionality test, both in practical and theoretical terms'.[79] In the UK context, Finnis notes that 'our courts [. . .] visibly treat the new, fourth step as in practice the most important of them all'.[80] Once proportionality is seen as a test oriented towards maximisation, it is easy to see why the final balancing prong of the test is pre-eminent. It is the one where the maximisation logic is expressed most directly. The other three stages, assessed independently from balancing, could be seen simply as evaluating the rationality of a measure (that it is not irrational in pursuing unworthy or unjust goals, or in deploying means not rationally connected with those goals, or sub-optimal). It is the balancing stage where the maximisation logic becomes explicit, by ending the enquiry with a quantitative comparison of gains and losses, to which all the previous stages are ordered.

Second, it can explain what the test *does not* direct judges to analyse. It is telling that though the test explicitly addresses the question of whether the measure that affects a right pursues a legitimate *aim*, it does not ask whether the measure is a legitimate *means* for furthering that aim. It assesses whether the means are adequate and sufficiently efficient (in comparison to other alternatives), and whether the realisation of the aim

---

[78] *Proportionality* 340.
[79] Klatt and Meister (n 24) 6.
[80] John Finnis, 'Judicial Power: Past, Present, and Future' (a lecture in Gray's Inn Hall, 20 October 2015), available at http://judicialpowerproject.org.uk/john-finnis-judicial-power-past-present-and-future/ accessed 20 January 2016.

is enough to compensate for the cost that the measure causes in a right. The legitimacy or moral soundness of the means as such (i.e., not by reference to the aim of the measure – whether they are apt for achieving the aim, whether the aim is worthwhile, etc.) is not directly assessed. This is remarkable, because the law is generally concerned with the evaluation of means, that is, of actions and choices generally: with whether they are, for example, unjust. The law reacts to unjust actions as such, regardless of whether they are pursued for a legitimate aim (the prohibition of certain forms of interrogation and law enforcement, of which the prohibition of torture is paradigmatic, are examples of this). But from the maximisation perspective it is perfectly reasonable to disregard the question of the legitimacy of means. If what is morally relevant in cases regarding human rights limitations is to maximise some property, then what matters is the probable consequences of the measure under review and its impact on human rights and the public interest.

But this is a big 'if'. In the following chapters I will offer mainly two critiques against the maximisation account of proportionality. In Chapters 4 and 5, I will argue that that there are no reasons for thinking that what morally matters in human rights cases is some form of maximisation. Rather, what morally matters in those cases is justice and rights, and these considerations are different from, and in some sense opposed to, considerations of maximisation. But first, in the next chapter I will argue that the kind of comparison that is crucial for the maximisation account cannot be undertaken, because it requires commensuration of incommensurables.

3

The Incommensurability Objection

A common objection against proportionality and balancing in human rights adjudication is that it is not possible to perform a quantitative comparison between gains and losses for rights or the public good by means only of rational criteria (as distinct from feelings, conventions or other sub-rational criteria). This is the incommensurability objection.[1] It is possibly the most underestimated challenge to proportionality reasoning. Proponents of the proportionality test, when they acknowledge the objection at all, often dismiss it quickly.[2] They rarely pause over it to assess its cogency and implications.[3]

Nevertheless, I believe incommensurability poses a serious challenge to some accounts of proportionality. The reason why the incommensurability objection has been underestimated is because it has often been misunderstood. Hence, I first provide a general account of the incommensurability objection, with the aim of making explicit its scope and limitations, and of dispelling some common misconceptions surrounding it. I devote special attention to how incommensurable choice can be supported by reason, as this has direct application in debates on proportionality. The incommensurability objection is narrower than it is commonly thought, since it does not claim that incommensurable choice is always irrational, and below I explore different ways in which it is reasonable to choose one alternative rather than another when the alternatives are incommensurable. Incommensurability only implies that, when confronted with an incommensurable choice, rational determinacy cannot be achieved through a quantitative comparison of the alternatives. Because such a comparison is exactly what the maximisation account of proportionality counsels,

---

[1] See *Negotiable Constitution* 89–100; and Stavros Tsakyrakis, 'Proportionality: An Assault on Human Rights?' (2009) 7 Int'l J Const L 468, 471–4.

[2] See, for example, Alexy and Barak's engagement with the incommensurability objection below at Section 3.3.

[3] Notable exceptions are articles by Paul Craig and Virgilio Alfonso Da Silva discussed below.

incommensurability does indeed ground a serious objection against that specific account of proportionality – but not against other influential accounts, and not against every legal method for choosing between incommensurable alternatives or that presupposes such a choice.

3.1 Incommensurability in General

3.1.1 Incommensurability and Incommensurability in Choice

Before addressing how incommensurability bears on balancing, it is useful to clarify some general issues about incommensurability. As will become clear in the following section, these issues are crucial for understanding in what precise sense incommensurability can ground a critique against the proportionality test. It is not necessary for our purposes to provide here an extensive account of the different understandings of incommensurability.[4] Here incommensurability will mean the following: two things are incommensurable with respect to X when X is not a property by which they can be compared quantitatively, that is, X is not a property by which it can be judged that one of the things is (overall, net) more or less X than, or just as X as, the other – whether or not there is a unit of measurement that can express X. To describe this type of situations we could use the term 'incomparability', and reserve the term incommensurability only for when there is no unit of measurement that can express X. In what follows I will generally use the term 'incommensurability' – which is the term used in the literature on balancing – and I will use it as a term of art in the sense I have just defined it. I will generally use the word 'compare' in a less committed sense, meaning simply to put the alternatives side by side, so to say, and evaluate each one in relation to the other.

It should be noted right away that whether two things can be commensurated or not depends on the property by reference to which one compares them. It is not a feature of things as such. There is always some property with respect to which it is possible to compare two things. I can compare my laptop and a friend by reference to which one is greyer, which makes those two objects of comparison commensurable with respect to greyness.

Incommensurability, in the context of human action, appears in choices. Incommensurability in choice exists and is relevant because human action

---

[4] See Ruth Chang (ed), *Incommensurability, Incomparability, and Practical Reason* (Harvard University Press 1997). On the relevance of distinguishing incommensurability from incomparability see below (n 40).

is ruled by reasons. When we are confronted with a choice, there are reasons that bear on the choice. These reasons are reasons for choosing in a certain way. It could be the case that different reasons that bear on an issue require that different properties be realised, which properties might not be reducible to each other, that is, it is not possible to translate one of the properties in terms of the other, or all of them into a single different one. When this happens, there will be incommensurability. Imagine I want to buy a house. Suppose the relevant question here is what is the best house for me to live in, and that this in turn depends on two variables: I want a house that is pretty, and that is big. Imagine that there are only two houses available, and that money is not an issue – I can have any house I choose, but I can choose only one (imagine, for example, that a benefactor will give me the house that I choose). House A is pretty but small; and house B is big but ugly. The two relevant properties (beauty and size) provide content to the idea of the kind of house that would be the best for me. The properties are irreducible to each other – a house does not become pretty by being very big, or big by being very pretty.

The first thing to note is that I can rank ordinally different houses by reference to each of the different properties, and even compare cardinally by reference to how big they are (since the property 'size' can be expressed in a measuring unit). I can say that house A realises more the property of prettiness than house B. But there is no unifying property that captures all that is relevant about my two properties for determining which is the best house, according to which I could rank my alternatives A and B *in terms of which realises the property more and which less*. 'Best overall house' ('X' in the definition above) is not such a property. The attributes of the houses that are relevant for establishing which is the best house are incommensurable with respect to what constitutes the best house for me, and therefore, if the houses rank differently along the different relevant properties (as they do in my example), the alternatives are incommensurable as well.[5]

[5] Here it may be useful to clarify my terminology. I speak of criteria, properties, attributes, alternatives, and choices. *Criteria* are the principles according to which we evaluate the alternatives; criteria are prescriptive (e.g.: choose the best house). *Properties* are that which criteria require to realise or not realise in choosing an alternative (e.g.: beauty). *Attributes* are these properties as they are instantiated in the different alternatives (e.g.: the beauty of house B). *Alternatives* are the concrete objects of choice (e.g.: house B). And *choice* is a situation in which a decision between alternatives is to be made. Two criteria can be different, and when it is not possible to translate one of the criteria in terms of the other, or both into a third, we say that they are *irreducible*. We say the same of properties. We can also say of properties that they are incommensurable, in that, for example, the beauty of houses, in the abstract, cannot be compared quantitatively to the size of houses, in the abstract, for

3.1.2   *Incommensurability and Rational Underderminacy*

In the example above, the fact that there is no single relevant property along which I could rank the different houses as 'better than' the others could mean that my decision between the houses is *rationally underdetermined*. A decision is rationally underdetermined when there is not just one alternative that it would be reasonable to choose. Continuing with my example, if the only relevant criterion for choosing between houses A and B is to choose the best house, and if what constitutes the best house is determined by the degree of realisation of the two irreducible properties of beauty and size, then the decision will be rationally underdetermined.

The temptation is to think that when a choice is incommensurable, it will have to be rationally underdetermined precisely for that reason. But this is not so. Incommensurability only means that the two alternatives cannot be put into one kind of relation: one based on a quantitative assessment on which alternative realises to a greater degree a relevant property. But there are other ways, which are not quantitative, of justifying a relation between different alternatives. If the alternatives are incommensurable, then one cannot reasonably decide between them through commensuration. But the incommensurable attributes of the alternatives at stake might not be the only element relevant for choosing. In the example of the houses, there may be reasons for me to choose that are not related to which house is the best. I might have to choose house B because it is our old family house and I promised my mother at her deathbed that I would. This may provide a reason that is conclusive: a reason for choosing house B, regardless of the advantages of the other alternative.

---

the purposes of defining what is an ideal or the best house. Attributes we say are incommensurable. Thus, beauty is different from size, and they are irreducible to each other; and the beauty of house A is not more, or less, or the same than its size – it is incommensurable with its size. Alternatives are incommensurable if they (according to their attributes) are ordered differently – rank higher and lower than others – in relation to the different relevant properties, so that, for example, if two alternatives are assessed in relation to two properties, and one alternative ranks higher in relation to one property and another ranks higher in relation to the other property, they are incommensurable. A choice between alternatives of which at least some are incommensurable is an *incommensurable choice*. Therefore, I think it is more proper to use the words 'incommensurable' in relation to attributes, alternatives, and choices, and 'different' and 'irreducible', in relation to criteria and properties, as I do here. But for the purposes of this chapter nothing depends on the use of this terminology, since it is also possible to say that criteria or properties are incommensurable, in the loose sense that they are different and irreducible, and give rise to incommensurability. I make it explicit only to clarify the sense in which these words can be used and avoid potential misunderstandings.

We should be careful here. Incommensurability is always *with respect to something*, and not a feature of the alternatives as such: the same alternatives can be incommensurable in some respect, and commensurable in a different respect. In our example, the alternatives are incommensurable with respect to which house is the best for me to live in. But with respect to the requirement to fulfil my promise to my mother the alternatives are commensurable: choosing house B would fulfil that requirement completely, while choosing house A would not fulfil it at all.

What interests us most is the general moral perspective: what I am to choose *simpliciter*, or what is the most reasonable choice to make here. In our example, the two alternatives have some rational appeal, because both of them realise a relevant property whose worth provides a reason that bears on my choosing between the different alternatives. From this perspective, the choice is one regarding incommensurable alternatives. There is incommensurability between the competing advantages of the other house (its realising more than house B the property of being pretty) and whatever is good in fulfilling my promise to my mother. A further example can clarify this point. I have an absolute duty not to perform deadly experiments on my neighbour without his consent. Whatever the moral good that is brought about by complying with that requirement, it is a different one from the knowledge I would attain by experimenting on my neighbour. It is not the case that respecting my duty not to conduct such experiments on him would realise the value of knowledge to a greater or to the same degree than would be realised by conducting the experiments (or that knowledge and the good damaged by my performing the experiments are instances of some other good by which they could be commensurated), so that we could say that both alternatives realise the same value to different or the same degree, and so that the decision not to perform the experiment is the only sensible one, since it yields more knowledge, or equal knowledge plus something else valuable (respect for my neighbour's integrity, for example). If this were the case, one of the decisions would be sub-optimal. But this is not the case. Whatever is of moral relevance in each alternative cannot be reduced to what is of moral relevance in the other alternative. None of the alternatives yields 'more' of a single relevant property. Note that this does not contradict, nor is it in tension with, the idea that there is an absolute requirement on me, such that I ought to comply with a certain moral requirement (in this case, not to perform the deadly experiments on my neighbour). Whatever moral good is derived from complying with that requirement, this moral good is incommensurable with the value of knowledge, but it is still the case that that requirement makes a conclusive claim on me – and that the value of knowledge in this case does not: it simply gives me *a* reason to act in a certain way.[6]

It could be said that choices of this type (incommensurable but rationally determined) are not really incommensurable, because the criterion that makes them rationally determined excludes other alternatives, and thus there is not even a comparison between choices, and therefore incommensurability does not even arise. As a way of speaking, one can say that there is no real choice because alternatives were excluded, precisely because the decision is rationally determined. This is just another way of expressing the same moral reality. It seems clearer to me to use the word 'compare' in the sense I have been using it all along (meaning to confront the different alternatives for option, prior to moral reasoning as to whether they are to be chosen or not), and to say that the relation between the two alternatives is one of incommensurability even if the matter is settled by a conclusive reason in favour of one of them, if (and this is the moral phenomenon that my terminology makes explicit) it remains true that whatever intelligible advantages there are in the alternatives discarded, these advantages are not commensurable with the conclusive reason(s) in favour of the alternative adopted.

But in some cases no other criterion will exist that will enable one to decide according to reason between incommensurable options. In those cases we are confronted with a choice that is rationally underdetermined. Incommensurability can be part of the explanation for why a choice is rationally underdetermined.

So, the possibilities of overlap in a choice between incommensurability and rational underdeterminacy are the following four: (i) Incommensurable – Rationally underdetermined, (ii) Incommensurable – Rationally determined, (iii) Commensurable – Rationally Underdetermined, (iv) Commensurable – Rationally determined.

The first two have been explained above. With regard to choices of the type (iii), this is, choices that are both commensurable and rationally underdetermined, the obvious example is when two choices rank equally in fulfilling the relevant criteria according to which they are commensurated. When this is so, then commensuration does not determine choice,

---

[6] Of course, a utilitarian may challenge this. This is not the place to prove the utilitarian wrong. My purpose here is only to show what incommensurability means and the view of practical reason that is presupposed by talk of incommensurability, for the purposes of understanding in what sense incommensurability could be an objection to balancing tests in the context of human rights adjudication.

and thus the decision can be rationally underdetermined. Choices of the type (iv) require no special comment. Commensurability is a source of rational determinacy, which explains the attempts of many theorists to find commensurability in moral choices.

3.1.3 Incommensurability and the Possibility of Choice

The previous remarks shed light on the crucial question of how choice between incommensurable options can be made and justified. Does incommensurability imply that rational choice is impossible whenever incommensurable alternatives are at stake?

In the previous section I said that an incommensurable choice could be rationally determined or rationally underdetermined. If it is determined, then of course it is possible to choose and to justify choice even in the presence of incommensurability.

What if the decision, as it is often the case, is one between incommensurable alternatives, and it is also rationally underdetermined? It might seem that in these cases choice is always irrational: for choice to be possible it would have to be driven by instincts or whims, since there is no reason that could justify choice in these cases. But that is not so. A decision is *irrational* if it does not follow any reason. But there are reasons that can guide, motivate, and justify choosing each of the incommensurable alternatives. It is simply the case that other reasons guide, motivate, and justify choosing other alternatives, and there are no conclusive reasons in favour of any of the alternatives. But the fact that there are no conclusive reasons does not entail that there are no other reasons at stake, or that these reasons are not still reasons, and thus reasonably motivate, guide and justify choice. As Anscombe remarked: 'When I do action A for reason R, it is not necessary or even usual for me to have any special reason for doing-action-A-rather-than-action-B, which may also be possible.'[7]

What creates the incommensurability is that the criterion[8] or criteria that bear on the decision require the realisation of different irreducible properties. Realising each property is rationally appealing, but the properties are irreducible to each other (or to some other relevant property).

---

[7] GEM Anscombe, 'Philippa Foot on Double Effect: One Point' in Mary Geach and Luke Gormally (eds), *Human Life, Action, and Ethics: Essays by GEM Anscombe* (Imprint Academic 2005) 251.

[8] A single criterion could require the realisation of different properties, as in the example of the houses.

If realising each of the properties is rationally appealing, then this means that there is a reason for choosing to realise any of the properties – even if this reason is not a conclusive one. In the example of the houses, it is perfectly reasonable for me to choose to get a house that is pretty, and that attribute of house A is a good reason for me to choose that alternative. My choice is not an irrational one. It is guided by reason in that it is a choice to act in pursuit of an intelligible goal, that will deliver me a benefit, and when no other alternatives for my choice could realise that same goal to the same extent and deliver something more. Of course, I could also choose house B, and that would still be reasonable, since other benefits will come from that choice. In situations such as these, I can choose based on feelings or other (legitimate – it would be immoral to choose based on, for example, hatred towards people of a certain race) sub-rational motives ('I just feel like having a pretty house for once!'). The decision will not be irrational, because it is ultimately warranted by reasons – the different alternatives must be supported by reasons, for them to be incommensurable according to reason. The decision is *rational* (in that it is made for *a* reason) and *reasonable* (in that it is sensible to all the relevant reasons that bear on the situation).

3.1.4   *The Incommensurability Objection*

Equipped with these concepts, we can understand the idea of an incommensurability objection. Objections take place in an argumentative context; they are objections to something. The incommensurability objection is an objection against any theory or method that proposes or assumes that it is possible to commensurate what is in truth incommensurable – that proposes or assumes that one should choose the alternative that realises the different relevant properties at stake 'more' or 'to an overall greater degree', when the different properties are irreducible to each other (and to any additional one) and alternatives are ordered differently along the different properties, so that some realise more than the other alternatives one or more of the relevant properties, but less than the other alternatives some other relevant property or properties. The incommensurability objection is directed, then, against a particular kind of assessment of the different alternatives, which is characteristically quantitative. This kind of assessment of the alternatives seeks to find which alternative delivers 'more', in choices where incommensurability entails that there is no alternative that realises 'more' in the relevant sense, but 'different'. 'More' here means 'more of the same property that captures all that is required by the different criteria bearing on the choice'. But incommensurability describes a situation where the relevant criterion or criteria require the realisation of different properties, which are irreducible. This difference needs to be taken seriously. For practical reasoning, it implies that there can be no conclusive reason for choosing any of the alternatives that is based on a quantitative assessment in terms of 'which alternative realises more' of all the relevant properties.

The incommensurability objection opposes then any method that directly attempts to commensurate incommensurables. It claims that it is *senseless*, in the way it is senseless to ask whether a lot of happiness is more than a moderate amount of blue paint. The incommensurability objection also opposes any method for addressing incommensurable choices that does not explicitly commensurate the alternatives, but does compare the degree to which they realise different irreducible relevant properties and treats this comparison as a conclusive reason for choosing one over the other, thereby attributing a significance to this comparison that it does not have. It attributes to this comparison the significance it would have *if and only if these different realisations of different properties were commensurable*. The incommensurability objection claims that this method is *unfounded*. For example, in a choice between two alternatives, where the relevant criteria for choosing are to realise property X and to realise property Y, and one alternative realises a lot of X and the other realises not much of Y, the first alternative is chosen because the fact that it realises a lot of X while the other realises not much of Y *is treated as a conclusive reason for choosing it*. No explicit commensuration has occurred here, but the properties are treated as if they were commensurable, since this is what would be required for treating the greater realisation of X in relation to the realisation of Y as a conclusive reason for choosing the first alternative. But if the properties are not reducible to each other (or both to a third that captures all that is relevant about the properties at stake) the alternatives are incommensurable, and thus it is unreasonable to choose as if the alternatives were commensurable, because they are not – choosing in this way fails to take the difference between X and Y seriously.

As is clear from the discussion in the previous section, the incommensurability objection is not an objection against any decision that bears on incommensurable alternatives simply for bearing on incommensurable alternatives. Neither is it opposed to any method that presupposes a

decision between incommensurable options, or that provides a decision-
making procedure for choosing between incommensurable options. As
was shown in the previous section, there is nothing irrational in itself in
deciding between incommensurable options. [9]

---

[9] Alexander Aleinikoff, in his influential article on balancing in American Constitutional
Law, misses the point of the incommensurability objection. He claims that '[s]ome critics
of balancing surely overstate their case by claiming that balancing, because it demands
the comparison of "apples and oranges," is impossible [...]. [W]e seem regularly to reduce
value choices to a single currency for comparison [...]. We rarely hear objections that
legislatures are unable to value and compare competing social interests. Furthermore, we
expect courts to make exactly these kinds of judgments in crafting common law doctrine.'
T Alexander Aleinikoff, 'Constitutional Law in the Age of Balancing' 96 Yale LJ 943, 972.
For Aleinikoff the real problem is the following:

> The problem for constitutional balancing is the derivation of the scale needed to
> translate the value of interests into a common currency for comparison. The bal-
> ancer's scale cannot simply represent the personal preferences of the balancer [...]
> Moreover, a personal scale would undermine a system of precedent and provide
> little guidance to lower courts, legislators, administrators and lawyers and clients.
>   Balancing, therefore, must demand the development of a scale of values
> external to the Justices' personal preferences. But from where and what might
> such scale be derived? This is the problem that has bedevilled balancers for
> some time. Ibid 973.

Aleinikoff confuses two things that need to be distinguished. The first is the question of
incommensurability itself. He seems to suggest that it is a sign of commensuration that
decisions, and even reasonable decisions, can be reached in the face of incommensurable values. But the incommensurability objection challenges one particular method for
arriving at such decision, not any decision between incommensurable values or interests
(Sections 3.1.1–5; 3.7–8). Yet against that method the incommensurability objection poses
a serious challenge. It is remarkable that Aleinikoff, after having identified that no 'external
scale' was possible for a quantitative ordering of interests, failed to grasp that this was
merely an epiphenomenon of incommensurability. Since *reasons* apply to different persons,
an ordering based on reason will be 'external' in the sense that Aleinikoff seeks: it will be
an ordering that everybody can be reasonably expected to accept reasonably. On the other
hand, Aleinikoff notes that in some cases only 'personal' orderings are possible: this is also
an epiphenomenon of the fact that in those cases only non-rational orders are possible –
that is, orderings based on feelings or other such subjective preferences – and therefore
one cannot reasonably expect that others reasonably accept such orderings as 'the best',
'the correct one', and 'a reasonable one'. What this entails is precisely what Aleinikoff seems
to deny in his initial remarks on the incommensurability objection: that in some cases no
quantitative ordering along the lines of 'a common currency for comparison' is possible or
reasonable. With respect to balancing rights, the point is that these are situations where it
is not possible to strike such quantitative comparisons, unless one unreasonably reduces
the relevant considerations to those that can be quantified along a single property (as when
one measures only the economic cost of sacrificing to some degree one right versus the
economic benefit of realising some aspect of the public good). And this is why the problem
of creating 'a scale' for these cases 'has bedevilled balancers for some time'.

3.1.5   *When and How It Is Possible and*
Appropriate to Commensurate

It is generally possible to commensurate when we are concerned with the realisation of a single property, and legitimate to do so if this is a reasonable undertaking. As said above, most alternatives can be commensurated by reference to some property – but it is not always the case that that property captures all that is relevant for that choice. Nevertheless, it is useful to remember that there is an important area of human affairs in which it is not only possible but also legitimate to commensurate. For the purposes of this chapter it is useful to analyse only a few forms of legitimate commensuration, which are or could be relevant for the proportionality debate.

The first is commensuration by reference to prior commitments (see Section 3.6). I can be committed to finishing this book. If I have that commitment, I can commensurate different alternatives as more or less conducive or detrimental to that aim. The alternatives can still be incommensurable in some relevant respect (for example, in relation to their contribution to a good life), but be commensurated by reference to that commitment. There are often reasons for adopting and keeping commitments. For example, the achievement of some important goods requires commitment. A choice between alternative career paths may be an incommensurable choice, as the different career paths realise different and irreducible goods. But to achieve the goods promised by any of the alternative career paths, I must commit to one of them. Because there are reasons for adopting and keeping commitments, it may be reasonable on occasions to choose the alternative most consistent with a commitment, and thus to commensurate different alternatives *by reference to that commitment*. This does not deny that, from the perspective of the moral worth of the alternatives, the choice may still be incommensurable. Even if they are being commensurated by reference to the commitment, it remains true that (if this is a choice between incommensurable alternatives) an unchosen alternative will deliver something of value different from what is delivered by the alternative chosen for the sake of keeping the commitment. Here, as with all other incommensurable choices, the choice of whether to undertake and to keep a commitment may be incommensurable but rationally determined,

---

The second issue, the need for an 'external' standard for adjudication is, nevertheless, very important. This problem is neither specific to balancing nor related to incommensurability as such, and has a specific legal dimension. I return to this question in Chapters 7 and 8, in my critique of 'proportionality as unconstrained moral reasoning'.

and choosing one of the incommensurable alternatives can be reasonable even if the choice is rationally underdetermined (Sections 3.1.2–3).

Similarly, it is also possible, and in some cases reasonable, to commensurate artificially. This is often done in games, tests, sports, and other similar endeavours. There is no single criterion for establishing when it is reasonable to commensurate artificially, but in all the cases in which it is reasonable to do so, the reasons for it are not related to treating incommensurable attributes as if they were truly commensurable. It is more the case that for the purposes of a certain practice the incommensurability of different attributes is, in a sense, not relevant, because the point is not to compare the different alternatives with respect to their incommensurable attributes. The commonly discussed cases of legitimate artificial commensuration are not even about a choice between incommensurable alternatives. Take the example of a standardised test. A standardised test of English proficiency (such as the TOEFL test, for example) may be composed of different subtests, each of which measures one discrete aspect of English proficiency (reading, listening, writing, etc.), and assigns points based on performance on each of the subtests. Suppose these aspects are incommensurable between themselves with respect to English proficiency. Then it is not the case that the ability to read in English of a person who scores 30 points in the reading subtest is greater than the ability to understand spoken English of the person who scores 25 at the listening test. Even if there is incommensurability between the different aspects measured by the different subtests, it may be reasonable to produce an overall score by adding the points achieved in all the subtests. A doctoral programme requires a 110 combined score for its applicants who are not native English speakers. A person who performs in any of the subtests below a certain level could not achieve this score. The information given by the combined score may be enough for the purposes of the admission committee, which needs to know if someone is proficient enough in all the different aspects, and a lower performance in one area may not matter if it is above a certain threshold, which must be the case if the combined score is sufficiently high. Treating the different incommensurable aspects of English proficiency as commensurable in this precise way is reasonable. It is reasonable because it is helpful to have a summarised way of expressing performance in the test in the form of a single number (the combined score), *and* because this number is used in a way that it does not display unawareness of the incommensurability of the different aspects of English proficiency. If, for example, it was possible to achieve the required combined score performing in any of the subtests lower than what is required for undertaking the doctoral programme, then the reasonable thing to do would be not to accept the overall combined score (as we could do if the performances in the different subtests were really commensurable), but to impose a minimum requirement for each subtest.

What is relevant to understand for our purposes is that, as Finnis says, '[t]*his* sort of [artificial] cross-categorical commensuration has [. . .] only scant analogy with the problem involved in morally significant choices outside the frameworks of comparison established by prior commitments.'[10] Moral choices are about choosing alternatives or courses of action that are better or worse, more worthwhile or valuable, or less, just or unjust, etc. Precisely the kind of commensuration that would be needed in the realm of moral choice is the one that artificial commensuration such as the one commonly undertaken in tests or games cannot and does not attempt to perform. What would be needed is a commensuration that can establish which alternative is more and thus deserves to be chosen, or less and thus should not be chosen, and not the kind of ad hoc commensuration offered by artificial commensuration, at the service of a limited and artificially constructed purpose. As David Luban remarks: 'What we want is not an ad hoc rank-ordering, but a rank-ordering induced by some significant or even essential property of the items.'[11]

Finally, prices, expressed in terms of money, allow for a number of legitimate commensurations. Money is a highly abstract and universal means of exchange. It can be exchanged for any good in the market, and thus it allows for efficiency and speed of exchanges in society. The price of goods and services reflects their rate of substitution in relation to all the other goods and services in the market that have a price. Prices and money therefore allow one to commensurate things, precisely because what is being commensurated is the same attribute of objects, expressed in the same unit of measurement. The unit of measurement is money, and the attribute that it expresses is the rate of substitution in the market of the different goods and services. Therefore, prices and money allow for comparisons of goods and services along one single criterion: their rate of substitution in relation to other things available in the market.

This kind of commensuration is rational, in that what is commensurated is something that can be commensurated. It is also a reasonable undertaking, so long as what is relevant for evaluating and choosing from a set of

[10]   John Finnis, *Philosophy of Law, Collected Essays IV* (Oxford University Press 2011) 363–4 (emphasis in the original). Finnis is referring here to a similar example of artificial commensuration, the decathlon.

[11]   David Luban, 'Incommensurable Values, Rational Choice, and Moral Absolutes' (1990) 38 Clev St LR 65, 67.

alternatives is only their rate of substitution for other goods and services. I can intelligibly say that this painting is worth less (in money) than a yacht, if by that I mean that its price is less than the price of a yacht. And I can say that this painting is worth 45,000 pounds. But it is not reasonable (because not true) to think or act as if this price was the only element relevant in the comparison, and thus one cannot say that an accomplished work of art such as the painting is less valuable all things considered than the yacht, or that the value of the painting is only an economic one expressed in its price. To do so is to miss much of the value in many different alternatives or goods that have prices.

3.1.6   Value Incommensurability

I will expand on value incommensurability, since debates on balancing and proportionality commonly refer to comparisons between values.

I will understand value incommensurability in the following sense: 'value' is not a single property X, such that in a choice regarding options that instantiate two or more different non-instrumental values[12] (or instrumental values that serve different non-instrumental values), it is possible to rank the options based on whether they realise more or less or equally X in relation to the other options.

Value incommensurability is premised on the idea that certain values are irreducible to other values. It is worth fleshing out this idea. Whatever is good in realising one value, it is not the same as what is good in realising another one. It is not the case that all that is of value ultimately realise a supreme value, in relation to which all realisations of value are instrumental; or that all realisations of value are different manifestations of the same value, realising that value to the same or different degrees. One can have a word to capture a state of general value-realisation (well-being, happiness, common good, etc.), but this is not a higher value to which the other values are merely either means to, or manifestations of. What words such as well-being capture is a situation of realisation of different values – and aspects of values – which are not reducible to each other, or to any other

---

[12] The incommensurability of different values does not entail commensurability of different instantiations of the same value. Finnis, for example, holds that there can be incommensurable instantiations of the same basic good. Finnis (n 10) 357. For ease of exposition I will refer only to incommensurability of different values, though everything that I say of this type of incommensurability could also be said of incommensurable instantiations of the same value.

value to which they all are subordinated either as means or as instances of it.[13] If this is the case among a set of values, then there will be value incommensurability between the values in the set.

3.2 Incommensurability and Proportionality

Does incommensurability ground an objection against the proportionality test? Recall the *Quila* case mentioned in the previous chapter (Section 2.1). The court framed the issue as concerning a quantitative comparison between the detrimental effect of the measure on unforced marriages, and the deterrent effect on forced marriage. Yet how can these two different effects on very different interests protected by different human rights be compared quantitatively, as the court's framing of the case requires? How many forced marriages must be effectively deterred in order to compensate for the burden on the thousands of young married couples in the situation of the claimants? When can it be said that the former is 'less' or 'more' or 'equal' (or other similar terms denoting a quantitative comparison, such as 'far from', 'vastly exceeds', and 'almost the same') than the latter?

I will address these questions by focusing on Robert Alexy's theory of proportionality, which, of the main theories of the maximisation account of proportionality, is the most influential and paradigmatic of proportionality reasoning. My argument applies to the other theories of the maximisation account of proportionality as well.[14] In Alexy's theory, as said above

---

[13] It is possible to say that all values are such by sharing the property of contributing to, say, human fulfilment, in the same way that it is possible to say that all medicinal drugs share the property of contributing to human health. But this does not deny that what different values contribute to human fulfilment is essentially different, not reducible to a common property, in the same way that different medicinal drugs have different active ingredients, which produce different effects in our organism, thus contributing in different ways to health that are not reducible to each other. There is no common property shared by values in virtue of which they are all 'valuable', in the same way that there is no one active ingredient shared by all medicinal drugs in virtue of which they can all contribute to human health.

[14] Below I engage with Barak's specific argument against the incommensurability objection (Section 3.3). David Beatty's theory is premised on the idea that what morally matters in the human rights cases for which proportionality is applied is satisfaction of preferences or subjective interests (see Section 2.2.2). It could be argued that subjective interests or preferences are commensurable in principle. It is possible that a particular alternative for choice satisfies more and/or stronger preferences or interests than other alternatives. Computing the strength or quantity of these interests or preferences will be challenging, and in some cases perhaps even impossible. But in others it might be possible to compute them. And, in any case, in practice it might be hard to commensurate interests, but that does not make them incommensurable. Nevertheless, there will be incommensurability when different and irreducible criteria for satisfying preferences or interests apply to a

(Section 2.1.1), human rights are understood primarily as principles, this is, as optimisation requirements – 'norms which require that something be realised to the greatest extent possible given the legal and factual possibilities'.[15] Principles, though, typically provide different and irreducible criteria for evaluating alternatives. The different principles prescribe that different properties be realised, which are not reducible to each other. A 'conflict of principles' is one where, if there are two alternatives, one alternative ranks higher than the other in relation to realising one principle, but lower in relation to realising the other principle. As seen in the previous section, in these cases there is incommensurability. This is the case with Alexy's examples of collisions between principles: one principle requires realising freedom of expression, while another requires realising the rehabilitation of an offender, or the respect for the personality of a person offended; and one requires realising the freedom to pursue one's own profession, and the other the health of the population.[16] If principles are optimisation requirements of something that is incommensurable (realisation of irreducible principles or values), the incommensurability objection will apply to attempts to determine which alternative yields greater value or principle realisation in cases of conflicts between principles.

There is no explanation in Alexy's theory of how incommensurability can be overcome (with the exception of the brief remarks on commensurating by reference to the constitution: see below Section 3.3). As seen above (Section 2.2.1.1), for applying what he calls the 'substantial Law of Balancing', Alexy proposes a scale of light, moderate, and serious (l, m,

---

given situation, as I explain in this section. If, for example, a particular alternative satisfies a greater number of preferences or interests, but another one satisfies fewer but stronger preferences or interests, the alternatives will be incommensurable. Also if by 'interests' we refer not to subjective interests (desires or preferences) but to objective interests, that is, things that are in the interest of someone, that are good for someone, then these things can be incommensurable: whatever is good for me in being able to (say) hold religious beliefs without being offended for that, it is different from the good that you derive from (say) being able to express your opinions freely and display the product of your creative work. If it is not true that those two kinds of interests can be reduced to a common property, or one to the other, then there will be a problem of incommensurability in human rights cases where those or other similar interests are at stake. In any case, in the following chapters (see Chapters 4 and 5) I raise other objections to proportionality that apply more directly to Beatty's theory.

[15] *Theory* 47.
[16] According to Alexy, these are the principles at stake in the *Leebach* and *Titanic* cases, and in the decision on health warnings of the German Federal Constitutional Court. See *Theory* 54–6, 100, 105 (on the *Leebach* case), and *Balancing and Subsumption* 437, 438 (on the *Titanic* and health warnings cases).

and s), in relation to which to assess the intensity of interference with each principle.[17] Alexy 'breaks the balancing process down into three steps', the first two consisting in establishing the intensity of interference with each principle at stake.[18] After analysing these two steps, Alexy says: '[T]he question is now how the third step can be carried out, in which the evaluations are to be set in relationship with each other.'[19] If incommensurability is taken seriously, this is the difficult question to answer. Alexy does not engage with this question, but rather, asserts, immediately after posing the question, the circumstances under which one principle takes precedence over the other. As seen in the previous chapter, what Alexy's specification of these circumstances ultimately amounts to is that a principle takes precedence over another when it has more at stake than the opposing principle, that is, when it would be satisfied to a greater degree than the opposing principle by a decision in its favour. But if this is a choice between incommensurables, this conclusion is unwarranted. The choice is still one between realising (more or less) of one principle, and realising (more or less) of a different principle.[20] Both alternatives can contribute something different. The point of incommensurability is that this difference needs to be taken seriously.

To be clear: the comparison that Alexy's method requires so far – that is, comparing the degrees of satisfaction and non-satisfaction of the opposing principles – is an intelligible one. It is possible to say that a principle has been interfered with very much, and that another has been interfered with little. The problem is in the priority rule for establishing which of the conflicting principles has precedence, according to which the principle that should prevail is the one that has more at stake. This comparison of degrees of satisfaction of principles does not have the significance Alexy attributes to it, and therefore the priority rule posited by Alexy lacks justification. This priority rule would be justified only if the degrees of satisfaction of the principles at stake were commensurable, since, if this were the case, realising the principle that would be satisfied to a greater degree would yield 'more' of the same relevant property than realising the rival

---

[17] *Theory* 405–6. As said in previous chapter, we must not be distracted by Alexy presenting the balancing exercise as assessing the weight of the 'intensity of interference' that the measure produces to one principle, and the 'degree of importance' of satisfying the opposing principle in the way the measure does, since what it is meant by the latter is no more than the degree of satisfaction of the principle. See *Theory* 406–7, and above Section 2.2.1.1.

[18] Ibid 407.

[19] Ibid.

[20] A similar point is made by Webber in *Negotiable Constitution* 92–3.

principle. But since the degrees of satisfaction of the competing principles are incommensurable, the priority rule is not justified. Recall: the incommensurability objection also opposes any method for addressing incommensurable choices that compares the degree to which they realise different irreducible relevant properties and treats this comparison as a conclusive reason for choosing one over the other, thereby attributing a significance to this comparison that it does not have. It attributes to this comparison the significance it would have *if and only if these different realisations of different properties were commensurable* – but they are not. (I return to this issue in Sections 3.5 and 6.)

A different source of incommensurability arises from the different criteria proposed for making the comparison between the different alternatives. Defenders of quantitative balancing à la Alexy specify this comparison as one between one or more of the following criteria: the abstract importance of the conflicting (usually different) principles, the degrees of satisfaction or non-satisfaction of the principles in the possible outcomes of the case (if the measure is implemented or allowed to subsists, or if it is not), the reliability of the empirical assumptions regarding the satisfaction or non-satisfaction of the principles, and the reliability of the classification of the alternatives at stake according to the previous criteria.[21] The problem is how to bring into relation the different orderings of the alternatives that the different criteria require. What if the different alternatives ranked differently according to the different criteria? If this happens, then there is no single property that could capture all that is relevant in the different criteria, so as to produce a single ordering of the alternatives in terms of which of them realise the property more and which less.

None of these incommensurabilities can reasonably be resolved through artificial commensuration (see Section 3.1.5). Alexy undertakes this kind of commensuration in explaining what he calls the 'Weight Formula'. Above I explain the Weight Formula in some detail (see Section 2.2.1.1). The Weight Formula 'expresses the weight of a principle under the circumstances of the case to be decided',[22] this is, it expresses whether a principle is 'weightier' than (i.e., should prevail over) the rival principle at stake in that concrete case. In the formula the different considerations that are balanced (the degree of satisfaction or non-satisfaction of the conflicting

---

[21] All these criteria are explained in Matthias Klatt and Moritz Meister, *The Constitutional Structure of Proportionality* (Oxford University Press 2012). See especially the 'Weight Formula in its complete form', at 11.

[22] *Balancing and Subsumption* 444.

principles, their abstract weight, and the reliability of empirical premises regarding the satisfaction or non-satisfaction of the principles) are given numerical expression. The Weight Formula is a division that, once a number has been given to all the variables, yields a quotient. Depending on whether the quotient is more, less, or equal than one, one of the principles at stake prevails over the other, or they are thought to be of equal weight and thus discretion is granted to the primary decision-maker.[23]

But this artificial commensuration will not do: it commensurates using numbers that represent different things. Three dragons are more than one dragon, but not more or less than, or equal to, 33 years, and it makes little sense to add them or do some other mathematical operation with them. Of course, one can create an ad hoc category in relation to which one commensurates artificially, as in the example of the English test. But this, as explained above (Section 3.1.5), is not something that can be rationally done in moral choices. Here, incommensurability matters.

If the considerations at stake are incommensurable, then it makes no sense to treat them as commensurable and pretend that there is a conclusive reason for choosing one way or the other on the false ground that one alternative yields 'more principle realisation' than the other – as if it contributed everything that the other does, plus more. This is not the case when the alternatives are incommensurable. Sound practical reasoning chooses differently, based on different methods and considerations, when it faces incommensurable choices than when it faces commensurable ones (see generally Sections 3.1.2–5). If the values and principles at stake in human rights cases are different and irreducible to each other, creating incommensurable choices, sound practical reasoning needs to acknowledge this incommensurability, instead of ignoring or obscuring it.

3.3   Is There a Common Criterion for Commensuration in Proportionality Cases?

Robert Alexy and, more recently, Aharon Barak have provided a similar argument for the commensurability of rights, principles, or values.

Alexy claims that incommensurability is not a problem because one can compare human rights and public interests by reference to 'their importance for the constitution'.[24] Barak also rejects the incommensurability objection, because for him 'a common denominator' exists 'in the form of the marginal

---

[23] Ibid 440–8.
[24] Ibid 442.

social importance in fulfilling the public purpose and the marginal social importance in preventing the harm to the constitutional right.[25]

Neither Alexy's nor Barak's account escapes the incommensurability objection. As Timothy Endicott notes, in replying to this argument, '[i]dentifying a single criterion does not eliminate incommensurability, if the application of the criterion depends on considerations that are themselves incommensurable.'[26] Alexy's argument fails because it is the constitution that establishes the conflicting incommensurable values: applying the constitution to solve the question simply reproduces the problem of incommensurability. On Barak's account social importance is derived from normative sources such as philosophical traditions, social evaluations, and the legal system. It includes not only the importance of pursuing a public purpose, but also the importance of the rights that are involved.[27] If the values at stake in human rights conflicts are incommensurable, these sources will express those values, which will still be incommensurable. Being able to capture them with a word does not make them commensurable.

3.4   Strong and Weak Incommensurability

Some defences of proportionality have relied on Jeremy Waldron's distinction between strong and weak incommensurability. Thus, Klatt and Meister have seen in this distinction support for the idea that establishing an ordering of competing principles requires balancing.[28]

For Waldron,

> [s]trong incommensurability is a radical and disconcerting prospect. It suggests that two considerations, A and B, figuring on opposite sides of a practical decision-problem might be genuinely incomparable. The true state of affairs might be as follows: it is not the case that A carries more weight than B, and it is not the case that B carries more weight than A, and it is not the case that they are of equal weight.[29]

[25] *Proportionality* 484. The notion of 'social importance' in Barak's theory is explained above at Section 2.2.

[26] Timothy Endicott, 'Proportionality and Incommensurability' in Grant Huscroft, Bradley Miller, and Grégoire Webber (eds), *Proportionality and the Rule of Law* (Cambridge University Press 2014) 311, 318.

[27] *Proportionality* 365.

[28] Klatt and Meister (n 21) 62–3.

[29] Jeremy Waldron, 'Fake Incommensurability: A Response to Professor Schauer' (1993) 45 Hastings LJ 813, 815.

When faced with strong incommensurability, 'there is no basis in our knowledge of value to say that one decision rather than the other was the correct one'. Waldron insists that strong incommensurability 'is the sort of incommensurability that can leave us paralysed, not knowing what to choose' and that it 'leads to agony and paralysis in the face of immiscible values'.[30]

Weak incommensurability, on the other hand,

> is usually expressed in terms of a simple and straightforward priority rule. The claim that considerations A and B are incommensurable in this second, weak sense connotes that there is an ordering between them, and that instead of balancing them quantitatively against one another, we are to immediately prefer even the slightest showing on the A side to anything, no matter what its weight, on the B side.[31]

Waldron contrasts this 'ordering' with 'utilitarian-style weighing and balancing',[32] and holds that the ordering can be explicated in at least three ways: as one value trumping the other, as side constraints imposed on the attainment of values, and as a lexical priority between values.[33]

The difference between strong incommensurability and weak incommensurability is that in the case of strong incommensurability 'the competing values cannot even be brought into relation with one another. They are genuinely incomparable in the practical realm';[34] whereas in the case of weak incommensurability 'the values can be brought into relation'.[35] The lack of commensurability in values that are weakly incommensurable 'refers only to the absence of a common dimension of measurement that would allow trade-offs between them in either direction'.[36]

Waldron's distinction conveys an important truth, which supports my account of incommensurability in general. We might be confronted with a choice between two alternatives where, because they realise two values that are incommensurable, it will not be possible to decide between them by choosing the alternative that realises more overall value (Waldron's 'balancing alternatives quantitatively'). Nevertheless in some cases it will be possible to order the different alternatives and establish precedence of one over the other.

---

[30]   Ibid 816.
[31]   Ibid (emphasis in the original).
[32]   Ibid.
[33]   Ibid 816–17.
[34]   Ibid 817.
[35]   Ibid.
[36]   Ibid.

I think that the kinds of choices Waldron describes with the ideas of weak and strong incommensurability can be more clearly expressed in terms of incommensurability and rational underdeterminacy. This is so because the latter ideas articulate more explicitly the features in the kind of choices that Waldron is concerned with that make it possible or impossible to rationally order or rank the different alternatives.

Waldron's weak and strong incommensurability refer to the two different types of choices where incommensurability is present, which are characterised in turn by whether they are or are not rationally underdetermined. Strong incommensurability refers to choice situations where there is incommensurability between the different alternatives available, and the decision between them is rationally underdetermined. The features according to which Waldron characterises strong incommensurability do not show that it is 'strong' because there is more incommensurability present in the decision, but because of the absence of some other rational criterion that can determine what is to be done – that is, the decision is rationally underdetermined. When this happens, there is no need to characterise the situation as leading us 'to agony and paralysis'.[37] 'Paralysis' is not the right word here, because the incommensurable values at stake provide reasons for action, and thus each can rightly motivate choice (see Section 3.1.3). 'Agony', again, is not a necessary feature of incommensurable choices that are rationally underdetermined. Whether there is agony will depend on how dramatic the choice is, but not on incommensurability. And one can face a dramatic choice even when one knows what is the right thing to do: like Jean Valjean's choice between letting an innocent man be imprisoned in his place, or becoming an outlaw again.

Weak incommensurability refers to choice situations where there is incommensurability between the different alternatives, but the decision is not rationally underdetermined, because there is some moral principle at work – which can be expressed in the language of trumps, side-constraints, or lexical priority, or in some other way – that serves as a conclusive reason for choice and action.

Waldron's strong and weak incommensurability refer to two of the four possible combinations of incommensurability/commensurability and rational determinacy/underdeterminacy (see above Section 3.1.2).

It is important to highlight here that in deciding between two 'weakly incommensurable' values, one does not decide by reference to some form of commensuration of the values at stake. This is why 'weak

[37] Ibid 816.

incommensurability' is still 'incommensurability'. When it is possible to determine the ordering between alternatives for a given choice situation, it is through practical reasoning that does not consist on commensuration between values. 'Balancing', in the way it is understood in the maximisation account of proportionality, plays no role here.

3.5   Comparisons of Degrees of Satisfaction

Virgilio Da Silva has offered an important argument against the incommensurability objection – one on which a number of proponents of proportionality rely on to dismiss the incommensurability objection.[38] Da Silva claims that the debate on incommensurability is 'marked by several terminological misconceptions, which blur many of its conclusions'.[39] Da Silva is particularly concerned with authors confusing incommensurability and incomparability, or thinking that the former entails the latter.[40] On his account, 'two goods are incommensurable if there is no common measure that can be applied to all of them'.[41] But even if two goods are incommensurable, we might still be able to compare them, 'for in order to compare goods or values it is not necessary to rank them cardinally. It is enough if we are able to rank them ordinally.'[42] Da Silva claims that 'the thesis of incomparability between basic values is not important'[43] since

---

[38] See TRS Allan, 'Democracy, Legality, and Proportionality' in Grant Huscroft, Bradley Miller, and Grégoire Webber (eds), *Proportionality and the Rule of Law* (Cambridge University Press 2014) 222; and Klatt and Meister (n 21) 63. Vicky Jackson relies on a similar argument, also referring to the possibility of comparing absent a common metric, and to Luban's discussion of large/small trade-offs. See her 'Constitutional Law in an Age of Proportionality' (2015) 124 Yale LJ 3094, 3156–7.

[39] Virgilio Alfonso Da Silva, 'Comparing the Incommensurable: Constitutional Principles, Balancing and Rational Decision' (2011) 31 OJLS 273, 276.

[40] Ibid. Da Silva is right in pointing out, following Ruth Chang, that not all comparisons are made by means of measuring the compared objects. Ruth Chang, 'Introduction' in Chang (n 4) 1–2. In my use of the term, as well as in Waldron's, incommensurability is a term of art that refers to more than lack of a common measuring unit, extending also to the kind of comparisons of trade-offs that Klatt and Meister, and Da Silva propose. It is appropriate to use the same word for referring to both types of situation, since it points to a similar feature in them: that there is no property by reference to which it is reasonable to compare the different alternatives so as to decide a situation where they are in conflict by reference to a quantitative assessment concerning which alternative realises the property to a greater degree.

[41] Da Silva (n 39) 283.

[42] Ibid.

[43] Ibid 285.

comparisons and balancing are always made among concrete alternatives
and not among abstract values. When one balances between basic constitutional rights, she [sic] does not intend to compare the abstract values of,
say, freedom of expression and privacy, or of economic development and
protection of the environment. What one intends is always to compare the
numerous possibilities of protecting and realising such rights in a concrete
situation and to weigh among them.[44]

This, for Da Silva, presents an opportunity for commensuration.
Following Alexy, Da Silva claims that 'what is at stake' is the 'degree of
satisfaction and non-satisfaction in this specific concrete case' of values
or principles.[45] Degrees of satisfaction and non-satisfaction can be compared. For this he uses Alexy's scale of degrees of interference, which cat-
egorises interferences as 'light', 'moderate', or 'serious'. For Da Silva, what
Alexy shows with his scale is that 'no matter which principles are at stake,
what should be compared is the trade-off between the satisfaction of one
principle and the non-satisfaction of the other one'. Da Silva concludes
that this kind of 'trade-off analysis [. . .] makes comparisons easier and, by
creating commensurability between what is to be compared, leads to the
possibility of rational choices'.[46]

Da Silva's argument fails to undermine the incommensurability objection. Grégoire Webber has argued that the degrees of satisfaction and non-
satisfaction of each principle are 'taken only from the perspective of the
principle being evaluated'.[47] Therefore, 'one should not assume that [for
example] a light interference with one principle is of the same measure as a
light interference with another principle'.[48] Da Silva's reply to this objection
is that they are in fact comparable. To illustrate this he provides a hypothetical based on a case mentioned by Webber: a conflict between the wish
of some religious people to display religious signs in their houses, and a
contractual prohibition of decorations, alternations, and construction on
the balconies of co-owned property.

> Imagine that wearing a kippah or a veil would [. . .] be strictly forbidden,
> and in such a scenario, praying might also be forbidden if it might be heard
> from outside the flats. The goal of this clause would be, say, to promote
> equality among residents. Since not every resident has a religion and since
> not every religion has external signs, let us imagine that it was decided

---

[44] Ibid 286.

[45] Ibid.

[46] Ibid 287 (citation omitted).

[47] Grégoire Webber, 'Proportionality, Balancing, and the Cult of Constitutional Rights
Scholarship' (2010) 23 Can JL & Juris 179, 196, quoted in Da Silva (n 39) 289.

[48] Webber (n 47), quoted in Da Silva (n 39) 289.

that equality among residents would be better protected through a ban of every sign of religion inside the building. Let us suppose that several residents filed lawsuits against this clause. In its report, the court states that the interference with the freedom of religion was serious, while the degree of promotion of equality was practically irrelevant. Until this moment, no comparison has been made.[49]

For Da Silva it is obvious that the differences of satisfaction of the competing principles can be established. From this, he immediately draws the following conclusion:

> The evaluations of the degrees of interference and satisfaction were made completely independent of one another. Does this mean that we cannot compare them? Would it be irrational to decide that religious freedom should have precedence in this case? Webber's arguments are not convincing.[50]

It is intelligible to say that one value or principle would be more affected than another one if a certain choice did not favour it, in the same way that we can say that a person has more to lose in a given situation than another person.[51] But this does not undermine the incommensurability objection, because if the principles (or the values they promote) are incommensurable, the choice between them is still a choice between incommensurables. To choose between a lot of one value, and a little of a different one, is still to choose between incommensurables with respect to overall value-realisation. The temptation is to think that because the incommensurable values at stake are realised to different degrees, we can assert that one of the choices is somehow sub-optimal. That there is a net gain in choosing to realise the principle that has more at stake, instead of the principle that could be realised (or would be sacrificed) only a little. But this is not so. If it is still true that whatever is good in realising one of the values at stake is different from whatever is good in realising the other value, and that they cannot be reduced to each other or to some higher or common value, then there is no sub-optimal decision here. Therefore, as said above (Section 3.1.4), that one value could be realised to a great degree and another to a reasonably small degree is no conclusive reason for choosing any of the alternatives.[52]

---

[49] Da Silva (n 39) 290.
[50] Ibid 291.
[51] This does not entail that it is always possible to make this kind of comparison.
[52] Da Silva's example can be misleading, in that he presents the degree of promotion of one of the principles at stake (equality) as 'practically irrelevant'. If that were so, then there would be no opposing values at stake. See Section 3.6 on 'trivial benefits'.

Da Silva is right in claiming that establishing degrees of satisfaction and non-satisfaction is not a purely technical enterprise.[53] The problem is not that proportionality and balancing do not require any moral reasoning, but rather that they require the wrong kind of moral reasoning, one that is too narrowly focused on comparisons of degrees of satisfaction and non-satisfaction of values, which, while intelligible, treat as commensurable what is incommensurable, and thus, are open to the incommensurability objection.

3.6   False Commensurability and Large/Small Trade-offs

Some challenges to the incommensurability objection consist in pointing to examples of cases where our common sense intuition is that we decide by commensurating what incommensurability theorists would consider incommensurable values or principles. The force of this challenge is not clear. Intuitions can be wrong. Because of this, we test our intuitions through rational debate, and try to provide a rational justification of the judgements that we arrive at by intuition. A dissonance between rational conclusions and intuitions is a reason for *revising* one or the other or both,[54] but it is not a sufficient reason for abandoning the former. One theory is not preferable to another simply by virtue of being compatible with common sense intuitions, if rational scrutiny establishes that it is flawed. This amounts to the following for the purposes of the incommensurability objection: even if it were shown that some of our intuitions point against the incommensurability objection in some cases, that would not be a sufficient reason to abandon it, until there is a positive account of how moral reasoning proceeds by commensurating what incommensurability theorists regard as incommensurable.

In any case, I believe that attempts to present examples of commensurations that the incommensurability objection claims that we cannot perform ultimately fail. This is so either because the example at stake does not require commensuration, or because the example does illustrate a commensuration, just not of the type that the incommensurability objection rules out.

---

[53] Ibid 288.

[54] In the same spirit that a discrepancy between principles arrived at by a theory of justice and considered convictions of justice provides an opportunity for revising both, 'for even the judgements we take provisionally as fixed points are liable to revision' – as articulated by John Rawls' presentation of the idea of reflective equilibrium. See John Rawls, *A Theory of Justice* (rev edn, Harvard University Press 1999) 18.

The former is the case in an argument made by Da Silva. He claims that

> There are several examples which show that it is not only possible, but also necessary, to compare basic values. As for the example involving love and freedom [as involving two basic, and thus incommensurable and incomparable values], someone could be willing to forego a part of his freedom in order to live with the woman he loves, even if she lives in a country where human rights and basic liberties are not fully protected.[55]

But this reply misses the point. The incommensurability objection, as said above (Section 3.1.4), does not claim that it is impossible or unreasonable to choose between incommensurable values – it just claims that one cannot commensurate them (or compare them, in Da Silva's terminology). Da Silva's example is one of choosing between incommensurable values, not one of commensurating them. In the example there are two incommensurable values at stake. A mark of this incommensurability is that something is sacrificed: a degree of freedom. Whatever is gained in love does not compensate in kind the loss in freedom. Whatever reason one might have to make that decision, or the contrary, cannot be based on a method that attempts to quantify the potential gains derived from choosing each alternative, and determine which decision would yield a net gain. Nevertheless, as Da Silva rightly says, 'someone could be willing to' choose one of the alternatives, and assume the cost in terms of the sacrifice from the perspective of the other value. But this does not imply that the decision is based on commensuration.

There is a type of choice where our intuition seems to be that we decide between incommensurable values based precisely on there being a net gain on one choice rather than the other. This is the case of large/small trade-offs. Da Silva illustrates this quoting a hypothetical from David Luban:

> A college athlete, who has no intention of playing his sport professionally after graduation, finds that he can become very slightly more proficient by undertaking a new, very time-consuming training schedule. He is already proficient enough to play his sport at a high level. His academic counsellor warns him that the extra time spent on training will have devastating effects on his studies. Is it rational for the athlete to undertake the program?[56]

Da Silva treats as evident that in the example 'there is no trace of incomparability, and it seems that a rational choice is not only possible, but rather clear', since for most of us it would be obvious that the athlete would

---

55 Da Silva (n 39) 285.
56 Ibid 287, quoting from Luban (n 11) 65.

be irrational in doing the extra training. For Da Silva it is obvious that '[t]he reason for this is the existence of a clear large/small trade off'.[57]

But a closer look at Luban's hypothetical shows that it is far from supporting Da Silva's point. In Luban's example a particular commitment is presupposed by characterising the athlete as someone 'who has no intention of playing his sport professionally after graduation'. As Finnis explains in his reply to Luban's paper:

> The commensuration we make or presuppose when we judge it irrational for this athlete to undertake the programme is made possible not by the size of the respective gains and losses in different basic goods, but by the plan of life which this athlete has already adopted (chosen) – by his commitments to whatever he needs his college studies for (medical practice . . . classical scholarship . . .). We could judge the very same gain in athletic proficiency and loss in scholastic performance rational if we were told that this young man is in college in order to get into the pro's.[58]

Once a particular life project is chosen, one can rank alternatives according to which ones are more helpful in realising that project. Luban's hypothetical illustrates commensuration *by reference to commitment* – and not a large/small trade-off that rationally determines an incommensurable choice, as Da Silva suggests. Note that the alternatives are only commensurable by reference to a particular commitment. It is not the case that commitments, or more generally, life projects, provide a general way to commensurate all alternatives. Sometimes alternatives can be incommensurable by reference to a commitment (if I have a commitment to fulfil criteria A and B, and my two alternatives rank differently along the two criteria). In other cases, it may not be reasonable to follow one's commitments or life projects, and therefore, it may not be reasonable to commensurate by reference to them. Commitments play an important but limited role in dealing with incommensurable choices. As said above, sometimes it is reasonable to adopt and to keep a commitment, and therefore to commensurate alternatives by reference to that commitment, but this does not eliminate the incommensurability of the alternatives from the perspective of their moral worth (see above Section 3.1.5).

It could be objected that there are indeed large/small trade-offs that rationally determine incommensurable choices, even if Luban's hypothetical is not an example of them. Take the hypothetical of the houses mentioned above. House A is prettier, but house B is bigger. The properties

[57] Da Silva (n 39) 287.
[58] Ibid 362.

relevant for determining which house is better are beauty and size (and the two properties have equal importance). This decision is one where the alternatives are incommensurable. Now, suppose house B is an always growing house, which becomes bigger and bigger each day (in an harmonic way, so that the increase in size adds value to the house: it grows in number of rooms, closet space, and so on), until someone chooses it. The beauty of both houses and the size of house A remain constant. Is there a point where we can say that house B is so much bigger than house A that it would be unreasonable not to choose it?[59]

Some people's intuitions are that there is such point where house B simply becomes a better house than house A, and therefore it would be unreasonable to choose house A, if one should choose the best house. Below I suggest that this view is implausible and that upon reflection it is not intuitively appealing. But, leaving intuitions aside, the idea that even in this case the options are incommensurable is supported by the account of moral choice and action explained in Section 3.1. The believer in large/small commensurations may remain unconvinced. He may understand the argument behind the incommensurability objection, but realise that it challenges so frontally some of his moral intuitions that he is not prepared to accept it. He may suspend judgement until he arrives at a positive account of how large/small commensurations of otherwise incommensurable alternatives are possible. This may be a reasonable thing for him to do. But none of this amounts to an intellectual challenge to the incommensurability objection.

Here we can introduce a weaker form of the incommensurability objection. The 'weak incommensurability objection' claims the following: proposals in favour of quantitative balancing must be abandoned unless they are accompanied by an account of how it is possible to commensurate the different rights and public goods at stake, and why this commensuration is morally relevant. What is at stake in the debate on balancing tests and proportionality is the important question of when it is justified to limit a human right. The 'weak incommensurability objection' is grounded on the idea that any controversial method for deciding such an important matter must be backed by reasons – particularly since reasons have been offered against it. It cannot be simply supported by the intuitions of those defending it.

Nevertheless, it is true that we have a sense that there are large/small trade-offs. Thus, it is useful to explore the ways in which it may seem that a decision is based on commensurating incommensurable alternatives.

---

[59] I thank Timothy Endicott for this hypothetical.

In some cases legitimate commensurations are hidden. This happens, for example, when the goods at stake have market value, such that the set of incommensurable alternatives could be improved by a series of transactions. This I will call 'improving alternatives'. The example of the houses is artificial, because we know that houses have market value, and that the decision is never limited absolutely (say, to house A or B), but commonly limited by budgetary considerations. Suppose I am buying a house, and if I had more money, my choice would be between houses A' and B', each better with respect to every relevant criterion than houses A and B. This can help understand why in the hypothetical above, where house B is presented as a growing house, *there could be a reason* to choose that house over the other, if we make more realistic some of the features of the hypothetical. This is not because there is a commensuration between the size of house B and the beauty of house A. It is because choosing house B can be part of a set of actions aimed at producing a general improvement of the choices, so that one can end up with an overall better house than the ones offered by one's initial alternatives. This will be so when, for example, the bigger house B is (within certain limits?), the greater its market value. If the question is presented as a choice between houses A and B, and one imagines that house B 'grows', and that regardless of its growth I can still choose it, then there may come a point where choosing a house of the size of house B can be part of a course of action that yields an overall better alternative: *ex hypothesi* I can still afford house B, whatever its size (which means that the price at which it is offered to me cannot rise above a certain level), but there must be a point where its growth in size has increased its market value considerably. The overall best house is not the now huge house B in relation to the prettier house A, but houses A' or B', which become live alternatives only through buying and selling house B for a profit, when house B is big enough to have an economic value that could match house A' or B'.[60]

The commensurations in a comparison such as the one between house A and the now very big house B ground no challenge against the incommensurability objection, because there is no commensuration between the incommensurable attributes of the houses with respect to which house is better – not even between large/small realisations of the relevant properties. *This* commensuration is still impossible. This becomes clear when we think about choices involving different intrinsic values. It is better to have more true friends than few, and it is better to have a great ability to

---

[60] Analogous legitimate commensurations can take place when one of the alternatives entails a general worsening of future alternatives.

appreciate music than to have it in a small degree. Having three friends but being able to appreciate music only to a small degree is not better or worse than, or equal to, having only one friend and a great ability to appreciate music. What about having a million true friends? Can we imagine a point where a certain quantity in the realisation of friendship could become 'better' than the alternative of having only one friend but also a great ability to appreciate music? If these were alternatives for choice, could someone really say that there is a point (say, at 10 million real friends) where the first alternative is the only reasonable one, and choosing to have only one friend and a great ability to appreciate music would be an unreasonable choice? Here, it seems to me that there is not even the appearance of commensuration. No alternative seems better, and no increase in the realisation of the value of friendship offered by the first alternative could provide a conclusive reason for choosing that alternative instead of the other. But then again, someone could say 'I do not share *that* intuition', and we would have to set aside the hypotheticals and their appeal to intuitions, and engage in theoretical debate on incommensurability.

Another type of situation that may seem to involve commensuration of incommensurable values is what I call 'value overflow'. It takes place when one alternative realises one value, and the other realises that value plus something. There is no incommensurability here, since the same value is realised by both alternatives, and one of them realises some additional value. This is commonly the case when instrumental values are considered. You can choose to have a job that does not allow you time to work out – which would contribute to your health – but pays very well, or a job that allows you time to work out, but pays considerably less. So, the decision might seem to be one between certain amounts of money and a particular instantiation of the value of health. But if accepting the job will allow you to afford excellent healthcare, which, in your concrete circumstances, has a greater impact in your overall health than working out regularly (perhaps because you have some illness), then the decision is not between incommensurable alternatives: both realise the value of health, one to a greater degree than the other.[61]

'Value overflow' can also take place in a choice between different alternatives that directly realise different values, but for one of the alternatives the benefits of realising one value are such that, as a consequence, some other values are realised as well, including those that would have been

---

[61] Though if, for example, the value of working out goes beyond its contribution to your health, the choice can be incommensurable.

realised by the other alternatives, which are realised equally or to a greater degree by the former alternative. For example: a student could keep a very demanding study schedule, and lock herself in the library, thus realising the value of knowledge. Or she could have a less demanding study schedule, and allow some time to meet some other students and make new friends. So one alternative directly realises the value of knowledge, and the other the value of friendship. But the second alternative may also realise the value of knowledge, because it allows her to participate more fully in an academic community, having interesting discussions about scholarly topics, getting information on interesting talks that she might have otherwise missed, etc. Suppose the second alternative realises the value of knowledge to a similar or greater degree than the first.[62] In this kind of situation the alternatives are commensurable, and there are sub-optimal alternatives, but the commensurability is hidden precisely because the values more directly at stake are in fact incommensurable, and one needs to imagine or calculate the indirect consequences of a decision (something we perhaps do as a habit, unconsciously) to see the possibility of commensuration.

Another type of situation that may mislead one into thinking that it involves commensuration of incommensurable values is what I call 'successive value realisation'. It is based on the idea that one chooses and participates in different values during a lifetime, and plans general schemes of action that allow one to participate in those values more fully given one's concrete circumstances. I could stay a few more hours at my desk and seize this rapture of inspiration for completing a poem, or I could go outside and contemplate the sunset. But the sunset will be there tomorrow while the conditions of inspiration that will allow me to make this a good poem might not present themselves again. Whatever is good in writing a good poem, it is not the same as and does not deliver whatever is good in watching the sunset, so, there can be no commensuration between writing a good poem or watching the sunset. Here the values at stake are still incommensurable. But there is no need to choose: on one course of action both values could be realised at different moments (today and tomorrow), and on the other only one of the values. At times we can confuse these situations for large/small trade-offs, because it is easy to confuse 'large' with 'exceptional' (they are often companions) and 'small' with 'ordinary'. But what justifies our sense that this choice is rationally determined is that on one course of action we could instantiate both values (seizing the

---

[62] It could also be that what is at stake are incommensurable aspects of the same value (different and irreducible forms of knowledge) – and then the choice is incommensurable.

exceptional opportunity for instantiating one of the values now, leaving the ordinary opportunity for instantiating the other later), and on the other we could only instantiate one (the one that could be instantiated by the ordinary opportunity). Nevertheless, if there were a need for choosing to instantiate only one value (say, this will be the last sunset), it would be a choice between incommensurable alternatives. And sometimes the opportunity to do something later will not allow for the realisation of the same value, or to the same degree, and there will be no 'successive value realisation'.

A different way in which a decision can seem to be rationally determined in the way the idea of large/small trade-offs suggests is when the benefits derived from one alternative are so small that they become 'negligible' or 'trivial'. These terms, or other similar ones, are common in descriptions of purported large/small commensurations.[63] This situation is the reverse of 'value overflow', and I will refer to it as 'trivial benefits'. It is true that when there are 'trivial benefits' there is no incommensurability. But this is not because the incommensurable values can be commensurated, but because in this case there is not really a choice between different instantiations of value. Negligible or trivial benefits are no benefits at all. Those words mean that the benefits they designate, literally, do not matter. This is what 'trivial' means, and what 'negligible' (that I can treat as if it did not matter) implies. So, if I am confronted with two options, and one of them realises a value to a negligible degree, and the other realises a value, period, then I am not really confronted with a choice between incommensurable values, because one of the alternatives does not realise a value at all. The decision is clear and one of the alternatives is sub-optimal. There is no real trade-off. This can be illustrated with the example of the student athlete: is it worth it to decide to train when one can improve one's performance only to a trivial degree (assuming that the value of training is in improving performance), sacrificing study? Of course it is not, because there would be no value in the first option. But if we introduce some value in that alternative (for example, the benefit of forming character by training a bit harder), the choice stops being intuitively obvious, because we will be confronted with a real choice between incommensurable values.[64]

---

[63] Da Silva (n 39) 290; Endicott (n 26) 321.

[64] It is worth insisting that my point here is completely analytical. Words such as 'trivial' or 'negligible' imply that there is no realisation of value. I do not argue that in some cases that we think we are realising some value to a small degree we are actually not realising any value, or that small realisations of value do not matter. I only argue against a way of speaking of certain alternatives for choice as if they instantiated some value, when in effect it is meant that (and they are treated as if) they did not.

There is no reason to think that it is possible to commensurate incommensurable values in the presence of large/small trade-offs. There is no good theoretical explanation for this possibility, and our examination of examples of situations where we seem to commensurate in the face of large/small trade-offs shows that they can be explained as instances of commensuration by reference to a commitment (itself not justified by reference to commensuration of the values at stake), 'improving alternatives', 'value overflow', 'successive value realisation', or 'trivial benefits'. To this we should also add those cases where, despite incommensurability, there is a conclusive reason that bears on our choice, so that the decision is rationally determined (see Section 3.1.2). I do not know whether these categories exhaust the ways in which it seems that we decide by commensurating incommensurable alternatives. But they at least deal with the kinds of examples that are discussed in the literature on proportionality. Further examples might be provided for discussion, but it is the burden of those challenging the incommensurability objection to present them, and to show that those examples are in fact examples of commensuration of the kind ruled out by the incommensurability objection.

3.7 Cleaning the Augean Stables?

Paul Craig has noted that many legal doctrines either consist in a choice between incommensurable values, or allow courts to choose between things that are incommensurable. He argues that if the reason for abandoning balancing is that the alternatives between which the test needs to decide are incommensurable, then we should also abandon many other established legal doctrines.[65]

But the incommensurability objection does not claim that one cannot or should not choose between incommensurable alternatives (Sections 3.1.3–4). So, if some legal doctrines rely on a choice between incommensurable alternatives, or establish a procedure for choosing between incommensurable alternatives, this is not in itself challenged by the incommensurability objection. Accepting the incommensurability objection commits one to reject a particular method for establishing what to choose when confronted with certain incommensurable alternatives, but it does not commit one to reject any choice between incommensurable alternatives.

---

[65] Paul Craig, 'The Nature of Reasonableness Review' (2013) 66 Current Legal Problems 131, 150–5.

3.8   Incommensurability in Law

In relation to the many legal cases where some form of incommensurability bears on the decision of the court, Timothy Endicott argues that '[l]egal
systems justifiably – and, in fact, necessarily – authorise judges to recon-
cile incommensurable considerations'.[66] He presents as example of this the
fact that courts need to determine compensation for civil damages (e.g. to
establish how much money would compensate for physical suffering) and
criminal sentencing (to establish exactly how much time in prison a person should spend as punishment for a particular offence).

The general point underlying Endicott's remarks is correct: we sometimes need legal systems to specify what reason leaves underdetermined
(whatever explains why the issue is rationally underdetermined, be it
incommensurability or some other feature of the situation). Does this save
quantitative balancing from the incommensurability objection?

It does not. As said above (Sections 3.1.2–3), it is possible to choose
reasonably in cases where there are incommensurable alternatives. But
balancing tests do not only provide the opportunity for choosing, but
also a method for doing so. If this method presupposes that the alternatives are commensurable when they are not, it is an unsound method.
Furthermore, if proportionality and balancing simply provided the opportunity for choosing between incommensurable alternatives, it would still
be open to criticism. In the legal context, proportionality and balancing
tests are not institutions established by the law to provide for an authoritative decision in cases where there is a rationally underdetermined choice
to be made. They are used in the context of judicial review of what others have determined. Methods for judicial review must meet a burden
that decisions of primary decision-makers need not meet. The latter can
be justified simply by reference to the need for an authoritative decision
in a particular matter, even when this decision is rationally underdetermined. It is no argument against this reason for granting authority to a
decision-maker to settle the issue that the decision between the different
alternatives is rationally underdetermined, if there is still need for a decision to be made. But a method for judicial review claims to do more than
to settle matters that are rationally underdetermined. It claims to establish
whether the decision of a primary decision-maker that settles the issue is
somehow deficient. Proportionality and balancing should be evaluated on
these terms. The incommensurability objection shows one way in which

---

[66]   Endicott (n 26) 324.

a particular method for judicial review fails in serving judges to establish whether a particular decision of a primary decision-maker was deficient, because it commits them to an unsound method that presupposes a commensuration of incommensurables.

Note that my argument does not amount to a general critique of judicial review. Its implications for judicial review are more modest: it only criticises a particular way of understanding what is morally at stake in human rights cases. Whether there should be judicial review, and the form it should take, depends on what are the relevant moral requirements at stake, and whether the institutional interaction that best fulfils these requirements is one that includes judicial review. Requirements of justice, the application of which does not depend on such a quantitative assessment, may be the most relevant moral consideration bearing on human rights cases (see below Chapters 4 and 5). My account of incommensurability leaves room for such requirements of justice. As shown above, incommensurability does not rule out the existence of reasons that determine choice in favour of one of the alternatives, and, therefore, incommensurability does not rule out the existence of requirements of justice that have the peremptory normative force often associated with human rights. Now, the best institutional arrangement to secure these requirements may be one that includes some form of human rights judicial review. This question of institutional design depends on the concrete circumstances of a particular society. The argument of this chapter does not settle these issues.

3.9   Conclusion

According to the view of incommensurability presented here, the incommensurability objection is narrower in scope than some have thought. It does not challenge every choice between incommensurable alternatives, and it does not even claim that every choice between such alternatives is rationally underdetermined. Nevertheless, the incommensurability objection is still relevant. It is an important challenge to a widespread account of proportionality – the maximisation account of proportionality – and it dispels the illusion that some form of technical commensuration of rights and public goods is possible. This does not mean that human rights cases cannot be decided reasonably. It only means that a certain method for deciding them is unsound: any method (commonly aimed at maximisation) in human rights cases that attempts to commensurate between incommensurables, be they human rights, public goods, interests or preferences, constitutional values or principles.

Why Proportionality?

In this chapter I present the following objection to the maximisation account of proportionality: even if it were possible to strike a comparison of the kind proposed by theories of the maximisation account between a human right and a conflicting human right or public good, there would still be no reason for treating this comparison as a morally decisive criterion for deciding human rights cases. It is one thing for a criterion to be capable of application, another for it to be the appropriate criterion for deciding a particular matter. The criterion will be appropriate if it captures the relevant moral considerations that bear on the situations to which the criterion is to be applied, and the relations between these considerations. This question is at the heart of what I have called 'the moral perspective': what is it that is of moral relevance in the human rights cases to which proportionality is applied? In particular, are the comparisons proposed by the theorists of the maximisation account of proportionality all that is morally relevant, or even part of what is morally relevant, in human rights cases?

4.1 Is Proportionality 'Rational'?

Much of the debate about the proportionality test revolves around the question of whether proportionality is a rational form of adjudication, or, on the contrary, is an arbitrary one. Bernhard Schlink argues that 'the balancing of rights, interests and values [. . .] is unavoidably subjective'.[1] Jürgen Habermas claims that because 'there are no rational standards' for bringing values associated with constitutional rights into a 'transitive ordering with other values from case to case [. . .] weighing takes place either arbitrarily or unreflectively'.[2] Proportionality would fail to provide

---

[1] Bernhard Schlink, 'Proportionality in Constitutional Law: Why Everywhere but Here' (2012) 22 Duke J Comp & Int'l L 291, 299. See also Bernhard Schlink, 'Proportionality (1)' in Michel Rosenfeld and András Sajó (eds), *The Oxford Handbook of Comparative Constitutional Law* (Oxford University Press 2012) 725.
[2] Jürgen Habermas, *Between Facts and Norms* (William Rehg tr, MIT Press 1996) 259.

judges with a method that can be rationally applied for arriving at a decision in human rights cases.

Alexy's well-known defence of his theory against these objections focuses on showing that proportionality does provide a method for addressing human rights cases (and thus does not amount to free, open-ended moral reasoning), and that this method is rational. As seen above (Section 2.2.1), in the basic application of Alexy's method for balancing,[3] the question is whether the non-satisfaction of one principle is compensated by the satisfaction of the competing principle. Alexy addresses this by evaluating whether the degree of non-satisfaction of the principle affected by the measure under review is greater than the degree to which the measure satisfies the competing principle. In his reply to Habermas, Alexy notes how it is possible to rationally establish the different degrees of satisfaction or non-satisfaction of the principles at stake (whether the satisfaction is 'high' or the non-satisfaction or interference 'light', etc.) in different cases. Alexy concludes that: 'The assumptions underlying judgements about intensity of interference and degree of importance are not arbitrary. Reasons are given for them which are understandable.' For Alexy, '[t]his disproves the thesis that balancing in the final analysis permits anything because it lacks rational standards. To that extent the Law of Balancing survives Habermas' objections.'[4]

What Alexy seems to attempt to establish is that his method can be rationally applied, that is, that the method can inform a process of reasoning towards the solution to the case, without recourse to feelings, prejudices, or other irrational grounds that eventually decide the matter; and, thus, that the correctness of the application of the method can be rationally assessed. This is what Alexy means by his theory of proportionality being 'rational'.

But this debate misses a more fundamental question – one that is already suggested in my treatment of the incommensurability objection, but is worth now spelling out. Is it reasonable to apply the proportionality test to human rights cases?

Proponents of the maximisation account of proportionality have not explicitly addressed this problem. The debate on rationality and balancing, which takes as a point of reference Alexy's theory, raises the question

---

[3] This is, when the different principles at stake are not of different abstract weight, and when the empirical premises regarding their satisfaction or non-satisfaction are equally reliable. Alexy's 'elementary version' of the Weight Formula expresses the degrees of satisfaction or non-satisfaction of the relevant principles. See *Balancing and Subsumption* 444.

[4] *Theory* 405.

of whether proportionality is a method that can be applied by reasoning, yielding an outcome that is rationally determined by the method. But there is one sense of 'rationality' that this debate has not addressed, for which some may prefer to use the word 'reasonableness'. This sense is not about whether the method can be applied by reason, but about whether it is reasonable to apply that particular method in addressing a certain type of problem. Suppose I have a method for deciding which watermelon I will buy when I go to the market. I simply choose the biggest. This is a rational method in the sense that I can establish through rational means which watermelon is the biggest. Other people can reconstruct my reasoning in choosing watermelons by applying my same method, and a mark of this is that they will be able to predict my decisions. Now, am I unreasonable in choosing watermelons based on their size? Probably not. But if I choose books on proportionality based on that same method, that would be unreasonable. This is not because reason cannot apply the method to decide which book to buy, or judge whether the application of the method is correct or not, ultimately having to rely on feelings or prejudices. People can assess which book on proportionality is the biggest in the store, and there is nothing subjective about that process. Yet it is wrong – unreasonable, if not totally unguided by reason – to use that method because there is no reason that justifies using that method for buying books on proportionality. Unless I want a book on proportionality to fill a gap in my shelf with books on proportionality, using that method would fail to capture the relevant considerations that apply to such a decision. Thus, using that method would be unreasonable even though it is true both that the method itself can be applied through reasoning and that the correctness of its application (whether the decision is really warranted by the method) can be rationally assessed.

4.2 Quantitative Comparisons and Rights Adjudication

The question here is not whether it is possible to engage in the kind of quantitative analysis of which the balancing stage of the proportionality test (on the maximisation account of proportionality) is representative. The question here is rather whether proportionality, as understood in the maximisation account of proportionality, is appropriate for deciding cases regarding limitations of human rights. This, in turn, depends on whether proportionality is able to capture the morally relevant considerations that should bear on the kinds of cases that we are assessing. As said before (Section 2.2), the maximisation account of proportionality is aimed at maximising values, principles, interests, or preferences. This supposes that what morally matters in human rights cases is precisely to maximise that which the proportionality test is aimed at maximising. But, is it?

The point relates to the kinds of quantitative comparisons that the proportionality test, and especially its balancing stage, is designed to perform for evaluating whether a purported interference with a human right is justified or not. In the previous chapter the claim was that generally in human rights cases it is not possible to perform those comparisons. Here I will argue that it is not morally pertinent to attempt to do so.[5] The two problems – whether it is possible to balance and whether it is pertinent to do so – are obviously related. The point of incommensurability theories is not that there is nothing commensurable between two different potential objects for choice. The point is rather that some considerations are incommensurable, and if these considerations are the relevant considerations in a particular choice situation, then the choice may be between incommensurable options, if the different options rank differently according to the incommensurable considerations. The considerations that are relevant for a given choice are not necessarily the considerations that can be commensurated. Whether they can or cannot be commensurated is not a criterion of relevance. Therefore, it is possible that the considerations that are relevant are incommensurable. Here, the question is whether the considerations that maximisation accounts of proportionality try to capture (whether they can be commensurated or not, or compared on some level) are the properly decisive considerations for deciding human rights cases.

As in my example above, if I have to choose to get a book on proportionality, and can only choose a limited amount (say, one), I will normally be confronted by a number of alternatives that are incommensurable, since they realise to different degrees properties that are relevant for my choosing (some books are more original, some are more rigorous, some more exactly pertinent to my topic, etc.). But I can adopt as a criterion for choosing books on proportionality 'always choose the biggest book you can afford'. That criterion makes commensurable alternatives that could otherwise be incommensurable, and allows me to produce one ranking of the alternatives, categorising each alternative in terms of bigger or smaller than, or of equal size to, each other. So this criterion solves the problem

---

[5] Kai Möller has previously manifested doubts about the pertinence of balancing in *Challenging Critics* 719: '[i]t is not clear that even in cases where there is indeed a common scale balancing the conflicting goods on that scale is appropriate. [. . .] I believe that there are many cases where balancing on a common scale, while possible, would be inappropriate: but I cannot prove this point here.'

of incommensurability, and has many of the advantages that theorists of proportionality praise about the test:[6] it provides rational determination for choice, and as a consequence, provides predictability in the decision-making process, objectivity (it does not depend on me but on an impersonal standard), transparency (the decision-making procedure can be rationally reconstructed by an observer), and neutrality (because the procedure is fact-based the personal values of the person applying it do not come into play). The problem is that it is a silly criterion to apply. There is no reason for me to make that choice based on that criterion. I have better reasons to decide on the irreducible properties that specify desirable aspects of a book on proportionality.

This applies to adjudication as well. Imagine that my eating a diet rich in vitamins is in conflict with your plan to travel to Patagonia (perhaps because you have a contractual obligation of providing the healthy vegetables that I need, and I cannot get them otherwise, but you cannot travel if you have to provide me with my vegetables). Suppose we can commensurate my subjective interest (the strength of my desire, for example) in eating vitamins with your subjective interest in a trip to Patagonia. Even if we could compare the stringency of those interests and arrive at an intelligible account of preference satisfaction or optimisation in the concrete case, it is not clear why this would be relevant for moral or legal discourse.

This is why the attempts made by defenders of the maximisation account of proportionality to defend the possibility of balancing are incomplete in an important respect. Showing that there is something comparable, or that there is a formula that allows for deciding between incommensurables, is not enough. They need to prove both that something can be balanced in the way they claim, *and* that balancing is the relevant criterion to solve the particular case. Why would the morally decisive consideration be, as Alexy's substantial Law of Balancing prescribes, the degree of satisfaction or non-satisfaction of the principles at stake, so that we should consider 'disproportionate' a measure that greatly interferes with a principle, but satisfies to a moderate degree a different one (that, probably, benefits a different group of people)? Why would the morally decisive consideration be, as in Beatty's theory, which party has a greater interest or stronger preference in the decision?

Alexy has provided a *doctrinal* explanation why we should apply the proportionality test to cases involving constitutional rights, that is, a reason based on implications of positive law or settled aspects of legal

---

[6] See David Beatty, *The Ultimate Rule of Law* (Oxford University Press 2004) Chapter 5.

practice that are taken as given. This doctrinal explanation is based on the idea, crucial in Alexy's theory of rights (see above Section 2.2.1), that constitutional rights and the public interest are principles, and principles are requirements to realise something 'to the greatest possible extent'. From this it follows that when two principles collide, there is a need to solve the conflict through proportionality, which is designed precisely to try to optimise both principles.

I agree with Kai Möller that Alexy's doctrinal explanation for applying proportionality does not follow.[7] But, in any case, my argument here is not that there is no doctrinal reason for applying proportionality. What I am looking for is a different kind of reason: a *normative* or moral reason for applying proportionality in certain cases. By this I mean a reason that shows that the test is not arbitrary – that it captures what is of moral relevance in those cases to which the test is to be applied. If what the test captures – some form of maximisation – is all that morally matters, or the decisive moral consideration in those cases, that would be a sufficient reason for applying that test to those cases.

There are two obstacles for this enterprise of proving that what is morally relevant in human rights cases is maximisation of interests or preferences, as in Beatty's theory, or satisfaction of wide-ranging principles, as in Alexy's theory.[8] Firstly, if what is to be maximised are the interests or preferences of the parties, some of the interests or preferences could be unworthy of satisfaction. What reason would support the need to further the interests that a racist has in promoting people from his race as morally superior? Vicky Jackson has shown how Beatty's account of proportionality cannot deal with this issue – unless one introduces an account of what interests are legitimate.[9] Similarly, broad principles such as those associated with constitutional rights in Alexy's theory can include many

---

[7] See Kai Möller, 'Balancing and the Structure of Constitutional Rights' (2007) 5 Int'l J Const L 452, 453.

[8] As shown above (Section 2.2.3), Barak's theory is ambiguous as to what precisely does proportionality assess, in particular the last balancing subtest. In the previous chapter I showed why Barak's method of balancing by reference to 'marginal social importance' runs against the incommensurability objection. Nevertheless, if he were to correct that aspect and accept that 'social importance' is nothing more than an empty concept that includes whatever is morally relevant in the case (and at times he seems to suggest this: see *Proportionality* 489–50), the objections I make in this chapter could not be directed against Barak's theory. Nevertheless, it would be open to the objections I make in part II of this book.

[9] Vicky C Jackson, 'Being Proportional About Proportionality' (2004) 21 Const Commentary 803, 828,

different interests, actions, and situations, some of which could also be unworthy of satisfaction.[10] Below (Section 4.2), and in the next chapter (Section 5.6), I address this point in more detail in connection with the relation between rights and values, and with Stavros Tsakyrakis' argument against proportionality.

Secondly, and more important for the purposes of the law, legal cases are typically not about maximisation (and morality does not command something different – not even for sophisticated utilitarian accounts of legal adjudication).[11] Why should we expect that cases involving human rights be different?[12]

We should not. We can illustrate the point with a hypothetical. Take a paradigmatic human right, like the right not to be subjected to torture. Suppose we are in a situation where we can torture a terrorist so that he provides information necessary for rescuing two journalists held hostage by a terrorist organisation. If we fail to rescue them soon, the journalists will be tortured by the terrorist organisation. So, in a case like this, there is something we can commensurate: one 'torture' against two 'tortures'. But the relevant criterion for deciding the case is not how to maximise lack of torture in the world, but whether we are entitled to use torture. Human rights documents provide for an absolute prohibition of torture precisely because the morally relevant criterion that applies to this case is that we are not entitled to treat a fellow human being in certain ways, and torture is one of those ways.[13] The aspects of the case that can be commensurated and maximised – outcomes considered as events and experiences, not precisely as deeds as such – are not morally decisive.

There is no reason to think that maximisation is the aim of the practice of legal adjudication, or that of human rights adjudication. Particularly if this aim is the one succinctly captured in the traditional formulation of doing 'justice according to law'. Justice is not about aggregating or maximising

---

[10] See *Theory* 397, referring to 'the fact that the field of constitutional principles is practically unlimited'.

[11] See John Rawls, 'Two Concepts of Rules' (1955) 64 The Phil Review 3, 6–13.

[12] Da Silva realises the greater complexity of cases involving not only one person deciding between incompatible goods for herself, but adjudicating between different persons. But he only analyses whether this different situation affects the possibility of comparing the different values at stake, leaving unaddressed the question of whether this more complex situation may be ruled by a criterion that renders irrelevant such comparison. Virgilio Alfonso Da Silva, 'Comparing the Incommensurable: Constitutional Principles, Balancing and Rational Decision' (2011) 31 2 OJLS 273, 284–5.

[13] See Jeremy Waldron, *Torture, Terror, and Trade-Offs: Philosophy for the White House* (Oxford University Press 2010) 232–4.

preferences or interests effectively or efficiently, but about distribution, that is, about who is entitled to what.[14] Legal adjudication is about establishing what in justice belongs to each party according to the law.[15]

This would still be the case even if one were to argue that human rights cases are not about maximising interests but *values*. Below I challenge the link between values and rights presupposed by this position. Here I wish to note that cases that involve rights are not only about realising a particular good outcome or a value. Sometimes what conflicts are two legitimate interests such that, independently of the conflict, the satisfaction of each of them would be good for the party whose interest it is, and valuable for society generally. Rights, it must not be forgotten, are about justice, and justice supposes the question of 'what is due to each person' – and thus, in the context of adjudication,[16] supposes allocation of goods between different persons.[17] The question is not about maximising benefits for one person (even if this were possible), but to give what is due to each. This is crucial. Private law rights help illustrate this point: if I promised to pay Jane an amount X for a service that she did for me on the conditions agreed upon, then I have to pay her X if the conditions are satisfied. It is unjust for me not to pay her X. If I fail to pay, it would not be reasonable to ask whether there will be more marginal social benefit in me paying my debt than in not doing so, or to ask which contending party has a stronger interest over the amount owed. It is just that I pay Jane as promised for the service she performed and unjust that I do not. In case of non-payment,

---

[14] See Jeremy Waldron, 'The Primacy of Justice' (2003) 9 Legal Theory 269, 276–8.

[15] Note that it is not controversial that after there is a moral assessment of what justice requires in a case, we can find commensurable alternatives when trying to establish how to best fulfil the standard set by criteria of justice. This can happen, for example, when the debtor is insolvent. In bankruptcy cases the judge or some other impartial third party, such as a liquidator, might be given some form of administration over the goods of the debtor in order to pay the different creditors. It could be the case that under some alternatives the liquidator will raise more money and thus will be able to fulfil to a greater degree the obligations of the debtor. In this case some alternatives are commensurable. But this is comparability by reference to a standard that is set with independence from any maximising exercise, since what is owed to the creditors is not grounded on any maximising inquiry, but on other considerations, such as fulfilment of contractual or familial obligations and pro rata equality between the creditors.

[16] See *NLNR* 179: '[T]he act of adjudication itself is always a matter for distributive justice. For the submission of an issue to the judge itself creates a kind of *common* subject-matter [...] which must be allocated between the parties.' (Emphasis in the original.)

[17] The idea was highlighted by an oft-quoted brief remark by John Rawls with relation to utilitarianism: 'Utilitarianism does not take seriously the distinction between persons'. J Rawls, *A Theory of Justice* (rev edn, Harvard University Press 1999) 24. I expand on this in Section 5.4.

if the court were to choose on the basis of considerations of maximisation of values, it would be shifting its focus away from the requirements
of justice in the case. The law typically acknowledges this and commands
payment, and does not allow for a general defence based merely on the
stringency of the interest of the debtor, or on inquiries into what would be
more valuable for which party or for society at large.

The point is not that human rights have necessarily the same structure
as rights in private law (which are in themselves quite complex), but that
conflicts involving justice are not simply about how we can attain certain
goods or values, but about who should have precedence in a particular
conflict, or which goods are to be given to whom, or who deserves to be
deprived or given a particular good, etc. The question is rarely in law how
to maximise some value or set of values, but what does each party deserve
according to the law.

If this is so, we can conclude not only that a reason needs to be provided
for applying proportionality to human rights adjudication. If this depends
on whether proportionality gives expression to what is morally relevant in
the cases to which it is applied, proportionality cannot be the appropriate
method for deciding human rights cases: in those cases considerations of
justice are the determinant ones, and not those relating to maximisation
of interests, values, or principles. In the next chapter I further expand on
how proportionality filters out considerations of rights – the kind of considerations of justice more closely related to human rights cases. But now
I want to return to the weaker claim: that there is no reason to apply the
proportionality test to human rights cases. In the following section I shall
assess a potential reason for considering that human rights cases are about
maximisation after all, and that therefore a method aimed at maximisation, such as proportionality, is appropriate for deciding those cases.

4.3 Legal Rights Are Not Values

4.3.1 Values in General

I am interested here in one particular property that moral values are taken
to have in debates on proportionality. Values are seen as unqualified goods,
such that it is always better if there is more presence or realisation of that
good. Values thus, according to this conception, 'are, like utilities, goods
which are sought to be maximised according to some choice rule'.[18] If, as

---

[18] Paul-Erick N Veel, 'Incommensurability, Proportionality, and Rational Legal Decision-
Making' (2010) 4 Law & Ethics of Human Rights 177, 198.

for Alexy, human rights are principles, and principles are the counterpart on the normative level of values in the axiological level,[19] then the link between rights and values could be a reason for maximising rights. Courts sometimes refer to human rights as ultimately consisting in values.[20] If human rights are values, then balancing could be addressing the relevant moral considerations: the values involved and the requirement to optimise them (though if the values are incommensurable, this would still rule out any kind of quantitative method for deciding between them by reference to which alternative realises more or less 'overall value': see Section 3.1.6). Here I do not intend to take issue with this characterisation of values. My claim in this section is that even if (at least some) values are indeed to be understood as characterised above, human rights are not values.

We first need to distinguish between values and that (types of conducts, institutions) which typically realises or protects those values. Even if it were true that it is always better to realise a particular value more, and thus that there are reasons to maximise participation in that value, from that it would not follow that we have reasons to maximise that which typically realises that value. Friendship, for example, is a value. Calling someone to inquire about his health when he is ill is an action that typically instantiates and fosters friendship. But maximising the instances of calling someone who is ill to inquire about their health would be absurd, and potentially detrimental to friendship itself. Moderation, opportunity, and the manner in which one performs particular actions are central considerations to bear in mind when deliberating over a concrete course of action aimed at realising a value. Finding the virtuous mean is not about maximising – and it is harder.

Furthermore, it would be a logical mistake to assume that, if a particular value can be realised through a particular conduct of the type X, any time that someone does X the particular value is realised or engaged in some

---

[19] *Theory* 92–3.

[20] See e.g. *Campbell v MGN Ltd* [2004] UKHL 22, [2004] 2 AC 457 [16]–[17], referring to 'values encapsulated' or 'enshrined' in articles 8 and 10 of the European Convention on Human Rights; *Re S* [2004] UKHL 47, [2005] 1 AC 593 [17], referring to how 'the values under the two articles [the same articles 8 and 10] are in conflict'; *MGN v United Kingdom* (App No 39401/04) (2011) 53 EHRR 5 [142], referring to the court's task of 'verifying whether the authorities struck a fair balance between two protected values guaranteed by the Convention which may come into conflict with each other in this type of case, freedom of expression protected by art 10 and the right to respect for private life enshrined in art 8'.

way. Not every time someone calls another person to inquire about his health is the value of friendship engaged.[21]

All this applies especially to the relation between values and legal institutions, particularly since the law works with types of conducts. As Hart put it: '[T]he law must predominantly, but by no means exclusively, refer to classes of person, and to classes of acts, things, and circumstances.'[22] A type of conduct may be promoted or protected by the law, and this might be justified by some instantiations of that conduct realising a value.[23] But depending on how vaguely the law refers to the conduct protected, it can include in its scope acts that do not realise that value. To be sure, vagueness is not always a deficiency: precisely the need for tailoring the description of the action or situation to the value in the particular case might counsel some vagueness so as to accommodate new facts that the lawmaker might not be able to foresee, or some other valuable aims that might be involved in the situation.[24] Relatively vague and general language might also be necessary for the law to guide effectively (since too detailed a regulation might be difficult, if not impossible, to apprehend and apply by those subject to it).[25] Law-making is difficult among other reasons because one needs to closely limit legal propositions so as to make them precise enough to guide action effectively in a way that realises the values one is trying to protect through that norm, without encroaching on the realisation of other or the same values; while at the same time leaving some room for adjustment when necessary and avoiding unnecessary complexity. Thus, it is not surprising to find a law that is aimed at, say, protecting certain actions which under certain circumstances express or promote certain values, but because of the way that law is crafted, its semantic reach goes beyond those actions that actually realise that particular value, encompassing other

---

[21] One could of course specify an action so precisely as to make its description always refer to conducts that realise the particular value. That would depart from common parlance. And it might be an impossible task – but for the trivial way of doing it by incorporating the notion of the realisation of the value into the act-description itself ('calling a friend realising the value of friendship'). There is no guarantee that our limited language can provide the resources that we would need in every case, and our relative ignorance of facts, particularly of the way certain conducts (or institutions, etc.) can engage certain values now and in the future, casts further doubts on whether this enterprise is possible. In any case, my argument is not affected by the possibility of further specifying the relevant act-descriptions. It is enough that the argument holds when the description of an act does not perfectly match with the realisation of the value – as is largely the case in law.

[22] HLA Hart, *The Concept of Law* (2nd edn Oxford University Press 1994) 124.

[23] The same could be said, *mutatis mutandis*, of conducts that harm values.

[24] See Hart, *The Concept of Law* 128 ff.

[25] See Timothy Endicott, *Vagueness in Law* (Oxford University Press 2000) 190.

actions that can fall under the same legal act description, but which do not realise that value or any value at all. The greater the semantic reach of the law, the greater the possibility that actions or situations that fall under it do not realise the same value, and that some do not realise a value at all.

The distinction between a value and that which typically realises it applies to human rights as well. When two actions fall under the semantic reach of a particular human rights norm, it is not necessarily the case that both realise the same value, or that they realise a value at all. When human rights are formulated in very broad terms, it is unlikely that the semantic reach of the human right will match the realisation of a single value by the type of action or situation comprehended in the semantic reach of the human right thus formulated.

Freedom of expression provides an illustrative example. If the right is formulated in general terms, so as to refer simply to 'expression', then it will reach semantically all sorts of different forms of expression. It will include political criticism, and it will include, say, sports commentary and child pornography as well. These three forms of expression might fall within the semantic reach of the right to freedom of expression. But they do not realise the same value, and one of the examples does not realise a value at all.[26,27] For example, political criticism realises the values associated

---

[26] It could be objected that the value is something like 'self-expression'. But why would this be a value, with independence of the content of what is expressed? What one expresses, as with what one believes, can be good or bad for oneself and others, depending fundamentally on the content of the expression or belief. When the racist expresses the racism deeply enshrined in his heart, isn't he both expressing a message that is detrimental to society, and affirming for himself a belief that degrades him as a person? If so, then posing a putative value of self-expression is not a viable alternative to assessing (among other things) the content of an expression for the purposes of establishing its moral value. What if the value pursued is pleasure, or simply satisfying one's interests? As Alexy concedes, not every interest (and pleasure) one pursues is valuable (see *Theory* 87 n 162). I engaged above with the question of 'maximisation of interests', in evaluating whether it is the morally relevant consideration in human rights cases. Below (Section 5.6) I further analyse it in relation to Tsakyrakis' argument for the exclusion of spurious interests. Note that all this relates to the question of what is the particular link between a right and some value. It is a different question whether and under what conditions the state is allowed to affect an individual's autonomy.

[27] Some hold that one of the points of having human rights is to establish certain spheres of freedom that do not depend on the authorities' evaluation of whether the acts performed in exercise of those freedoms are morally valuable or not (see below Kumm's account of the 'antiperfectionist' aspect of rights in the liberal tradition, at Section 6.2). If this is the case, then we have already abandoned the conception of rights as values, the conception whose deficiencies I am trying to show here, and have replaced the value-maximisation enquiry with some other kind of Kantian-inspired inquiry aimed at establishing the spheres of freedom that one can have that are compatible with the same sphere of freedom

with democracy and good government. Sports commentary and child pornography do not realise those values. There is no reason to assume as a matter of logical or practical necessity that it is one and the same value that is always at stake in all the actions protected (or forbidden) by a particular human right.[28]

Thus, it would be unsound to maximise every instance of a right as if one were maximising a single value. If the reason for maximising human rights is that values ought to be maximised, then a more discriminating approach would be needed – one that could distinguish the value at stake in different human rights instantiations, and, crucially, those situations where there is no value at stake on the side of the right. This is crucial, because one problem associated with proportionality is its inability to filter out illegitimate interests (Section 5.6). This is not surprising, given the wide acceptance of the simplistic rhetoric of rights as values and interests. It is obvious why maximisation of interests can include illegitimate or spurious interest – since there are such things as illegitimate and spurious interests. It is less obvious why maximising rights as values would fail to filter out illegitimate considerations. The problem lies in the confusion between values and the rights that protect some types of conduct that can realise values. Some conduct falling under a legally defined type of conduct can realise the value commonly realised by some instantiations of that type of conduct, while other conduct of the same type cannot. As Stavros Tsakyrakis has argued, this leaves plenty of room for spurious and illegitimate considerations to creep into reasoning about human rights.[29]

Legal rights are not values. They are technical institutions of positive law, institutions the articulation and enforcement of which attempt to express and enforce a particular requirement of practical reason (see

---

for everyone else. For some of the problems with a position committed to only limiting liberty for the sake of liberty, see HLA Hart, 'Rawls on Liberty and Its Priority' (1973) 40 University of Chicago LR 534.

[28] An additional example can be found in Rawls' discussion of the right to private property. Only certain forms of private property (personal property) are connected to [the values of] self-respect and a sense of personal independence. For Rawls private property over the means of production, for example, is not necessary for the realisation of those values (and through them, to what Rawls calls 'the moral powers'), and thus that particular conception of property will not be chosen as a basic liberty in the original position – whether it should be adopted by society is a question to be decided at the constitutional or legislative stage. John Rawls, *Political Liberalism* (Columbia University Press 2005) 289.

[29] Stavros Tsakyrakis, 'Proportionality: An Assault on Human Rights?' (2009) 7 Int'l J Const L 468, 482–3.

below Chapter 9). The right is not exactly the value (or any of the values) at stake. The closest it can come to a value is in promoting or protecting instantiations of the value. Rights are ways to promote and protect, or prohibit, certain typical ways in which one instantiates or violates that value. Furthermore, what was said in the previous section applies here as well: sometimes rights can distribute something among different parties, something that would be valuable for both parties and society as well, because it is right for one party to have that particular good or opportunity.

4.3.2   Political Values

There are further difficulties in identifying rights with specifically political values, such as liberty and equality. Even if rights could be identified with these values in the relevant way, the problem would be that these values are clearly not the kind of goods that one would like to maximise indefinitely, as, for example, friendship. Take the example of equality. We can imagine different states of affairs in a community, in some of which people are more equal than in others. The most equal one is one where everybody dresses the same, has the same kind of job, the same number of friends, the same hobbies, and so on. If values are to be maximised precisely because they are unqualified goods, so that 'the more of them the better', then equality is not such a value, and thus is not to be maximised. Before maximising equality, we need to have a more precise and concrete understanding of the value as oriented to a specific state of affairs. For example: equal treatment under the law; or equality of opportunities; or some material form of equality, as for example equal access to education and health care. Shaping the value of equality into a more precise conception is a necessary and important part of any serious attempt at realising that value. Simple maximisation will not do.

Something similar happens with liberty. We can imagine a state of affairs in which there is complete lack of state coercion. People have the liberty to kill or harm other people, as well as the liberty to say whatever they want and hold whatever religious belief seems right to them. But again, it is not clear that one should move towards this state of affairs. Here there is a complexity that is not present in the previous example, in that one could argue that such a state of affairs is not more 'free' than one where one is protected from attacks from other people. The promotion of liberty requires the absence not only of state coercion, but also of coercion exerted by private individuals. Since the latter cannot be contained without some state coercion, one needs to find some sort of balance. If this is true, then one is freer in some situations where there is some state coercion than in other situations where there is none.

But this argument is troublesome, since there is no way to show that one has actually 'more' liberty when one is not constrained by the state than when one is. Talk about 'more' liberty suggests that there is some sort of quantitative calculus going on; it sounds as if for one particular state of affairs we could add the liberties of all the different individuals, and then discount the encroachment on their freedom by private coercion, and then compare this net result with some other alternative state of affairs – so that after all this, we could say in which state of affairs there is more liberty. This obviously cannot be done.[30] If liberty means, for example, the ability to choose unconstrained, then we cannot calculate whether one has more of this ability or less in a situation in which there is no state coercion. To pass a moral judgement on whether this is a state of affairs we have reasons to pursue, we need a qualitative assessment of the kinds of options that we think are valuable and just, and those that are not. But if this is so, then, again, liberty is not something to be simply maximised. If liberty is understood as referring only to absence of state coercion, it is simply wrong, because there is a threshold starting from which we would not want more liberty thus defined. If liberty includes not only absence of state coercion, then the idea of maximising liberty, at least past a certain threshold, is senseless, because it requires a quantitative assessment that reason cannot perform.

In both cases of political values there is need for moral reflection on matters such as in what aspects we want to be equal, and up to what point, and for what particular decisions we want to be free, what options should we have, and what options we think no one should have. The maximisation account of proportionality is premised on maximising a certain property, but debates about political values are not aptly portrayed as concerned with maximising those values, because the relevant question is about specifying those values. Once they are properly specified, the values can be maximised (though political values and even instantiations of the same value are often incommensurable, and, if so, in cases of conflict it is not possible to decide between them by some form of quantitative method

---

[30] Berlin notes this in relation to the value of freedom, pointing to five factors on which 'the extent of my freedom seems to depend' and concluding that 'it may well be that there are many incommensurable kinds and degrees of freedom, and that they cannot be drawn up on any single scale of magnitude'. Isaiah Berlin, 'Two Concepts of Liberty' in *Liberty* (Henry Hardy ed, Oxford University Press 2002) 177 n 1.

aimed at commensurating them. The incommensurability objection still applies here: see Section 3.1.6).

Nevertheless, even once political values are properly specified, one cannot assume that they will correspond to human rights, so as to ground the claim that conflicts regarding human rights are about maximisation. This is for the reason already mentioned in relation to values in general: a value is different from that which typically promotes the value. Once political values are specified (so that it is clear what kind of equality or liberty we should aspire to, for example), we need to create legal rights and duties (among other institutions) that promote and protect those values by attaching certain legal consequence to forms of behaviour that typically promote (or harm) those values. The right is not the value and thus, even if the value should be maximised, this is not a reason for maximising everything that falls under the domain of the right. And, again, distributive considerations might be relevant so that the morally relevant question is not so much how to realise more value, but who deserves something valuable in this case.

From the preceding remarks we can draw two conclusions. Firstly, the idea of values as something to be maximised does not provide a justification for turning human rights adjudication into a matter of maximisation. Even if values are to be maximised, that which realises the value is not necessarily (and not commonly) to be maximised. If rights are not values, then it is wrong to claim that rights are to be maximised because values are to be maximised.[31] The objection made in this chapter still holds: even if the incommensurability problem could be overcome, there is still no reason to apply a maximisation method for deciding conflicts involving human rights. And secondly, we should be aware that rights typically include in their semantic reach actions or situations that do not realise a value, or do not realise a value that deserves protection as a human right. Identifying the right with the value risks treating actions or situations that do not engage the relevant value, as if they did. A method of adjudicating human rights must be able to cope with these differences – to which maximisation is blind.

---

[31] One cannot get around this objection by claiming that 'the promotion and protection of fundamental rights is always valuable'. The claim is true, but it says nothing relevant about the content of those rights. In particular, it says nothing about whether they call for some form of maximisation or not.

4.4   Conclusion

Despite the attempts of some defenders of proportionality to establish the rationality of the version of the test they defend, and in particular, of the balancing subtest, they have failed to prove a more basic point: that proportionality is pertinent for addressing human rights cases; that it is reasonable to apply the method they propose to the decision of human rights cases. This depends in turn on whether the method they propose captures what is morally relevant in the cases to which it would be applied. Since the method is premised on the postulate that some form of maximisation is what is relevant, the question is whether in human rights cases the morally decisive consideration, or the only relevant consideration, is maximisation in the form specified by any of the theories of proportionality. There is no reason to think that this is the case. Legal cases are typically not about maximising, but about what is due to each, that is, about justice. Furthermore, the relation between human rights and values does not justify the use of a method oriented towards maximisation, such as the version of the proportionality test discussed in this part of the book.

Proportionality, Rights, and Legitimate Interests

In the previous chapter I argued that the theories of the maximisation account of proportionality fail to show that the proportionality test captures what is morally relevant in the human rights cases to which it is applied. I suggested that there is at least one type of consideration that is typically crucial in legal cases that the maximisation account does not capture: considerations regarding what is due to each party, that is, considerations of justice.

In this chapter I attempt to show more concretely how the maximisation account of proportionality fails to capture the special force of human rights – which is the specific way in which it fails to capture considerations of justice at the level of human rights. Here, I present my own positive account of rights, their role in practical reasoning, and their special force. This account is sufficiently general so as to be compatible with a range of theories of rights. I argue that the maximisation account of proportionality does not capture the specific kinds of reasons in which rights consist. There have been ingenious efforts in recent literature to harmonise proportionality and rights reasoning though, I argue, all these efforts ultimately fail. Finally, I draw on Stavros Tsakyrakis' critique of the legal practice of proportionality in the European Court of Human Rights to illustrate how the absence of proper rights reasoning can be manifested in human rights cases.

5.1   Distinguishing Debates: Rights, Rationality, and Balancing

Is proportionality, and, crucially, its last balancing stage, sensitive to the special kinds of reasons that rights are? There is a sense in which it obviously is. A method for deciding about the limitations of rights is often embedded in a larger theory that provides also an account of what rights are. An account of proportionality can be part of a larger theory that provides an account of *legal* human rights that is compatible with that particular account of proportionality. Perhaps the more prominent example of this is Alexy's theory. Alexy's understanding of proportionality is not only compatible but it is also required by his particular account of constitutional rights (see Section 2.2.1). When I say I want to explore whether proportionality is compatible with rights, I do not mean that I want to analyse the relation between rights and proportionality in this sense. It is critical, then, to clarify what kind of claim I am making, and what is at stake.

First we need to distinguish two levels: that of doctrinal analysis, and that of moral analysis. One can make a claim about what rights require at both levels. At the doctrinal level, one makes a claim about what a certain legal system requires. One can make the claim that a particular set of *legal* rights (say, constitutional rights) requires such and such. At the doctrinal level one grounds these types of claims ultimately on the relevant legal sources in the ways characteristic of the legal craft: by interpreting the relevant texts, by analysing the relevant cases, etc. What is characteristic of the doctrinal level is that the claims made at such level are claims about what is required by legal sources – claims about what our law requires.

At the level of moral analysis one thinks of reasons that bear on different situations – the relevant moral considerations that bear on a type of situation, and how these different considerations relate to each other. To assert at this level that there is a certain right and that this right requires such and such, is to say something about the *moral* requirements that bear on a situation. What one calls 'a right' in this context is a particular type of moral reason. Once one identifies a type of reason, it may be useful to name it, but what is crucial is not how it is referred to, but to achieve clarity on the relevant moral requirement.

Legal categories and methods can be analysed at each of these levels. One can explore, for example, whether our law adopts a particular understanding of proportionality. And one can explore whether this understanding of proportionality captures relevant moral considerations. Analysis at the different levels can be combined, as when one attempts to determine which legal method is the most responsive to the relevant moral requirements of those that fit enough the relevant legal sources[1] (or vice versa).

These distinctions are not novel. What is seldom explicitly articulated is that there is a certain priority of the moral level, in that legal categories are expected to be reasonable and not arbitrary. This means that they are expected to correspond to what morally matters in the cases to which they apply, so as to order action according to justice and other requirements of practical reason. Legal categories that fail to do this (that are blind to the

---

[1] As in Ronald Dworkin's theory of legal interpretation. See his *Law's Empire* (Harvard University Press 1986).

relevant considerations, or even conspire against them) are deficient, and need to be corrected by the appropriate institution in charge of improving the law in that area. What I want to assess is whether a particular legal method aptly captures a relevant type of moral reason that bears on the kinds of conflicts to which that legal method is applied. If there are such things as moral rights, and these are reasons of the special normative force that is commonly attributed to them in moral and political theory as well as in public discourse, then does proportionality (and particularly its last balancing stage) aptly reflect this type of moral requirement?

If a legal method for adjudicating human rights cases is blind to the specific way in which rights are a relevant moral consideration that bears on those cases, then that legal method is flawed. The reasonable order of precedence is this: the legal method should capture what morally matters in the choice-situations where the method will be applied. It is easy to lose sight of this truism, and think that what the method captures *is* what matters. This, as we will see below, is a mistake made by some defenders of proportionality.

5.2   Rights and Maximisation

Rights entail a way of looking at a certain conflict. To address a conflict from the perspective of the rights at stake is a distinctive way of addressing that conflict. Rights are distinctive moral concepts, and the perspective they entail is distinctive as well. This view is not wholly uncontroversial. It is well known, for example, that Bentham characterised 'natural' (as opposed to 'legal') rights as 'nonsense upon stilts'.[2] But if one does not wish to do away with rights, then one must accept that rights are distinctive, that is, that rights are not just a way of calling some other consideration under certain circumstances (e.g. the calculus of utility when it is systematically consistent with a particular favourable treatment for a certain person), but rather that they are different from other typical moral considerations – in particular, different from considerations of value realisation, interest satisfaction, utility maximisation, etc.

Rights have a distinctive structure: they consist in a requirement seen from the point of view of the person entitled to its fulfilment.[3] As for their

---

[2] Jeremy Bentham, 'Nonsense Upon Stilts' in Stephen G Engelmann (ed), *Selected Writings* (Yale University Press 2011) 318.

[3] This formulation is ambiguous enough to be compatible with both 'interest theories' and 'will theories' of rights.

content, they are generally associated with matters of justice: the requirements on which rights consist of are requirements of justice – regarding what is someone's due, what is owed to someone.[4] This much is hardly disputed. Rights are characterised as having a particular force, a certain pre-eminence. As Waldron notes, what the main accounts of rights share is an understanding of 'their strength, their urgency, their peremptory character'.[5] Rights do not just provide reasons, but provide especially strong, and many times conclusive reasons.[6] There are different views regarding how to better characterise this pre-eminence of rights. Below I focus on the idea of rights as trumps, as side-constraints, and as having lexical priority (the characterisations of rights proposed by Ronald Dworkin, Robert Nozick, and John Rawls, respectively). For now, I focus on more general features of rights reasoning, which are valid for all these and many other accounts.[7]

---

[4] This is true of moral rights. Legal rights can be grounded on other requirements. It may be the case that allocating certain rights to certain people would allow for greater efficiency or some other such value, thus providing a reason for the law to grant that particular legal right.

[5] Jeremy Waldron, 'Introduction' in Jeremy Waldron (ed), *Theories of Rights* (Oxford University Press 1984) 14, quoted in *Negotiable Constitution* 117.

[6] Though, some would add, not necessarily absolute, always undefeated, reasons. See below (n 32).

[7] In making the case for the benefits of the proportionality test for a democratic culture, Stephen Gardbaum treats this peremptory force of rights as entailing an important institutional consequence regarding the competence of legislatures. Referring to the limits that constitutional rights pose on ordinary law-making, he asserts: 'The conception of constitutional rights as trumps demands that such limits be peremptory or categorical; that in the face of a valid constitutional rights claim, politically accountable decision making is totally disabled.' Stephen Gardbaum, 'Proportionality and Democratic Constitutionalism' in Grant Huscroft, Bradley Miller, and Grégoire Webber (eds), *Proportionality and the Rule of Law: Rights, Justification, Reasoning* (Cambridge University Press 2014) 271. In this chapter my point is more modest than defending an idea of constitutional or human rights as trumps: if human rights cases involve moral rights, then a sound legal method for addressing those cases needs to be sensitive to considerations of moral rights, because legal categories in general should capture what is morally relevant in the cases to which they are applied. Below I defend a conception of human rights as narrow and indeed of peremptory *legal* force (see Chapter 9). In any case, Gardbaum's claim in the above quoted passage seems to me unwarranted. One issue is the force and content that rights have in moral and legal reasoning. A different matter is the attribution of competences in different organs for the different tasks associated with rights (enacting rights in law, specifying them, applying and enforcing them, etc.). From the idea that constitutional rights have some form of peremptory legal force a particular form of judicial review of legislation does not follow. The question is which institutional design best secures the fulfilment of such rights so as to better realise the requirements of justice that ground them, as well as other relevant values. And even where there is already some form of judicial review of legislation in place, courts

There is a tight link between the role rights play in moral discourse (grounding claims regarding what is owed to the person that holds the right) and their special moral force (their pre-eminence as reasons for action). The paradigmatic situation in which questions regarding what is someone's due arise is when different persons have conflicting claims about something, as, for example, when A, B, and C all claim to be the exclusive owner of X. Suppose X is owed to A; it is A's due to be acknowledged as owner of X and to be respected in his ownership of X. One can present this in terms of A's claim over X having precedence over B and C's claims over X, a precedence that can be expressed in different ways: A's claim has priority over B and C's, or it 'trumps' them, or it somehow constrains B and C's actions in relation to X (or the actions of a third party intent on improving the situation of B and C). A prescription regarding what is due to someone can often be aptly presented in terms of that person having a particular claim that enjoys some form of pre-eminence over the conflicting claims of others. The special moral force of rights consists in their pre-eminence, and this pre-eminence in turn is a function of their role in moral discourse.

If rights are distinctive, then to address a problem from the perspective of rights is a distinctive way of addressing that problem. If one believes that rights are relevant in a particular situation, then in assessing that situation one should attempt to establish what the relevant rights require. One addresses the problem attempting to understand how the different facts involved trigger rights claims, and what these claims demand in that particular situation. This is what adopting the perspective of rights means. When one addresses a conflict from the perspective of rights, the crucial question is: 'what is due to each party involved in the conflict, according to his or her rights?' Relevant issues that typically arise in answering this question are: 'do the parties have a right to what they demand?', 'What rights do they have?', and 'What is the scope of those rights?' To look at a situation from this perspective affects the analysis of the facts involved: from the perspective of rights, only some of the perhaps countless facts

---

can be deferential to the judgement of legislatures as to the limits and force of constitutional rights understood as trumps, accepting that legislatures play an important role in the specification and protection of constitutional rights; and courts can be quite invasive in their review of whether legislation that affects what they take to be broad *prima facie* considerations is ultimately justified or not, seeing in every piece of legislation a potential threat to fundamental rights that requires the judicial *imprimatur*. In all this, the important democratic considerations that Gardbaum mentions in his article are relevant, regardless of the understanding of rights that one adopts.

involved will be relevant, and only under some of the potentially infinite descriptions of those facts. Once the perspective of rights is adopted, and the relevant facts are assessed in the light of the applicable rights, one has a practical conclusion as to what is required by rights in a given situation. Because rights provide reasons for action, one has a reason to act in the way determined by rights reasoning.

One remarkable aspect of rights reasoning is its claim to pre-eminence: to be a controlling perspective, so that human choice and action in situations to which it bears ought always to consider this perspective and be consistent with it, regardless of the proposed courses of actions suggested by reasoning according to other perspectives. This is a function of the above-mentioned special force of rights. Not all perspectives make such a claim to pre-eminence – indeed, very few do.[8]

The perspective of rights is different from, and irreducible to, other perspectives: for example, it is different from and irreducible to the perspective of maximisation of, say, interests or values. There is a difference between addressing a conflict by asking, 'which outcome satisfies to a greater degree the interests of the parties', and addressing it by asking 'who has a right to a certain outcome in the dispute'. The perspective of rights and the perspective of maximisation are distinct: by addressing a particular question from the perspective of rights one does not address it from the perspective of maximisation, and vice versa. One perspective does not entail or include the other. None of the perspectives can be translated in terms of the other. Neither can the perspectives be decomposed into a common simpler form. Each perspective demands its own form of reasoning about the issue, and yields its own solution. Of course, one can think of a problem in terms of both perspectives, but this requires that one conducts two separate inquiries, one from each perspective. To address an issue from the perspective of maximisation only entails not to address it from the perspective of rights, and vice versa. When each perspective is treated as sufficient, the other is not considered. The perspectives can work in tandem, so to say. One can first address an issue from one perspective and, if that leaves open two or more options, one can then address the issue from the other perspective to choose between those options. But the application of each perspective remains autonomous from the other perspective. Because the perspectives cannot be conflated into a single

---

[8] Religious precepts often make such a claim, for example.

unified perspective, only one can be controlling of the issue.[9] The different perspectives are pertinent in different types of situations, as I will explain below. For now, we need only this basic characterisation of each perspective and its irreducibility to the other.

5.3   Rights and Proportionality

Proportionality is often understood to be oriented towards maximisation. This, as we saw, is how theorists of the maximisation account of proportionality understand the test (see Section 2.2). The method is aimed at establishing whether adopting or not adopting the measure produces a greater satisfaction of the principles, values, or interests involved: if adopting the measure, then adopting it is legally warranted. If not adopting the measure produces a greater satisfaction, then the measure is legally deficient.

Does such a method reflect the special normative force of rights? Here the distinction between different perspectives for addressing a situation is useful. This understanding of proportionality is oriented towards maximisation. It therefore assumes the perspective of maximisation characterised in the previous section. This perspective is predominant and controlling. While the perspective of maximisation is assumed, other things not related to maximisation are moved out of the picture. Considerations of what is due to someone according to his or her rights – which demand adopting the perspective of rights – are an example of considerations that are moved out of the picture. This is why the special force that rights are taken to have is not captured in the proportionality analysis as proposed by Alexy and others, and in legal decisions adopting the maximisation account of proportionality. As explained in the previous section, rights, as distinctive considerations that have a distinctive structure and force, demand that one looks at a certain issue from the point of view of

---

[9] For example, issues regarding child custody seem to require paying attention to different perspectives. Here, the 'interests of the child' are not just a relevant consideration, but typically the paramount consideration in many jurisdictions. Both rights satisfaction and interests satisfaction are relevant and related in the following way: the child has a right that his or her interest is considered paramount. Here the controlling perspective is that of rights. The issue is framed as regarding what is due to those involved, and what decides the issue is a right of the child. The maximisation inquiry comes in once the rights issue is settled independently, and it is completely shaped by the controlling right. The issue is not decided by reference to what outcome yields the greatest net amount of interest satisfaction for the relevant persons; the claims of the child are seen as paramount, and maximisation is only relevant regarding the child's claim, that is, the claim established as dominant by rights reasoning.

this type of consideration, that claims to be – at least to a considerable extent – controlling. Even if considerations related to maximisation satisfied in some cases the same interests as those promoted by rights, the perspective of maximisation could not capture the special protection granted to those interests by rights.[10] If a legal method adopts the perspective of maximisation as the defining one for solving a type of case, it will not address considerations of rights and their specific moral force. The maximisation understanding of proportionality does not capture rights, simply because it is not *about* rights.

This explains why critics of proportionality have noted time and again that proportionality reasoning somehow fails to engage properly with rights. For example, in an influential article, Stavros Tsakyrakis argues that proportionality reasoning typically displays little interest in assessing the pre-emptive force of the rights involved (see below Section 5.6). Grégoire Webber makes a similar case against proportionality. He argues that 'the discourse of "competing *interests*", "competing *values*", and "optimising *principles*" suggests that the place of rights under the received approach is never secure, indeed never truly important or special'.[11] This way of conceiving rights 'obfuscates the merits and moral worth of rights'.[12] It is not surprising that in a case like *Quila* (see Section 2.1) the perspective of rights is notoriously absent from the judgement. Neither the majority nor the minority engaged directly with questions such as: what is it the parties are due as a matter of their human rights? What does the government and the community owe persons in the situation of the plaintiff with regard to residence permits as a matter of their human right to privacy? What does the government and the community generally owe actual and potential victims of forced marriage as a matter of their human rights? Instead, the crucial issue becomes whether the beneficial effect of the measure in deterring forced marriages is large enough to justify the negative effects on young couples seeking to reside in the UK, and it is this sort of question (including subordinate questions such as whether the government's reasoning in adopting the measure considered the relation between its negative effects and its positive effects, how intrusive should the court be

---

[10] As Webber notes, for proportionality reasoning 'no right is controlling *as a right*'. Grégoire Webber, 'On the Loss of Rights' in Grant Huscroft, Bradley Miller, and Grégoire Webber (eds), *Proportionality and the Rule of Law: Rights, Justification, Reasoning* (Cambridge University Press 2014) 136 (emphasis in the original).

[11] *Negotiable Constitution* 123, emphasis in the original.

[12] Ibid.

in assessing the impact of the measure and the reasoning of the government, etc.) that shapes the reasoning of the court.

This is to be expected. If proportionality is conceived from the maximisation perspective it is not oriented towards rights but towards something else. Part of the appeal of proportionality is that it seems manageable, objective, not overly complicated, and apt to yield the greatest satisfaction of all the principles involved. This is because it is oriented towards maximisation, and maximisation requires mostly a quantitative comparison, which, at least in principle, is more likely to have the advantages just identified (see Section 4.2). Rights reasoning can only muddle this picture. As Tsakyrakis points out, it requires substantive moral reasoning, not reducible to quantification. But, if rights are relevant moral considerations that bear on human rights cases, there is no alternative to taking them into account properly.[13]

5.4   Utilitarianism of Rights

It could be argued that balancing does take rights into account, but in a different way: rights ground certain requirements that should be satisfied, but when these requirements collide with other requirements (requirements grounded on rights, or on other relevant considerations), then the question is how to satisfy these different requirements to the greatest degree. Proportionality, and balancing in particular, can be understood as methods for assessing precisely this. They do not need to be interpreted as requiring maximisation of individual or social interests, or of values directly (though some important accounts of proportionality that follow the maximisation logic do this; see Section 2.2.2). They could be interpreted as requiring maximising the satisfaction or fulfilment of constitutional requirements, and particularly of rights. Robert Alexy's account of proportionality lends itself to this interpretation:[14] it requires the maximum overall satisfaction of *principles*, which can be understood as optimisation requirements regarding the realisation of particular requirements associated with rights. On this account, proportionality is not oriented towards maximisation of

---

[13] There are different ways in which legal adjudication can be sensitive to rights, the kind of open-ended moral analysis advocated by Traskyrakis and other scholars being only one of them. A superior alternative is to understand adjudication in the context of the characteristically legal practice of crafting and applying relatively precise and differentiated legal categories. See below Chapters 7 and 9.

[14] See Alexy's distinction between the mode of principles and the mode of values in *Theory* 92. But see ibid 99 and 107 (referring to 'balancing interests').

overall value satisfaction. It requires a more bounded maximising exercise: to maximise realisation of the constitutionally protected rights and public goods at stake in the case. It could be affirmed that Alexy's method is one that takes rights thoroughly into account, by attempting to realise rights to the maximum degree.

This way of understanding rights and proportionality is attractive. It seems to bring together the perspective of rights and the perspective of maximisation. Engaging with this understanding of rights is fruitful beyond the mere dialectic against opposing theories. It sheds light on an important element of the characterisation of the perspective of rights and the perspective of maximisation, namely, when is it *pertinent* to apply each of the aforementioned perspectives.

The understanding of proportionality just described fits well the insightful characterisation provided by Robert Nozick of what he called 'utilitarianism of rights'. Nozick explains it thus:

> [A] theory may include in a primary way the nonviolation of rights, yet include it in the wrong place and the wrong manner. For suppose some condition about minimizing the total (weighted) amount of violations of rights is built into the desirable end state to be achieved. We then would have something like a 'utilitarianism of rights': violations of rights (to be *minimized*) merely would replace the total happiness as the relevant end state in the utilitarian structure. [. . .] This still would require us to violate someone's rights when doing so minimizes the total (weighted) amount of the violation of rights in the society.[15]

Nozick provides a brief argument against utilitarianism of rights: utilitarianism of rights is deficient because it fails to respect the inviolability of persons.[16] The rights of some may not be violated for the sake of the overall greater realisation of the rights of society, because 'there is no *social entity* with a good that undergoes some sacrifice for its own good. There are only individual people, different people [. . .]. Using one of this people for the benefit of others, uses him and benefits others.'[17]

This may seem an extremely individualistic position, but I believe the underlying point is correct and not especially controversial. To show this we need to add an additional element to Nozick's insight. The relation between a society and the individuals that compose it is not that of, say, an individual and the parts of his or her body. In both cases one can talk of a relation of a whole to its parts, but this relation is very different for

---

[15] Robert Nozick, *Anarchy, State, and Utopia* (Basic Books 1974) 28.
[16] Ibid 31.
[17] Ibid 32–3.

each case. The latter relation (that of an individual and the parts of his or her body) is one where the parts have no meaning or intrinsic value other than as parts of that whole. To destroy without good reason a hand or a foot is wrong because it is *someone's* hand or foot.[18] Therefore, if I consider sacrificing, say, the health of my foot for the sake of improving the health of my hand, I can assess the sacrifices and improvements by reference to the well-being of a single entity that is the sole source of the value of this foot and of this hand: me. The opposite is the case in the relation between persons and the societies to which they belong. Persons do have intrinsic value, independent of their belonging to a society. Each person is an independent *locus* of value and concern. And this is where problems with utilitarianism enter the picture: the intrinsic value of persons resists being computed in terms of 'overall social value', precisely because said value does not reside in society, but in human persons as such. Utilitarianism's ability to provide a straightforward criterion for resolving complex choices involving different potential outcomes for different people rests characteristically on aggregating the different realisations of a relevant property (e.g. interests satisfaction, utility realisation, value realisation, rights fulfilment) for the different persons affected by the decision, for each possible outcome, and then comparing which outcome yields a net gain in the relevant property. The crucial move is the aggregation of results for each *locus* of value and concern. In doing this, the issue is treated *as if* it concerned *only one locus* of value and concern – one strives to maximise the relevant property for a single entity. The different *loci* of value and concern are treated as parts of that single entity *for which one tries to find the result that yields the greater gain.* This is what aggregation entails. For the net aggregate result to express something worth controlling practical deliberation, it must be the case that what matters in the different realisations of the relevant property for different individuals should be referred to the same entity, as, for example, the good of the different parts of the body is good insofar as it constitutes the good of the person whose body it is. It is because of this that Rawls deemed the decisive deficiency of utilitarianism (and rights utilitarianism has this same deficiency) that it 'does not take seriously the distinction between persons'.[19] Rawls thought characteristic of utilitarianism that it 'extends to society the principle of choice for one

---

[18] And, if it is not, and these are random hands and feet lying down in the street, then it would be less wrong to destroy them, and, arguably, wrong to the extent that they were someone's hands and feet and one owes some respect to those people, which has as its typical manifestation the respect for the forms of burial.

[19] John Rawls, *A Theory of Justice* (rev edn, Harvard University Press 1999) 24.

man', conflating all desires or interests into one net sum.[20] The principle of maximising the net balance of satisfaction is only pertinent if those things that are to be balanced correspond to a single entity. Therefore, a crucial question[21] in deciding whether some such maximising method is to be applied is whether the different goods, interests, or claims to be weighed are best represented as goods, interests, or claims of a single entity.

Rights, on the other hand, are seen as harmonious with the separateness of persons. For Nozick, rights are better understood not as part of some end state to be achieved, but as side-constraints to human action: 'the rights of others determine the constraints upon your actions'.[22] On this account, rights have a greater normative force, as they impose effective limits that cannot be dissolved by considerations of greater realisation of some other principle or value. The special moral force of rights as side-constraints means that they cannot be balanced away, and they cannot be balanced away because they 'express the inviolability of other persons'[23] – an inviolability that prevents overall weighing of the conflicting rights of different individuals. In this, Nozick and Rawls agree. For Rawls, '[e]ach member of society is thought to have an inviolability founded on justice or, as some say, on natural right, which even the welfare of every one else cannot override. Justice denies that the loss of freedom for some is made right by a greater good shared by others.'[24] Rights attest to the separateness of persons, to the fact that each person is an independent *locus* of value and concern.

It is not necessary to adopt all the particularities of the controversial theories of Nozick and Rawls to see the force of their insights in their assessment of utilitarianism. We can draw from their arguments to illuminate the question of rights maximisation in human or constitutional rights adjudication. It is important, first, to make explicit a link between these arguments and our distinction between the maximisation perspective and the perspective of rights.

Nozick and Rawls' point about the separateness of persons and the relation of society to the individual is a sound one, and serves as common ground between their otherwise opposing theories. This point can be

---

[20] Ibid 25. This is emphasised throughout Rawls' treatment of utilitarianism. See also ibid 21–4, 26, 163–7.
[21] Not the only relevant question. Another relevant question is whether the things to be weighed are commensurable. See Chapter 3.
[22] Nozick (n 15) 29.
[23] Ibid 32.
[24] Rawls (n 19) 24–5.

extended to the parties in a legal case concerning the limitations of human or constitutional rights. If the parties in such cases formed some kind of unity that captured everything of moral value in the parties and their claims, then it could be pertinent to address the issue by asking which outcome maximises the net balance of satisfaction of the claims of the different parties. Maximisation relies on the aggregate of satisfaction of different claims into one single net result. For the net aggregate result to express something decisive for practical deliberation, it must be the case that what is relevant in the different claims is common and can be referred to the same entity, as in the example of the good of the parts of the body, which is good in that it constitutes the good of the person whose body it is.

One can say that the parties in a case do form some kind of unity ('the parties'), or that they both belong to a greater one entity ('society'); but the relation of each party to the whole to which it belongs is not the one illustrated above with the example of the body and its parts. It is not the case that any of these unities ('the parties' as a group, or society) captures everything of moral value in each party and his or her claims. The moral value of each party and his or her claims is independent from the parties belonging to any such group. It is not pertinent therefore to maximise the net balance of satisfaction of their claims, as if these were claims of just one entity with whose only welfare we were concerned.

The parties cannot be reduced to a common entity, but rather have to be dealt with as separate, distinct, individuals, each an independent *locus* of value and concern. Therefore, the conflict between the parties needs to be framed in terms of putting them in an appropriate relation to each other. The problem is not one of maximising satisfaction for the sole entity that matters in the choice situation, but in determining a reasonable order for a plurality of entities, all of which matter in the choice situation. In establishing the right relation between different entities it is necessary to establish what is due to each of them, and particularly, what they owe to each other. Rights are moral concepts oriented towards establishing this. The perspective of rights is pertinent only when in a choice situation one needs to decide for different separate entities at stake, each an independent *locus* of value and concern, and therefore the distinction between them matters. When there is only one relevant entity at stake, it is useless to adopt the perspective of rights.

Utilitarianism of rights requires that one adopts the maximisation perspective. This is so in the legal context as much as in the political one. This perspective can only be pertinent (though not necessarily adequate) in choice situations where there is only one relevant entity, for whose sake one is to maximise. But, as seen above, in virtually all legal cases there is a plurality of relevant persons involved. Therefore, utilitarianism of rights cannot be a pertinent way of addressing such cases. If some version of balancing and proportionality is a method committed to maximising the fulfilment of different rights and goods of different persons, in the form of utilitarianism of rights, then it is not pertinent for addressing virtually any legal conflict.

5.5 Accommodating Rights into Balancing

There have been a number of proposals for accommodating the special normative force of rights into the maximisation understanding of balancing and proportionality. The proposals can be divided into two main groups: those claiming that ultimately all rights depend on balancing; and those claiming that the balancing methodology can express the special force of rights, and even the absolute force some rights are thought to have. In this section I explain these proposals, and argue that all of them fail. Engaging with them will shed light on further elements of the characterisation of rights reasoning in general offered here, particularly regarding the pre-eminence of rights and the structure of absolute rights. It will also clarify the role of proportionality and balancing in guiding legal reasoning and its implications for rights. All this will sharpen the contrast between the balancing methodology and rights.

5.5.1 Do Rights Depend on Balancing?

Some defenders of proportionality argue that the pre-eminence of rights is itself a function of an underlying balancing. This would follow from the idea, held by many defenders of proportionality, that the limits of rights are the product of an implied balancing.[25] Klatt and Meister, for example, argue that 'narrow definitions [of rights] rely on balancing'.[26] They illustrate this with the example of hate speech:

> Assuming that the right to freedom of speech is absolute and, by definition does not protect hate speech, then this definition is the outcome of a balancing test that takes both interests into account, namely, the right of

---

[25] See for example Matthias Klatt and Moritz Meister, *The Constitutional Structure of Proportionality* (Oxford University Press 2012) 21; *Theory* 209–10 and 74–6; Jud Mathews and Alec Stone Sweet, 'All Things in Proportion – American Rights Review and the Problem of Balancing' (2010) 60 Emory LJ 797, 869 (referring only to American case-law).

[26] Klatt and Meister (n 25) 21.

the freedom of speech, *and* the interests of the addressed person. It then overweighs the rights of the insulted person over the freedom of speech.[27]

Balancing is therefore considered 'unavoidable', and the question is only if it 'takes place in a hidden way' or openly.[28]

But from the mere fact that an ordering of interests or values has been established, it does not follow that balancing has taken place. This ordering could be a product of a different form of reasoning. Broadly speaking, there are two ways of resolving a conflict between different claims.[29] Suppose for the sake of simplicity that there are only two opposing claims. First, it could be argued that the reasons that ground the normative force of one of the opposing claims do not apply to the concrete circumstances of the conflict; therefore, there is no real conflict, since only one of the claims is really relevant. A second way of resolving the conflict is by acknowledging that there are two valid claims, and resolving which one is to prevail over the other in the concrete case. This can be done in a number of ways, being the kind of quantitative assessment involved in proportionality and balancing tests only one among many possibilities (see Sections 3.1.2–3). For example, I could choose A rather than B because, regardless of the value offered to me by each of them, I have a duty to choose A (I promised my mother in her deathbed I would choose A rather than B when the time came). The fact that an ordering was achieved does not imply that some balancing must have taken place, unless the word 'balance' is deprived of its more precise content, as specified by the maximisation account of proportionality, and it is taken simply to mean 'assessing the reasons in favour and against a particular ordering of interests, values, claims, etc'.[30]

Furthermore, the understanding of proportionality that we are concerned with here cannot reproduce the characteristic force that rights are taken to have. It is characteristic of this understanding that a limitation with a right is considered justified by reference to enough gains in some other right or public interest. Whether a right or an opposing right or public interest prevails may depend (as with Alexy's first Law of Balancing)

---

[27] Ibid.

[28] See ibid.

[29] I take this distinction from Jeremy Waldron's analysis of the conflicting claims in hate speech in his *The Harm in Hate Speech* (Harvard University Press 2012) 145–6.

[30] Note that Klatt and Meister are equivocal in this respect. They claim that a definition of a right must rely on balancing 'since the definition is based on reasons for and reasons against the protection'. See Klatt and Meister (n 25) 21. But this is not the idea of balancing proposed by their theory, which follows Robert Alexy's account of balancing, and thus refers to something more specific than merely considering 'the reasons for and the reasons against the protection'.

on which is affected to a greater degree; or (as with Beatty's theory) on which right or public interest in that case is more significant for the party that benefits from it (see Sections 2.2.1–2). For these accounts the protection granted by a right is contingent on the fact that under a particular set of circumstances the relevant properties (the degree of satisfaction of the principles, values, or interests at stake, or the significance of their realisation for the parties) are realised to a greater degree by respecting the right. But an increase in the degree to which the opposing principles, values, or interests realise the relevant property could alter the limits of the right – this increase could mean that the right does not grant protection in those particular circumstances.

But this is not what rights are about. The particular normative force that defines rights, and that links them with considerations of justice and dessert, is different from that of the unstable pre-eminence that a principle or interest has over another under the balancing model. Rights reasoning is *categorical*, qualitative rather than quantitative. Whether we explain rights as trumps, or as side-constraints, or in the form of lexical priority (to take the well-known accounts of Ronald Dworkin, Robert Nozick, and John Rawls, respectively),[31] the result is the same: rights are claims that need to be satisfied, regardless of certain types of opposing considerations. The right has pre-eminence over these considerations. It trumps them (under the rights-as-trumps model); or it signals that those considerations cannot be satisfied by measures that affect the right (and thus establish side-constraints to the satisfaction of certain goals); or it requires that the interest or value or claim protected by the right be satisfied first, and only then other considerations can be addressed. For our purposes what is noteworthy in all these different ways of accounting for the structure of rights is that they all operate categorically. The question is whether a particular interest or claim belongs to the category of interests or claims that are protected by a right, and whether the opposing considerations belong to the category of considerations that the right trumps, or that can only be satisfied respecting the side-constraint that the right consists in, or that can only be satisfied once the right has been satisfied.[32]

---

[31] See Ronald Dworkin, *Taking Rights Seriously* (Harvard University Press 1978) xi; Nozick (n 15) 29; and Rawls (n 19) 214.

[32] As has been noted, most authors stop short of claiming that rights can never be overcome by the opposing considerations that they are supposed to 'trump', constrain, or have priority over. Authors allow for the possibility of rights being overcome in, for example, cases of a 'moral catastrophe'. See Jeremy Waldron, *Torture, Terror, and Trade-Offs: Philosophy for the White House* (Oxford University Press 2010) 31. But this does not deny that rights

This kind of ordering, where one type of consideration has this pre-eminence over another, cannot be justified by reference to balancing, because balancing does not capture the qualitative dimension that is crucial for a mode of practical reasoning that works categorically, as rights reasoning does. Balancing cannot establish that a category of considerations has pre-eminence over another category, because the method of balancing (as is often understood in debates on proportionality, see Chapter 2)[33] is not one that singles out or uncovers the quality of things (determining to which category they belong) and their moral significance, but the quantity of things: what principle has been interfered more with, what interest has been more affected, what need is more stringent, etc. From a quantitative ordering one cannot produce a qualitative ordering. It is not surprising that, as seen above (Section 5.3), these categorical forms of reasoning have no place in proportionality reasoning. For the same reason – because balancing is not concerned with questions regarding categories of considerations that deserve

---

work in the categorical way described above. They do work like that in normal circumstances. Another way to put this is to say that rights describe moral requirements that are perfectly valid in normal circumstances. It is only expected that some requirements are no longer valid, and others take their place, in exceptional circumstances. Nevertheless, it is also not obvious that in exceptional circumstances, for example, in the face of a moral catastrophe, we would apply something like balancing reasoning. In any case, rights still can be rightly said to have their full normative force in normal circumstances, and that rights reasoning is to be distinguished from balancing in those circumstances.

It could be argued that rights can be compatible with trade-offs. So, for example, the idea of lexical priority does not exclude trade-offs between claims of the same level of priority. But note that the *characteristic operation* of rights *does* exclude trade-offs. Rights as lexical priority operate precisely when there are opposing claims, and one enjoys such priority over the other, and when this is the case, there is no trade-off between *those* claims. Lexical priority is not at work when there is no such priority, and thus when this is the case between two claims trade-offs are not excluded by the idea of lexical priority. Similarly, rights as trumps may be traded off in some circumstances, but the characteristic operation of a right as trump is *trumping*: it is defeating other consideration without regard to trade-offs. And the same could be said of a right as a side-constraint: its characteristic operation is to exclude some course of action for attaining a particular goal. When the specific operation of the right takes place, there is no trade-off, because the specific operation of the right does not consist on a form of trading off the right against some other claim, but in establishing the priority of the right against a rival claim, or in trumping a rival claim, or in constraining the attainment of some goal. Only in a theory such as Alexy's is the specific operation of rights understood as consisting in some form of trade-off (see Section 2.2.1).

[33] An alternative account of 'balancing' is the one offered by the theories of proportionality explained in Chapter 6, where balancing is not a specific method. This understanding of balancing and proportionality more generally is open to different objections (see Chapters 7 and 8).

some form of pre-eminence over other categories of considerations – rights cannot be grounded on an implied balancing test.

Even if we understood rights as having less stringent force, such as they have according to Schauer's conception of 'rights as shields', it would still be the case that the form of reasoning typically involved in proportionality and balancing assessment cannot justify even these weaker rights or reflect their strength. For Schauer, 'A right to Ø [. . .] *is* the right to have the state not restrict the ability to Ø without showing a compelling state interest or the like. [. . .] Rights, as shields, may be thought of as having genuine force, even though they may not be absolute.'[34] For Schauer these rights are distinguished from balancing in that usually their application is not a matter for balancing. Usual cases will still be – as he notes they commonly are – 'far more focused on the right and its contours, and far less on the interests that might conceivably outweigh it'.[35] It is only when there is some particularly strong justification that the right may be outweighed by these considerations, and thus some form of balancing can be undertaken.[36] Schauer's account presupposes 'a certain psychology of decision making' according to which 'a decision maker can presumptively, but not conclusively, ignore some factor', remaining 'open to the possibility that [that] factor might be relevant in a few extraordinary cases but still does not take it into account unless it appears to a particularly great degree'.[37] It seems to me that 'rights as shields' play a different role in practical reasoning, and thus possess a different normative force, than the kind of reasons I here call 'rights'.[38] Nevertheless, even this kind of softer pre-eminence that rights have under

---

[34] Frederick Schauer, 'A Comment on the Structure of Rights' (1992) 27 Ga LR 415, 429.

[35] Ibid 432.

[36] Ibid 428–30. Though it does not follow from Schauer's argument that this assessment of whether the right is legitimately interfered with should be undertaken through balancing in the way it is understood by the maximisation account of proportionality. As has been noted here, there are other forms of moral reasoning beyond balancing. In other works Schauer seems to support the different, incompatible, understanding of proportionality as 'unconstrained moral reasoning'. See Frederick Schauer, 'Balancing, Subsumption, and the Constraining Role of Legal Text' in Matthias Klatt (ed), *Institutionalized Reason: The Jurisprudence of Robert Alexy* (Oxford University Press 2012) 307.

[37] Schauer (n 34) 432.

[38] This does not deny the value of the idea of 'rights as shields', which can serve as a descriptive tool for elucidating the operation of some weaker type of legal requirement in a legal system, or as a specifically legal category to express in the law a weaker moral or prudential requirement, all of which is consistent with the existence of stronger requirements (e.g. rights in the traditional sense described above Section 5.2) and with their recognition in the law. I elaborate on how human rights should be expressed in a body of law in the last chapter of this book.

Schauer's model cannot be established through balancing. For one thing, it still relies on distinguishing a category of considerations for special treatment. Furthermore, it is framed explicitly as providing greater protection than mere balancing would provide – it is aimed at ruling out balancing in most cases. How could balancing itself justify this protection?

5.5.2   Can Balancing Express Rights?

One proposal for accommodating the special normative force of rights into the balancing test is to incorporate the special strength of the right into the assessment of the importance of the principles at stake. Allison Young, for example, has suggested this in a recent paper.[39] Taking Alexy's theory as a reference, Young notes that proportionality relies on an analysis of the importance of the rights and interests being balanced, as well as on an assessment of the degree to which these rights are infringed. If there are sufficiently strong reasons for giving greater weight to the right in this calculation, then these reasons would operate when proportionality is applied, to accord enough weight to the right in question so that it would nearly always override the restriction placed on it.[40]

The point can be most clearly expressed in terms of the 'Weight Formula', proposed by Alexy to represent all the considerations that affect the weight of a principle, explained above (see Section 2.2.1.1). Recall the formula:

$$W_{i,j} = \frac{I_i \bullet W_i \bullet R_i}{I_j \bullet W_j \bullet R_j}$$

where '$W_{i,j}$' means 'concrete weight of principle of principle i in relation to principle j'; 'I' stands for 'interference', or satisfaction or non-satisfaction of a principle, 'W' for abstract weight, and 'R' for reliability of empirical premises

---

[39] Though she does not develop this argument, as her main claim does not rely on proportionality being able to accommodate rights. Her main aim is to establish the appropriate level at which different versions of proportionality are pertinent. She claims that optimising accounts of proportionality can be used to define more conclusive rights, which then can have a priority grounded on balancing, lending themselves for application by a 'state limiting theory of proportionality'. Alison L Young, 'Proportionality Is Dead: Long Live Proportionality!' in Grant Huscroft, Bradley Miller, and Grégoire Webber (eds), *Proportionality and the Rule of Law: Rights, Justification, Reasoning* (Cambridge University Press 2014) 43. She relies on Rivers' insightful distinction between an 'optimising' and an 'state limiting' conception of proportionality, put to use in his doctrinal analysis of proportionality case-law, in Julian Rivers, 'Proportionality and Variable Intensity of Review' (2006) 65 Cambridge LJ 174, 177–82.

[40] Young (n 39) 43, 50.

as to the satisfaction or non-satisfaction of the principles. Letters 'i' or 'j' as subscript indicate the principle to which the variables I, W, and R apply. As explained above, if the quotient of the division is greater than 1, then it means that principle 'i' is of greater weight than principle 'j', and thus should prevail over it in that particular case. If the quotient is less than one, it means that the latter principle should prevail over the former. If the result is 1, it means that there is a stalemate and there is discretion for the primary decision-maker.[41]

Young is surely right that it is possible to guarantee, for example, that P_i is given peremptory force in the formula, by attributing to it a weight such that it can defeat P_j. This can be done by according to the variables in the formula a weight such that the numerator is higher than the denominator. This could be done in any individual case. It may also be possible to establish a general precedence of one principle (P_i) against another (P_j) by according to the variables W_i and W_j a value such that P_i will always prevail against P_j.[42] In particular, in thinking about the special force of rights as opposed to public interests, if P_i stands for a right, and P_j for some public good, it is possible to attribute to the variables related to P_i a value such that they will 'nearly always' prevail against P_j.

The main problem with this way of capturing rights in proportionality analysis is that it renders the balancing methodology useless. Balancing tests are supposed to help us determine which principle has priority over another in a concrete case, and not simply to express a result arrived

---

[41] See *Balancing and Subsumption* 444–5, and *Theory* 401–14.

[42] One could make W the potentially decisive variable by stipulating that greater or lesser values could be assigned to it than to the other variables. If the difference between the values potentially assigned to one variable and to the others is big enough, one of the variables could be decisive whatever values turn out to be assigned to the other variables. For example, if any value could be assigned to W, including infinite and minus infinite, and to I and R only values from the range 0.25 to 4, then W could be decisive, such that it is possible to establish that P_i will always prevail against P_j by assigning a sufficiently large value to W_i in relation to W_j, and a value sufficiently large to W_i in relation to the possible values of the other variables. Alexy's position is ambiguous in this regard. In the 'Epilogue' to *Theory* he says that the possible values for W are the same as those for I (2^0, 2^1, and 2^2, for serious [or important], medium, or light [or unimportant] respectively). See *Theory* 409–10. These values in turn are of a similar order of magnitude to those that he proposes for R (2^0, 2^{-1}, 2^{-2} for 'reliable', 'plausible', and 'not evidently false'). See *Balancing and Subsumption* 447. Thus no absolute priority could be established a priori between two principles by attributing a greater abstract importance to one of them. But later, in addressing the question of whether his method could reflect the special force of absolute human rights, Alexy says that an 'infinite' value could be assigned to W. See below Section 5.5.3. If so, and supposing that the range of values that could be assigned to I and R remains the same, then one could attribute absolute priority to one principle in relation to some other principle, by attributing a greater abstract importance to one of them.

at through a different method. It is the latter that Young's proposal can achieve, but only by sacrificing the former. The special normative force of rights can be expressed into the balancing formula by according to the variables that compose it values that guarantee a given result favourable to the right. But then balancing is not determining the result, but some other method; the results rendered by this other method are later merely expressed in the balancing methodology.

What is interesting is that Young's suggestion for accommodating rights into balancing further illustrates that the perspective adopted by balancing (if balancing is to determine the result of the case and not simply to express it) is different from the perspective of rights. The Weight Formula compares the potential sacrifice entailed by some measure in terms of a given principle (or set of principles), with its potential benefit in terms of realisation of another principle (or set of principles). The point of this comparison is not merely academic – a normative consequence is attributed to it. If proportionality is used as a sufficient test for deciding the issue, whether an interference with a human right is considered proportional and thus acceptable or not will depend on this comparison expressed by the formula. The moral premise of such a method is the idea that enough gains on one principle justify the interference with another one – an idea that is at the centre of proportionality analysis, as seen above (Section 2.3). This is what the formula reflects by comparing losses on one principle with gains to the other, establishing which principle prevails by reference to the quantity of these gains and losses. This understanding of proportionality, as I argue above (Section 5.3), does not capture the special normative force of rights. It is not a form or reasoning concerned with rights, but with the greatest net satisfaction of principles, values, or interests. Precisely for this reason, if rights reasoning is to decide the matter, it must do so with independence from the proportionality analysis. If nevertheless one still wishes to present the issue in terms of proportionality, there is no solution but to interpret the proportionality test as providing a framework so empty that one can incorporate in it a result arrived at through means that are completely independent from it, and which do not need to be expressed in terms of proportionality to be fully intelligible. This, far from dispelling the tensions between proportionality and rights, reaffirms them.

5.5.3   Balancing and Absolute Rights

The inability of the balancing model to reflect appropriately the special force of rights becomes particularly clear when we see the efforts made by defenders of proportionality to accommodate absolute rights (rights that allow for no exception) into balancing reasoning.[43] There are specific reasons for why balancing cannot accommodate absolute rights, beyond those seen in the previous sections with regard to rights in general.

For Alexy, absolute constraints (which he calls 'categorical constraints') can be 'grasped by means of the weight formula'. He argues that this can be done by 'giving them an infinite value'. Here, we would have reached the 'limits of balancing', though '[t]he fact that balancing has limits of this kind is not to say [. . .] that proportionality does not remain at the centre of rights analysis'. Alexy reminds us that '[p]roportionality analysis is, as the weight formula shows, a formal structure that essentially depends on premises provided from the outside'.[44] If moral reasoning establishes that some claim is absolute, then this can be reflected in balancing by attributing an infinite weight to that claim in the Weight Formula.

There are two problems with this view. First, even if true, it would make proportionality trivial in the way seen in the previous section. Second, the Weight Formula does not capture what absolute claims are about. Absolute rights reflect requirements that must always be complied with. Therefore, they are negative requirements: requirements of not doing something. They reflect things that should never be done to a person. The right not to be tortured or the right not to be forced to adopt a religious belief are paradigmatic examples. This kind of absolute claim is distorted when it is inserted into the Weight Formula. The Weight Formula, as seen in Chapter 2, is premised on the idea that enough gains on one principle justify the interference with another one. By simply expressing a claim (any claim) in terms of the Weight Formula, what is implied is that large enough gains can justify disregarding that claim in a concrete case. As a

---

[43] Though some defenders of proportionality have acknowledged that it cannot reflect 'deontological constraints', and thus should not be applied to cases where such constraints are at stake – which entails that it should not apply to cases where absolute rights or absolute duties are at stake. See Mattias Kumm, 'Political Liberalism and the Structure of Rights: On the Structure and Limit of the Proportionality Requirement' in George Pavlakos (ed), *Law, Rights and Discourse: The Legal Philosophy of Robert Alexy* (Hart Publishing 2007) 162–4, and *Proportionality* 471. Note that Kumm has since changed his position. See Mattias Kumm and Alec D Walen, 'Human Dignity and Proportionality: Deontic Pluralism in Balancing' in Grant Huscroft, Bradley Miller, and Grégoire Webber (eds), *Proportionality and the Rule of Law: Rights, Justification, Reasoning* (Cambridge University Press 2014) 68–9.

[44] Robert Alexy, 'Thirteen Replies' in George Pavlakos (ed), *Law, Rights and Discourse: The Legal Philosophy of Robert Alexy* (Hart Publishing 2007) 344.

matter of logic, the Weight Formula always allows for the possibility that a principle be justifiably interfered with.

But absolute rights reflect an incompatible moral requirement: that *whatever happens*, those rights must be fulfilled, regardless of the benefits that could be derived from a measure that infringes them. A comparison between the infringed right and the benefits derived from the measure that infringes it *is not pertinent*. A claim cannot be absolute in this sense, and at the same time, as the Weight Formula necessarily conveys, allow for the possibility of a justified interference with it (if the gains for a competing principle are large enough in a concrete case).

All this is not only of theoretical but also of practical consequence. Once human rights cases are seen as regarding not the specification of choices and actions that are regarded as unjust and therefore impermissible, but a comparison between degrees of importance and of satisfaction of principles, values, or interests, then it is not impossible that some principle or interest justifying the violation of the absolute right will be of equal weight to the absolute right *as specified by the balancing methodology*. For example: we could torture a person so as to get the location of a terrorist cell and prevent the torturing of two other persons. Torturing a person infringes the right not to be tortured (or the interests associated with that right) at least to the same degree as the torture committed by the terrorist over two persons. If so, then respecting the right not to be tortured in this case would be of equal weight to the principle for whose sake it is being infringed. Note that this is so even if we attribute to the right not to be tortured an infinite value. If we attribute to this right, following Alexy, infinite value, we should attribute to the rivalling principle the same value, since it is the same right that it is being affected in the same way. In this case there is a stalemate, and thus the decision-maker has discretion: he could choose whether or not to torture the terrorist so as to get the location of the terrorist cell. Therefore, infringing the right not to be tortured of the person interrogated would not be disproportionate – it would be legitimate. Of course, on Alexy's model the lack of reliability of premises regarding the likelihood of preventing the torture of the two victims of the terrorist cell could affect the balancing so as to tip the scales in favour of not allowing the policy. But in any case, this is not what absolute rights are about, which simply rule out certain actions and choices, regardless of the benefits associated with them or the likelihood of those benefits occurring.[45] Similar

---

[45] The point here is analytical, regarding the operation of absolute rights. Whether as a matter of substantive morality there is an absolute right not to be tortured (or not to be forced

examples (where the same right is being harmed and protected by a single measure) could be provided for other absolute rights, such as the right not to be forced to adopt or abandon a religious belief. The balancing methodology cannot reflect absolute rights.

For similar reasons Klatt and Meister claim that there are no absolute rights:

> That the state should not torture a person, to cite Webber's example, is only an apparently categorical claim, since we know for certain that in nearly all situations this claim is true. Still, 'in most extreme circumstances' the principle of human dignity might be outweighed. Thus, the absoluteness remains to be relative to colliding principles, rather than being absolute. There is no such thing as an absolute principle.[46]

For Klatt and Meister the reasons for this are to be found in the nature of balancing principles:

> To establish an absolute priority or unconditional precedence is, however, impossible, since it is impossible to balance principles abstractly, without referring to concrete cases. Rather, the very idea of establishing precedence among principles already buys in the dimension of weight, and, thus, balancing. Balancing, however, may only take place relativised to concrete cases.[47]

Klatt and Meister thus discard as 'futile' the idea of 'establishing unconditional priorities of purported absolute rights'. But what is 'futile' is not the idea of establishing unconditional priorities, but to attempt to express unconditional priorities through balancing. This shows a fundamental problem in the way Klatt and Meister argue for the method they propose. Instead of showing how their proposal can reflect the moral requirements that bear on human rights cases, they rule out as irrelevant the moral considerations that cannot be captured by the method they propose.

The contrary should be case: the fact that proportionality and balancing filter out morally relevant considerations counts against them. Even if proportionality were not applied to cases involving absolute rights such as the right not to be subject to torture, it will be applied to cases regarding other rights. If those rights possess a special force, a kind of pre-eminence, then proportionality will filter out that special force or pre-eminence. Defenders of the maximisation account of proportionality cannot claim

---

to adopt a particular religion, etc.) is a different matter. For a defence of absolute rights see *NLNR* 223–6.

[46]   Klatt and Meister (n 25) 31–2 (citation omitted).

[47]   Ibid 32.

that those rights are the product of proportionality analysis – this claim cannot be sustained because proportionality cannot justify those rights as claims possessing the said special force or pre-eminence.

5.6   Rights Reasoning and Proportionality Cases

Stavros Tsakyrakis argues that proportionality 'risks neglecting the complexity of moral evaluation', and, most importantly, 'among the moral concepts that [proportionality] is likely to distort are fundamental individual rights'.[48] He centres his objections on some cases of the European Court of Human Rights.[49] In doing this, he shows how the specific deficiency of the proportionality test analysed in this chapter can manifest itself in cases applying that test.

In *Otto-Preminger-Institut v Austria* the court had to decide whether the seizure and consequent order of destruction by the Austrian authorities

[48] Stavros Tsakyrakis, 'Proportionality: An Assault on Human Rights?' (2009) 7 Int'l J Const L 468, 475.

[49] In his reply to Tsakyrakis' paper, Madhav Khosla challenges Tsakyrakis' use of cases such as *Otto-Preminger v Austria* and *IA v Turkey* because in such cases the court typically applies the 'margin of appreciation doctrine', and, according to Khosla, 'it is this doctrine, rather than proportionality, that has created the outcome in both cases'. Madhav Khosla, 'Proportionality: An Assault on Human Rights?: A Reply' (2010) 8 Int'l J Const L 298, 303. It is true that the doctrine of margin of appreciation is doing much work in both of these cases. But that does not entail that proportionality is not at stake as well. In these cases we see in action the doctrine of what George Letsas has called the 'structural margin of appreciation', according to which the European Court defers to state authorities because it recognises that they are better placed to assess the relevant facts (see George Letsas, *A Theory of Interpretation of the European Convention on Human Rights* (Oxford University Press 2007) Chapter 4). But note that the court defers to state authorities because they know better the *facts* that are relevant for the case. These facts relate, for example, to what is considered offensive or contrary to positive morality in a particular society. But what makes these facts relevant is precisely proportionality analysis. Thus, proportionality is at stake in these cases, despite the use of margin of appreciation. Furthermore, the cases analysed by Tsakyrakis are representative of a considerable line of cases using margin of appreciation doctrine in connection with proportionality analysis. See for example: 'By reason of their direct and continuous contact with the vital forces of their countries, State authorities are in principle in a better position than the international judge to give an opinion on the exact content of these requirements with regard to the rights of others as well as on the "necessity" of a "restriction" intended to protect from such material those whose deepest feelings and convictions would be seriously offended.' *Wingrove v United Kingdom* (App no 17419/90) (1997) 24 EHRR 1 [58]. The same statement is repeated in *Murphy v Ireland* (App no 44179/98) (2004) 38 EHRR 13 [67], and a similar one in *Müller and Others v Switzerland* (App no 10737/84) (1991) 13 EHRR 212 [35], *Handyside v United Kingdom* (1979–80) 1 EHRR 737 [48], and *Otto-Preminger-Institute v Austria* (App no 13470/87) (1995) 19 EHRR [Hereinafter *Otto-Preminger*] [56].

of a film that was considered offensive to the religious beliefs of the great majority of Tyroleans was compatible with article 10 of the European Convention on Human Rights.[50]

A majority of six out of nine judges of the European Court chamber held that there was no violation of article 10, since they deemed the decision of the Austrian authorities proportionate to achieve the legitimate aim of protecting the 'rights of others', in this case, religious liberty.[51] The minority took the view that, considering the measures taken by the applicant and the protection of the Austrian legislation to those under 17, 'on balance [. . .] the seizure and forfeiture of the film in question were not proportionate to the legitimate aim pursued'.[52] Both majority and minority decisions relied on proportionality analysis.

Tsakyrakis notes that the court was rather quick in asserting that there was a legitimate aim for the prohibition, and that this aim was the protection of a *right*. The majority, says Tsakyrakis, 'seems to have treated this as little more than a kind of formal inquiry, as mere taxonomic exercise'.[53] The minority treated this point more ambiguously. They asserted that there was no 'right to protection of religious feelings', but at the same time, accepted that the aim sought by the measure was legitimate since 'the democratic character of a society will be affected if violent and abusive attacks on the reputation of a religious group are allowed'.[54] Both majority and minority agreed that the measure had a legitimate aim, and explicitly in the decision of the majority it is affirmed that that aim was the protection of a right.

But whether there exists such a right on the side of those that benefited from the Austrian authorities' measure, and its precise content, is a contestable matter. Is any expression that happens to offend or disturb a believer by reason of her faith a violation of religious liberty? Surely not. This would seem too broad an interpretation of religious liberty. For the court, there cannot be a general right not to hear one's religious beliefs being criticised, but there has to be some protection from some methods of opposition to religious beliefs aimed at inhibiting people from expressing and holding those beliefs.[55]

These are sound distinctions, but as Tsakyrakis points out, the court makes notably little effort to assess how the above categories apply to this

---

[50] Tsakyrakis (n 48) 477.
[51] Ibid [47–8], [56].
[52] Ibid (dissent) [11].
[53] Tsakyrakis (n 48) 479.
[54] *Otto-Preminger* (dissent) [6], quoted in Tsakyrakis (n 48) 479.
[55] *Otto-Preminger* [47].

case and what do they entail. For Tsakyrakis this is linked to a common feature of proportionality, which he calls 'the principle of definitional generosity'. According to this principle

> the interpreter assumes a broad definition of what can conceivably count as an instance of the exercise of a certain right [. . .] The interpreter's purpose, here, is merely to assess whether a given act or behaviour will be prima facie included within the ambit of a provision safeguarding, say, freedom of expression or freedom of religion.[56]

Furthermore, and this is crucial, not much seems to depend on whether the legitimate aim at stake is a right – and what kind of right, human or some other perhaps less important one – or some other public interest.

> Since the threshold is not demanding, the normative implications that such a specification of a right carries with it are correspondingly limited. The interpreter can be generous at the stage of specification, safe in the knowledge that all the crucial normative issues may be deferred to the balancing stage.[57]

This under-specification of rights is problematic, and it affects not only the scope of the right (e.g. is this particular form of speech protected?), but, crucially, its strength (e.g. can this act of speech be impaired? What reasons can justify the impairment, and what reasons cannot?). Tsakyrakis observes this in relation to the *IA v Turkey* case.[58] In that case the applicant ran a publishing house that in 1993 published a novel addressing a number of theological issues. He was convicted of blasphemy and sentenced to two years' imprisonment and a fine, but the prison sentence was commuted for a fine, so that the applicant only had to pay a total fine equivalent to $16. With respect to proportionality in the narrow sense, the Court said it was 'mindful of the fact that the domestic courts did not decide to seize the book, and accordingly considers that the insignificant fine imposed was proportionate to the aims pursued'.[59]

As Tsakyrakis notes, this form of reasoning risks 'losing sight of the battles of principle with which human rights law is so intimately intertwined'.[60] The reasoning of the court displays little interest in assessing the pre-emptive force that human rights are taken to have. On the contrary, 'the balancing approach [. . .] is committed to a view whereby everything, even

---

[56] Ibid 481.
[57] Ibid.
[58] *IA v Turkey* (App 42571/98) (2007) 45 EHRR 30 [hereinafter *IA*].
[59] *IA* [47].
[60] Tsakyrakis (n 48) 485.

those aspects of our life most closely associated with our status as free and equal, is, in principle, up for grabs.'[61]

The problems of lack of specification apply not only to rights. What counts as a public interest, deserving to be put on the scale against the engaged right (say, here, of freedom of speech and communication), is also treated by the court without much analysis (and we can use here 'public interest' as a working label that includes other similar concepts such as 'public order', and 'morals'). By adopting the principle of definitional generosity courts save themselves the effort of undertaking this task. And by doing so, illicit justifications can end up being 'weighed' together with other preferences, interests, and, rights, instead of being weeded out.[62]

Critics of Tsakyrakis, such as Kai Möller and Madhav Khosla, have pointed out that a bad application of proportionality does not count against proportionality itself.[63] It could be that a court applied the test wrongly. It could even be (as Tsakyrakis suggests) that some courts generally apply the test wrongly. None of this, they say, would count against proportionality itself. But my argument is more ambitious. There is a widespread understanding of proportionality that by its very nature systematically filters out considerations of rights. This understanding of the test is not the invention of a critic, but has been elaborated and defended by some of the most distinguished and influential theorists of proportionality.[64] Analyses of case-law such as the one offered by Tsakyrakis provide a valuable illustration of how the deficiencies of proportionality appear in concrete cases. The main points Tsakyrakis makes against some applications of the proportionality test by the courts can also be made against some general theories of the maximisation account of proportionality:[65] not any interest can be protected as a legitimate interest, and not any legitimate interest can be considered a 'public interest', since an interest must be connected somehow to the common good in order to be part of the latter.

---

[61]   Ibid 489.

[62]   See ibid 488.

[63]   See *Challenging Critics*, 710–11, 718, 722, and 728. For a similar argumentative strategy see Khosla (n 49) 302–6.

[64]   And thus it is understandable that Möller has set out to elaborate an alternative theory of proportionality that is substantially different from the more orthodox account analysed in this part, and thus not open to the same criticism. See *Global Model*. In the next part of the book I engage with this account of proportionality.

[65]   Though I have my reservations about Tsakyrakis' proposal for replacing the proportionality analysis with moral deliberation in adjudication, as will become clear in the next part of the book.

And, especially, not all interests and values (not even those legitimate or connected to the common good) deserve to be protected as human rights. Justice demands differentiation. It demands the protection of some interests in a special, stricter way. But not all interests that we have are linked to justice in this way. And those that are, have a certain pre-eminence over other considerations, as justice has a particular pre-eminence over other considerations related to interests.[66]

All this is a very basic but important part of our moral vocabulary, precisely because it allows for expressing some relevant moral distinctions. If there are certain particularly stringent requirements of justice that ground certain claims that everybody has in virtue of being human, then proportionality analysis fails by not considering the particular force these claims have. This is candidly acknowledged by Beatty, when he claims that proportionality 'makes the concept of rights almost irrelevant',[67] and that in the proportionality analysis rights 'have no special force as trumps [. . .] They are really just rhetorical flourish.'[68] Nevertheless, if there are such requirements of justice, then not acknowledging their importance is a deficiency of his theory. In the same way, if what proportionality maximises includes legitimate interests and preferences and illegitimate ones, and interests that should be protected as rights and others that do not deserve this protection, then this legal method is at fault for not distinguishing between claims that differ from one another in morally significant ways and deserve different treatment.

5.7 Conclusion: Abandoning the Maximisation Account

I have argued that proportionality, at least under a widespread understanding of it, cannot capture the normative force of rights. It is not a form of rights reasoning, and, therefore, when it is applied, rights are moved out of the picture. This is paradoxical, since it seems that rights talk, and especially human rights talk, is more pervasive than ever. But legal rights can be understood in all sorts of different ways. They are given concrete meaning by the generally accepted doctrinal methods used for deciding cases involving them. It could well be that much in human rights cases does not respond to the kind of reasons that we call 'rights' in moral parlance.[69]

---

[66] For a defence of the 'primacy of justice' thesis, see Jeremy Waldron, 'The Primacy of Justice' (2003) 9 Legal Theory 269.

[67] David Beatty, *The Ultimate Rule of Law* (Oxford University Press 2004) 160.

[68] Ibid 171.

[69] As noted by Möller in *Global Model* 1.

Now, my argument is not about the proper use of the word 'right'. One can call something a 'right', but treat it as a reason of a different type. What I want to call attention to is the moving out of the picture of a distinctive and important type of reason – one associated with requirements of justice and attributed a special normative force – often called 'right'. Because these are important considerations, sound moral and legal analysis should be sensitive to them, and it is a deficiency for a legal method to ignore considerations of this type when they are at stake. If such considerations of justice are involved in human rights cases, then a legal method for addressing those cases needs to be sensitive to those considerations. It is a matter of the utmost seriousness if the most widespread understanding of the most widely used test for addressing human rights cases fails to meet this requirement.

The maximisation account of proportionality fails. It is open to all the objections I have made in the previous chapters. It is open to the incommensurability objection, because it attempts to commensurate incommensurable rights or principles, and because it attempts to strike this comparison along variables that are themselves incommensurable (intensity and extension of interests; or degree of satisfaction of principles and reliability of premises regarding their satisfaction, etc.). Furthermore, there is no reason for applying the method proposed by the theories of the maximisation account of proportionality to human rights cases. Defenders of proportionality have not provided such a reason, and they cannot do so because the method filters out considerations that are morally relevant in the cases to which proportionality is applied. The different objections show that human rights cases are more complex than the maximisation account of proportionality supposes. They require distinguishing different kinds of interests and public goods, and all these from rights, and establishing relations of priority that cannot be reduced to or grounded on a single quantitative comparison.

In the face of the objections presented against the maximisation account, there has been a tendency in some authors to provide novel interpretations of the proportionality test. Proportionality is defended from its critics by way of reconceptualising it. This reconceptualisation attempts to abandon the problematic methodologies of the maximisation account of proportionality. Instead, it empties proportionality of distinct content as a legal test, and conceives it as a tool for demanding justification for a measure of a particular authority that affects a human right, and for allowing the court to assess this justification through open-ended moral reasoning, unconstrained by the law. If proportionality is conceived in this way, then it is not affected by the objections made against it in this and the previous chapters. Proportionality would be able to accommodate whatever are the morally relevant reasons. But this would come at the price of providing no legal direction – a hefty price to pay. I now turn to the analysis and critique of this different understanding of proportionality, in the second part of this book.

PART II

6

Proportionality as Unconstrained Moral Reasoning

As said in Chapter 2, the general structure of the proportionality test makes intuitive sense when seen from the prism of maximisation. Once the maximisation account of proportionality is discarded, can the test be saved by taking advantage of the vagueness of human rights language, and of the proportionality test in particular, to reinterpret it, so that it can incorporate the relevant moral requirements that bear on human rights cases, such as the special importance that rights are taken to have? An account of proportionality that has gained prominence in the writings of recent defenders of the proportionality test can avoid the objections made against the maximisation account of proportionality. This account I call 'proportionality as unconstrained moral reasoning'.

In what follows I will describe the main theories of this account, I will situate this account in the proportionality debate, and introduce objections to it, which will be developed in the subsequent chapters.

6.1 Theories of Proportionality as Unconstrained Moral Reasoning

The account of proportionality as unconstrained moral reasoning is adopted in most recent theories of proportionality, particularly in defending the proportionality test against criticism. The writings of the main proponents of this account have received considerable attention in discussions on human rights law and adjudication, and the influence of this account is growing. There are good reasons for this. An advantage of this account is its potential for providing a unified view of some peculiar features of the legal practice of human rights that have become widespread in recent decades, such as rights inflation and the relatively open-ended character of human rights adjudication. The characteristics of this account that I explain next correspond to global trends in recent human rights law; these are all presented as a unified whole at the centre of which is the proportionality test in human rights adjudication. This account provides a general reconstruction of the legal practice of human rights that is intelligible and appealing.

It is characterised by the following. First, the account presupposes an expansive view of human rights, according to which human rights are taken to encompass a great number of interests, including (on some accounts) trivial or even immoral interests. Second, human rights thus conceived can be limited by a government measure that aims to promote some other right or public interest; when rights are limited, they require that the government presents reasons that justify this interference with rights. Third, the proportionality test is used to assess these reasons. Fourth, proportionality is understood as allowing for any morally relevant reason to be assessed in establishing which of the values, principles, or interests in conflict should prevail; particularly the last balancing stage will demand not the application of a concrete method (such as the one proposed by the theories of the maximisation account of proportionality), but that the judge engages directly with the reasons given by the parties and assesses them through practical reasoning unconstrained by a particular legal method or other legal categories. The idea of justification is at the centre of the main theories of proportionality as unconstrained moral reasoning.

Thus, some theorists have claimed that one of the main advantages of proportionality is that it allows citizens to demand from public authorities justifications for their actions. Cohen-Eliya and Porat, in an influential article, see this feature as part of greater trend, a 'profound shift in constitutional law on a global level', which they characterise following Etienne Mureinik,[1] as 'a shift from a culture of authority to a culture of justification'.[2] A culture of justification would 'require that governments should provide substantive justification for all their actions, by which we mean justification in terms of the rationality and reasonableness of every action and the trade-offs that every action necessarily involves, i.e., in terms of proportionality'.[3] Proportionality thus is taken to be central to the enterprise of public authorities having to justify their actions before courts, which have to 'assess those justifications *on the basis of reason*'.[4]

---

[1] Etienne Mureinik, 'A Bridge to Where: Introducing the Interim Bill of Rights' (1994) 10 S Afr J HR 31.

[2] Moshe Cohen-Eliya and Iddo Porat, 'Proportionality and the Culture of Justification' (2011) 59 2 Am J Comp L 463, 466 [hereinafter *PCJ*].

[3] Ibid 466–7.

[4] Ibid 488 (emphasis added).

A culture of justification is opposed to a culture of authority. A culture of authority, it is said, 'emphasises the need for finality', whereas a culture of justification emphasises the rationality of decisions.[5] In a culture of justification the judicial methods used to evaluate government's measures have to allow for a direct assessment of justifications. Adherence to text is secondary and can be ignored if necessary to directly assess justifications.[6] Another feature of the culture of justification is that

> rights are viewed as values – substantive goods – that reflect aspirations to progress and rationality. Rights, to use a common philosophical terminology, are viewed in 'perfectionist' terms as positive values to be promoted and respected as much as possible by governmental action.[7]

The immediate effect of this conception of rights is 'the expansion in their scope',[8] which allows for an increase in the actions that can be taken to affect a particular right, and as such be challenged in court. Proportionality is assumed to be a highly flexible judicial method that allows courts to assess directly the reasons for a measure that affects a human right.

Kai Möller provides a similar account of proportionality and balancing. Möller argues for a general right to autonomy, which he defines as 'a right to everything which, judged from the perspective of the agent's self-conception, is in his interest'.[9] This right therefore includes not only important interests, but also trivial or even evil ones (as an interest a person can have in murdering another).[10] What this right amounts to is that it only serves to trigger a demand for justification, whereby the government is required to provide 'sufficiently strong reasons' for limiting a person's

---

[5] Ibid 479. Moshe Cohen-Eliya and Iddo Porat, *Proportionality and Constitutional Culture* (Cambridge University Press 2013) 112 [hereinafter *PCC*].

[6] 'In a culture of justification, the judiciary's role is to demand that the government justify its actions. Such a conception downplays the importance of the text. The text allows for "outward" legitimacy, and secures the public status of the court, but it is not essential to the court's authority to review governmental action and demand justification. This authority is derived directly from the court's function, and from the idea that government action is not legitimate unless it is justified.' *PCJ* 479. See also 490: 'While it is true that the texts of new constitutions direct judges to assess whether the limitations are "justified in a democratic society," this amounts to an authorization by the text to downplay the text, i.e., to engage in the assessment of justification, rather than textual interpretation.' See also *PCC* 120.

[7] *PCJ* 478, citation omitted. See also *PCC* 118.

[8] *PCJ* 478.

[9] *Global Model* 73.

[10] Ibid 78–9.

autonomy interest.[11] In this sense 'one can speak of the right to autonomy as a "right to justification"'.[12]

This approach is seen to have as its counterpart an institutional design where courts can review measures enacted by public authorities that affect persons' interests generally through the two-step analysis that is so common in many jurisdictions. The first step only asserts that there has been an interference with a right and the second whether this interference is justified. At the first step, human rights should be interpreted broadly, so as to include any autonomy interest. Therefore, for Möller, 'nothing would be lost in theory by simply acknowledging one comprehensive prima facie right to personal autonomy', instead of 'a set of distinct constitutional rights'.[13]

The second step concerns the justification of the limitation of the right. Because the first 'prima facie stage [. . .] does not operate as a filter [. . .] most of the hard analytical work, separating successful from unsuccessful rights claims, must be done at the justification stage'.[14] The doctrinal tool for deciding whether a limitation of a right is justified or not is the proportionality test. A policy that interferes with a person's autonomy 'is proportionate and therefore justified if it resolves a conflict of autonomy interests in a reasonable way'.[15] Proportionality and balancing are conceived as doctrines that, 'because of the high level of abstraction at which they are formulated, offer no immediate guidance as to what makes a measure disproportionate or how to conduct the balancing'.[16] Balancing, in particular, should not be equated with 'autonomy maximization'.[17] Instead, it 'ought to be understood in the sense of "balancing all the relevant moral considerations"'.[18] Möller provides a typology of different senses of the

---

[11] Ibid 86–7.

[12] Ibid 87.

[13] Ibid 89–90. Though Möller ultimately leans towards bills of rights based on two practical advantages they have: they can 'single out some particularly important aspects of personal autonomy', and can leave out 'those rights which will rarely or never survive the justification stage, thus avoiding to some extent unrealistic expectations'. Ibid 90. Note that these types of 'pragmatic' considerations provide reasons for establishing more precise legal positive human rights, which would challenge the model based on a general right to autonomy that Möller promotes. This will be explored in the next chapters.

[14] Ibid 178.

[15] Ibid.

[16] Ibid 100. This is contradicted by Möller's assertion that proportionality 'provides a *structure* which guides judges through the reasoning process'. See ibid 179 (emphasis in the original). Below I address this tension (Section 6.4).

[17] Ibid 141.

[18] Ibid 134.

word 'balance'.[19] Depending on the considerations that bear on the case, some forms of balance may be appropriate and not others. Deciding which form of balance is appropriate in a particular case is part of the moral reasoning that needs to be done by the judge applying the proportionality test at the balancing stage. The idea of balancing, as a technical doctrinal category, 'does not without further argument give us guidance other than that a moral argument about the correct balance between the competing values has to be made'.[20]

Möller and Cohen-Eliya and Porat draw important insights from the original account of proportionality provided by Mattias Kumm. Kumm too sees proportionality as allowing for a practice of demanding justification of government action – what he calls 'Socratic contestation'.[21] And he endorses a similar view of human rights. Rights have two characteristics, according to Kumm: 'First, a rights-holder does not have very much in virtue of having a right. [. . .] An infringement of the scope of a right merely serves as a trigger to initiate an assessment' of whether the infringement is justified'.[22] The second characteristic 'is the flipside of the first. Since comparatively little is decided by acknowledging that a measure infringes a right, the focus of rights adjudication is generally on the reasons that justify the infringement'.[23]

This dovetails with the proportionality test:

> The four prong structure of proportionality analysis provides little more than a structure which functions as a checklist for the individually necessary and collectively sufficient conditions that determine whether the reasons that can be marshalled to justify an infringement of a right are good reasons under the circumstances. Assessing the justification of rights infringements is, at least in the many cases where the constitution provides no specific further guidance, *largely an exercise of general practical reasoning, without many of the constraining features that otherwise characterise legal reasoning*.[24]

---

[19] Ibid 137–40.
[20] Ibid 140.
[21] See generally Mattias Kumm, 'The Idea of Socratic Contestation and the Right to Justification: The Point of Rights-Based Proportionality Review' (2010) 4 2 Law & Ethics of Human Rights 142 [hereinafter *Socratic*].
[22] Mattias Kumm, 'Political Liberalism and the Structure of Rights: On the Place and Limits of the Proportionality Requirement' in George Pavlakos (ed), *Law, Rights and Discourse: The Legal Philosophy of Robert Alexy* (Hart 2007) 131, 139 [hereinafter *PL*]. The same formulation is in *Socratic* 150 and in Mattias Kumm, 'Constitutional Rights as Principles: On the Structure and Domain of Constitutional Justice' (2004) 2 Int'l J Const L 574, 582 [hereinafter *CR*].
[23] Ibid. See also *Socratic* 150 and *CR* 582.
[24] Ibid. See also *Socratic* 150 and *CR* 582 (emphasis added).

Proportionality's 'open-ended structure' allows for a direct assessment of the reasons that would justify government authority – what he calls 'the turn from legal interpretation to public reason oriented justification'.[25]

It is not clear which, if any, of the traditional legal constraints would remain for this account of proportionality. Kumm says that 'arguments relating to legal authorities – text, history, precedence, etc. – have a relatively modest role to play', the 'heart' of most human rights cases being the proportionality test.[26] Text is not seen as constraining legal reasoning, since it 'typically provides very little guidance for the resolution of concrete claims',[27] serving 'merely as a basis for an authorization for courts to engage in open-ended inquiry'.[28] The ideal of a culture of justification 'downplays the importance of the text'.[29] Little is said about the status of precedent for this account. Cohen-Eliya and Porat do not mention the word at all in their article.[30] Similarly, Möller does not mention it once in his book providing the most comprehensive account of his theory.[31] Kumm mentions precedent only to contrast legalistic reasoning – described as 'strongly focused on text, history and precedent' – with the proportionality analysis that allows for Socratic contestation. He remarks that 'the conceptual structure of legal doctrine more often than not distorts public reasoning while it professionalizes legal discourse'.[32] It seems as if a practice of following precedent, or any positive legal source for that matter, could do little more than hamper the task of demanding and assessing reasons from public authorities – the task of Socratic contestation courts are to perform, and for which they are so well suited on Kumm's account.

All these accounts of proportionality have the same features described at the beginning of this chapter. They understand proportionality as a tool for realising the requirement of justification that applies to government's interferences with persons' interests, and as giving the opportunity for courts to evaluate those interferences based on a direct engagement with the reasons presented by government, unmediated by legal categories. In this sense, they conceive of the proportionality test as requiring

---

[25] *Socratic* 142.
[26] Ibid 144.
[27] Ibid 153.
[28] Ibid 146.
[29] *PCJ* 479.
[30] *PCJ*.
[31] *Global Model.*
[32] *Socratic* 157–8.

open-ended moral reasoning for the purposes of establishing the legitimacy of a measure that interferes with a human right.

This unconstrained aspect of proportionality can be further explored by engaging with Kumm's claim that proportionality is not incompatible with some of the characteristics that rights are taken to have in the liberal tradition. Even though I do not agree with all of Kumm's characterisation of rights,[33] I will not challenge it here. Instead, I will focus on the way Kumm can incorporate these characteristics of rights into the proportionality analysis. Engaging with his arguments helps illustrate how proportionality can deal with some of the moral requirements seen in the previous chapters, particularly with the special force that rights are taken to have. The way in which Kumm incorporates the moral force of rights into the proportionality scheme can be used to include whatever is considered relevant from the moral perspective. Therefore, the implications of his argument go beyond Kumm's liberalism and what he presupposes are the relevant moral considerations. Thus, it is important to understand this promising alternative.

6.2   Can Proportionality Reflect the Characteristic Features of Human Rights?

For Kumm there are three characteristic features of human rights, according to the liberal tradition. The first is that rights 'protect individuals from strong paternalist impositions relating to how they should live their lives. [. . .] It is not within the jurisdiction of public authorities to prescribe what the ultimate orientations and commitments of an individual should be.'[34] Reasons based on perfectionist values then should be excluded from justification of rights infringements. Kumm holds that proportionality can accommodate this aspect of liberal rights. It does so

> both at the first prong of the proportionality test, since [perfectionist ideals] are not a legitimate purpose that can justify infringements of individual liberty, and at the level of balancing, since furthering a particular perfectionist ideal is not a reason to weigh when assessing the proportionality of a measure furthering some other legitimate purpose.[35]

In Kumm's account, the idea of excluded reasons is not implied by proportionality. Rather, proportionality and the idea of excluded reasons are

---

[33] For example, I think it is imprecise to conflate perfectionism and paternalism.

[34] *PL* 142.

[35] Ibid 145.

'complementary structural features of rights in a liberal constitutional democracy'.[36] Furthermore, he concedes that focus on 'proportionality alone' can 'obscure' some 'core structural features of liberal constitutional practice' that the idea of excluded reasons helps illuminate.[37]

The second characteristic of rights in the liberal tradition according to Kumm is what he calls 'anticollectivism'. Rights 'are believed to enjoy priority [...] in relationship to collective goods or "the general interest"', though the priority cannot be absolute: 'under any plausible account of rights the liberty interest will have to yield at some point'.[38] For Kumm, proportionality can easily incorporate this characteristic of rights. Here, the open-ended structure of proportionality is presented as the crucial aspect of proportionality that allows for the priority of rights to be reflected in the proportionality analysis:

> The metaphor of 'balancing' should not obscure the fact that the last prong of the proportionality test will in many cases require the decision-maker to engage in a theoretically informed practical reasoning [...] At the level of evaluating the relative importance of the general interest in relation to the liberty interest at stake, the weights can be assigned and priorities established as required by the correct substantive theory of justice. The last prong of the proportionality test then *provides a space for the reasoned incorporation of an understanding of liberties that expresses whatever priority over collective goods is substantively justified.*[39]

The proportionality test can accommodate this second characteristic of rights because the balancing stage is understood as allowing for general practical reasoning in assessing which of the interests, values, or principles should have priority in a given case.

The third characteristic is related to what Kumm calls 'anticonsequentialism'. 'The basic idea is that there are restrictions connected to the idea of the inviolability of persons that impose constraints on actors seeking to bring about desirable consequences.'[40] This characteristic is fundamentally linked with the idea of 'means–ends' relationships. It involves not using persons merely as means, at least given certain circumstances. What is interesting for our purposes is whether proportionality can express these

---

[36] Ibid 147.
[37] Ibid 146.
[38] Ibid 148. This way of understanding rights is not the only one. For an account of rights as 'in all cases [...] absolute', see *Negotiable Constitution* Chapter 4.
[39] *PL* 148–9. Emphasis added.
[40] Ibid 153.

kinds of considerations. Kumm concludes that proportionality cannot reflect this characteristic of liberal rights. His reason is that

> proportionality analysis and the balancing test in particular [. . .] systematically filter out means–ends relationships that are central to the understanding of deontological constraints. Yet the nature of means–ends relationship can be key. Whether the claims made by the rights-bearer [. . .] are made as an enabler or a disabler [. . .] [is] often [a] morally decisive feature of the situation. These questions only come into view once the structure of the means–ends relationship becomes the focus of a separate enquiry.[41]

But there is an inconsistency here. The other two characteristics of liberal rights were incorporated on the grounds of their reasonableness. Because they are reasonable, they deserve to be incorporated in the proportionality analysis and shape or correct the maximising procedure. Why not incorporate everything reasonable? This would raise the question of whether proportionality as a technical category is formal enough to accommodate this type of absolute claim. But Kumm already showed how an aspect of liberal rights that establishes an absolute priority can be incorporated in the proportionality analysis – the antiperfectionist aspect of liberal rights. Whatever the gains in perfectionist values, that cannot justify a particular measure that affects a right. This is as absolute as deontological anticonsequentialist constraints.[42] If the last prong of proportionality can 'provide a

---

[41] Ibid 162–3. On the enabler/disabler distinction, see Alec Walen, 'Doing, Allowing, and Disabling: Some Principles Governing Deontological Restrictions' (1995) 80 2 Phil Stud 183, quoted in *PL* 154 n 50. The well-known trolley example helps him explain this distinction. A runaway trolley will kill five people if a bystander does not: (First scenario) divert it into another track, where it will only kill V. (Second scenario) push V into the track to stop the trolley. In the first case V's claim purports to 'disable the otherwise permitted scenario'. On the second scenario, 'V makes a claim that he should not be used [merely] as a means to enable the rescue of others'. The claims of disablers are weaker than those of enablers. For Kumm claims of disablers are subject only to proportionality, while those of enablers are protected by deontological constraints that forbid using a person as enabler, that is, merely as means. Aharon Barak follows Kumm in believing that proportionality can accommodate the two first aspects of rights according to the liberal tradition, but not the third. See *Proportionality*, 468–72.

[42] Someone could argue against this premise of Kumm's analysis: that anticonsequentialist constraints are absolute, that is, that they specify certain acts that whatever the consequences at stake, can never be done. Jeremy Waldron has noted that 'most philosophical theories which oppose routine trade-offs between rights and consequences nevertheless toy with the idea of some sort of "out" to avoid *ruat caelum* absolutism'. Jeremy Waldron, *Torture, Terror, and Trade-Offs: Philosophy for the White House* (Oxford University Press 2010) 31. Kumm himself seems to share these apprehensions with absolute moral requirements, when referring to a 'baseline' relating to 'torture and terrorist killings' as implying

space for the reasoned incorporation of liberties that expresses whatever priority over collective goods is substantially justified',[43] it can also 'provide a space for the reasoned incorporation of liberties that expresses whatever anticonsequentialist prohibitions on treating persons merely as means is substantially justified'. Proportionality could also accommodate this characteristic in the first prong of the test – legitimate aim – in the same way as the feature of 'excluded reasons' was accommodated within the test, and for the same reasons.

We can make an even more general point: any reasonable moral idea can be incorporated into the proportionality analysis. This is implied by the idea that proportionality as an open-ended structure allows for unconstrained practical reasoning, where all the relevant considerations are taken into account and related in the most reasonable way.[44] Any relevant consideration can be accommodated in the proportionality analysis in at least the same way that the second characteristic of liberal rights was, and for the same reasons.

This is why Kumm's conclusion in his article on *Political Liberalism and the Structure of Rights* shows an inconsistency. Kumm claims that 'a structure of rights that is *exclusively focused* on proportionality' does not *adequately reflect* two of the central commitments of 'the tradition of Political Liberalism'.[45] Those two 'central commitments' are the antiperfectionist and the anticonsequentialist aspect of Political Liberalism – though the former can be accommodated in the 'legitimate aim' and the balancing part of the test, as explained above.[46] 'The anticollectivist aspect [. . .] on the other hand, is *appropriately reflected* in the proportionality structure.'[47] But the expression 'adequately/appropriately reflected' is being applied inconsistently, according to two different criteria. Understanding the

---

'something close to' (but not simply 'a') categorical prohibition. See *PL* 163. If certain particularly dire circumstances could justify violating anticonsequentialist constraints, then the difference between those constraints and anticollectivist constraints would be only a matter of degree, and the 'change in the baseline' of which Kumm speaks would not be significant enough for excluding anticonsequentialist constraints from proportionality. For a defence of moral absolutes, even on the face of a (then realistic) catastrophe, see John Finnis, Joseph Boyle Jr, and Germain Grisez, *Nuclear Deterrence, Morality and Realism* (Oxford University Press 1987).

[43] *PL* 148.
[44] Ibid 140, 151, *CR* 582, *Socratic* 146, 147 n 12, 150, 174.
[45] *PL* 164.
[46] Ibid 145.
[47] Ibid 164 (emphasis added).

difference between the two is crucial for evaluating the idea of proportionality as allowing for unconstrained moral reasoning.

The two different criteria are designated by the verbs *express* and *accommodate*. A technical legal category can *express* or can merely *accommodate* a moral consideration. A legal category expresses a moral consideration when the legal category provides guidance as to how to act or decide in a particular case so as to comply with the moral consideration. A legal category can merely accommodate a moral consideration when the legal category is not guiding action in a way necessarily consistent or necessarily inconsistent with the moral consideration, so that the person applying the legal category can be consistent or inconsistent with the requirements of the moral consideration, without disregarding the legal category. A legal category can express or accommodate a moral consideration in different degrees.

With respect to the anticollectivist aspect of liberal rights, Kumm says that proportionality can adequately reflect it because proportionality analysis can *accommodate* that moral consideration. It is said that proportionality 'provides a *space* for the reasoned *incorporation* of an understanding of liberties that expresses whatever priority over collective goods is substantively justified'.[48] We can *incorporate* something only if in some way is not yet there. But with respect to the antiperfectionist and anticonsequentialist aspect of liberal rights, Kumm seems to set a higher standard. Proportionality does not adequately reflect these aspects of rights because it does not *express* them. This is particularly clear in relation to the antiperfectionist aspect of liberal rights, the relation of it to proportionality being one of 'complementary structural features of rights in liberal constitutional democracy'.[49] The antiperfectionist aspect can be accommodated into the proportionality analysis, as Kumm suggests. As seen above, the same could be said of the anticonsequentialist aspect of rights.

If proportionality requires considering all the relevant moral considerations that could potentially apply in the case, it can accommodate all these aspects of rights, and any other consideration. Proportionality thus characterised cannot be reductionist. Not surprisingly, Kumm's later work on the matter emphasised the unconstrained character of proportionality reasoning and omitted mentioning the purported limitations in capturing certain relevant moral considerations (viz., anticonsequentialist considerations) that proportionality was taken to have in his earlier work.[50]

---

[48] Ibid 148–9 (emphasis added).
[49] Ibid 147.
[50] See *Socratic*.

Later on, Kumm came to reject the idea that proportionality could not accommodate deontological constraints (what he called 'human dignity exceptionalism'),[51] since 'balancing [. . .] requires the decision-maker to take into account everything relevant that is not already addressed in the first three prongs of the proportionality test',[52] arguing that

> [h]uman dignity exceptionalism is false. Whereas it was right to insist that the structure of political morality is not automatically captured [i.e., expressed, in my terminology] by the four prongs of the proportionality test [. . .] the proportionality test and the idea of balancing in particular is flexible enough to allow [accommodate] for the structural complexities of political morality to be taken into account [. . .]. [T]he balance will have to make appropriate reference to constraints that arise out of what is required to respect dignity.[53]

6.3   Proportionality as Unconstrained Moral Reasoning and the Proportionality Debate

If proportionality is understood as allowing for unconstrained moral reasoning, it is immune to the objections made in the first part of this book against the maximisation account of proportionality. These objections ultimately amount to the claim that proportionality does not properly capture the relevant moral considerations that bear on human rights cases. It filters out some relevant moral considerations – such as the special force of rights, and, on some versions, the distinction between legitimate and illegitimate interests – and the method is problematic in that it relies on an implicit or explicit commensurability of considerations that are incommensurable. The way proportionality analysis can incorporate the morally relevant considerations is by opening its scope as a technical category. If proportionality allows for open-ended moral reasoning without committing itself to a particular method for addressing human rights, then it can, in principle, allow judges to address human rights cases considering the moral requirements that the maximisation account fails to capture in its methodology.

It is not surprising that for Möller the different objections made to proportionality are unsound. For him, they rest on mistakenly assuming that proportionality must rely on 'interest balancing' – maximisation

---

[51]   Mattias Kumm and Alec Walen, 'Human Dignity and Proportionality: Deontic Pluralism in Balancing' in Grant Huscroft, Bradley Miller, and Grégoire Webber (eds), *Proportionality and the Rule of Law* (Cambridge University Press 2014) 67, 69.

[52]   Ibid 88.

[53]   Ibid 69.

of interests – while instead it demands 'balancing as reasoning'.[54] Thus, Möller can easily dismiss some of the main objections raised against proportionality: for example, that proportionality pretends to be technical and morally neutral.[55] Quite the contrary, it calls for moral argument and reasoning.[56] Or that proportionality does not discriminate between legitimate and illegitimate interests (and, we could add, between these and rights). On the contrary, sound practical reasoning should consider these distinctions.[57] He can also dismiss the objection that proportionality requires commensurating incommensurables. There is no need for doing this commensuration if proportionality is not committed to maximisation, and thus Möller rightly stresses that two alternatives that instantiate different values can be put into relation to each other, and one can be understood to have priority over the other based on general practical reasoning.[58] Panaccio has proposed a similar response to critics of proportionality. Proportionality cannot be accused of being a merely technical test that ignores the need for moral reasoning in human rights, since, as a test, it is 'substantively vacuous', requiring 'a normative theory to breathe life into it'.[59] It is a 'heuristic tool for practical-moral reasoning'.[60] Proportionality can therefore accommodate any moral theory, including those postulating incommensurability.[61]

All these objections, as the ones made in the first part of this book, are objections to proportionality as such. This must be distinguished from objections made to concrete applications of the proportionality test by courts. Möller also engages with objections of this kind. Stavros Tsakyrakis argues that proportionality 'gets the moral questions wrong'.[62] This critique is based on analysis of cases where Tsakyrakis thinks courts do not properly assess the moral questions involved. But for Möller one cannot

---

[54] *Challenging Critics* 715.
[55] Möller engages with this argument as presented by Tsakyrakis and Webber. I do not argue for this objection because I agree with defenders of proportionality that at least on Alexy's and Barak's version of proportionality some moral evaluations are necessary.
[56] Ibid 716–18.
[57] Ibid 718.
[58] Ibid 719–24. Though one may call this 'weak commensuration' (see Section 3.4). Regardless of the terminology, it is a different kind of method from the aggregative and maximising one that the incommensurability objection is aimed at.
[59] Charles-Maxime Panaccio, 'In Defence of Two-Step Balancing and Proportionality in Rights Adjudication' (2011) 24 1 Can JL & Jur 109, 118.
[60] Ibid 119.
[61] Ibid 118.
[62] On Tsakyrakis' objections, see above Section 5.6. Möller's defence is in *Challenging Critics* 718.

'blame the principle of proportionality for this'. One can only blame a court for not applying proportionality properly.[63] The same applies to the charge that proportionality is impressionistic, that is, that proportionality decisions do not articulate the reasons that justify them. Möller answers that the fact that certain decisions that apply proportionality are impressionistic does not mean that proportionality as such must be so; further, he argues, moral reasoning is not easy and sometimes courts must rely on their intuitions if they are to reason on their own about what is the morally best outcome of the case.[64]

All this has an important consequence for the proportionality debate. When proportionality is conceived as unconstrained moral reasoning, all the objections that were aimed against proportionality as such seem to lose their force. This is because they were aimed at a different account of proportionality, and also because proportionality as unconstrained moral reasoning does not propose a substantive test for addressing conflicts involving human rights. One cannot point to any intrinsic shortcomings with the way it addresses conflicts involving human rights, because it does not propose any distinctive way of addressing those conflicts. All the possible deficiencies one can find in applications of proportionality are just that: a court failed to 'balance reasons' properly, that is, failed to understand the reasons at stake in the case and act accordingly. And these deficiencies in applications of proportionality seem not to count against proportionality as such, but only against a particular decision. Assuming that a bad application of proportionality does not count against proportionality itself justifies Möller's insistence on distinguishing critiques of a decision or a version of proportionality and critiques of proportionality as such.[65]

6.4   How much Guidance Does the Proportionality Test Really Give?

So far I have emphasised the open-ended aspects of the idea of proportionality as allowing for unconstrained moral reasoning, since these aspects are the most prominent in the writings of the theorists that defend proportionality, and the ones that allow this account to avoid the objections made to the maximisation account of proportionality. Nevertheless, at

---

[63] Ibid.

[64] Ibid 727–30.

[65] See Ibid 710–11, 718, 722, and 728. For a similar argumentative strategy see Madhav Khosla, 'Proportionality: An Assault On Human Rights?: A Reply' (2010) 8 Int'l J Const L 298, 302–6.

times some authors suggest that there is another aspect to this account of proportionality: proportionality would be composed of tests that provide relevant legal direction for solving human rights conflicts. Thus, Möller claims that 'proportionality guides judges through the reasoning process as to whether a policy does or does not respect rights,'[66] quoting Kumm, who claims that proportionality can be seen as a 'check-list of individually necessary and collectively sufficient criteria that need to be met for behaviour by public authorities to be justified in terms of reasons that are appropriate in a liberal democracy.'[67] Möller further claims that proportionality allows judges to 'be *analytical*, that is, breaking one complex question ("Is the interference with the right justified?") into several sub questions that can be examined separately.'[68] It would seem that even though the balancing stage consists of open-ended moral reasoning, and thus, it would require reasoning that is unaided by legal direction, the previous stages do provide at least some guidance, so that 'in many cases, important moral work has already been done when reaching the balancing stage.'[69]

But there is a tension between guidance and opportunity for engaging in open-ended moral reasoning. Because constraint is the necessary consequence of guidance (if the law guides the judge towards a particular solution to the case, then other alternative solutions are excluded), the more specific the guidance provided by proportionality, the more it will constrain the reasoning of the judge, and thus the less it will allow for open-ended moral reasoning oriented towards justification. Defenders of proportionality as unconstrained moral reasoning never directly address this tension between guidance and unconstrained moral reasoning. But if proportionality did provide specific guidance, then it would not allow for open-ended 'balancing as reasoning', nor would it make any sense to talk about a 'turn from legal interpretation to public reason oriented justification,'[70] since the solution to the issue would be provided (at least to a considerable degree) by the law, and would thus depend on the interpretation of the relevant legal materials.

Note that the whole structure of the proportionality test (according to its doctrinal formulation as a four-pronged test) by focusing on means–ends rationality, and then on a comparison between the gains of the different possible policies, presupposes that interferences with the right

---

[66] *Challenging Critics* 726. See also *Global Model* 179.
[67] See *Socratic* 144, quoted in *Challenging Critics* 726.
[68] *Challenging Critics* 727 (emphasis in the original).
[69] Ibid.
[70] *Socratic* 142.

must and can be justified *by reference to the gains achieved by some other right or public good*. It is telling that though the test explicitly addresses the question of whether the measure that affects a right pursues a legitimate *aim*, it does not ask whether the measure is a legitimate *means* for furthering that aim. The issue is about consequences: whether the measure is adequate and necessary to pursue the aim, and whether bringing about that aim compensates for the loss on the side of the right. As said above (Section 2.3), this links the proportionality test with the maximisation account of proportionality: the less open-ended we conceive the test to be, the more it will invite judges to the kind of maximisation inquiry that was the target of the objections raised against proportionality, which Möller and other theorists of proportionality wish to avoid.

And they succeed in avoiding these objections, precisely because on their account, proportionality is understood as a particularly flexible test, allowing for open-ended moral reasoning. Despite Möller and Kumm's remarks suggesting the contrary, their version of proportionality offers almost trivial aid for addressing the issues to which it is applied, far less than what the law generally offers (or aims to offer) judges. This is the case with the balancing prong, of course, which on their account requires assessing the reasons in favour and against the justification of a measure. What about the other prongs?

In assessing the tension between open-endedness and guidance in the theories of proportionality as unconstrained moral reasoning, we need to bear one crucial distinction in mind. It is one thing what proportionality as a technical legal category directs us to. It is another what are the morally relevant requirements that, for some theorist, should bear on human rights cases and thus should be taken into account in the proportionality assessment.[71] Take the legitimate aim prong. What counts as a legitimate

---

[71] This is why it seems to me that the version of proportionality proposed by George Letsas is not substantially different from the one I describe in this chapter. Letsas presents his account as attempting to elucidate whether proportionality 'picks out a moral principle that is capable of justifying human rights or limits to them'. George Letsas, 'Rescuing Proportionality' in Rowan Cruft, S Matthew Liao, and Massimo Renzo (eds), *Philosophical Foundations of Human Rights* (Oxford University Press 2015) 318. For Letsas this moral principle is the right to equal concern and respect, and its more concrete manifestation in requirements to fair and just treatment, and that government does not act on certain reasons. Ibid 330–40. But he does not show how the proportionality test (the three- or four-part test described in Section 1.2) reflects these considerations, other than by allowing courts to assess any relevant consideration through open-ended moral reasoning. Of course, it is also possible that in some cases courts use a different set of legal requirements, but do so under the guise of proportionality; for this to be the case it is not necessary that these requirements relate in any way to the proportionality test and its different subtests.

aim is not determined by proportionality. It is typically not determined with precision by limitation clauses, which, if at all, refer to broad categories of social goods such as national security, protection of morals, and rights of others. Webber has further noted that in a given case there are commonly 'different possible characterisations' of the legitimate aim at stake, but the proportionality test does not offer guidance as to which of these characterisations should be used for the purposes of applying the test.[72] Möller's own examples regarding abortion and euthanasia show this. What counts, for example, as a legitimate aim for the purposes of banning euthanasia or abortion? Legal sources do not tell us. Möller goes some way, as does Kumm, into identifying considerations that would fail the test, relying on John Rawls' idea of public reason.[73] But antiperfectionism – which is still quite abstract – is one moral position among others.[74] As a technical category, proportionality would allow judges to follow that moral position, or other moral positions – as they have done on different occasions.[75] The antiperfectionism of Möller and Kumm is not trivial, though. If they are right, a judge applying proportionality should follow their proposals. But, as it stands, a judge following proportionality is not directed (guided and bound) by the law in this respect. And even if they were bound by some form of antiperfectionism, this still would be too abstract to provide effective guidance in most cases, since being within the domain of public reason, even Rawlsian public reason, is a minimal requirement and not a seal of reasonableness or correctness. That something falls within the confines of Rawlsian public reason does not mean that it is right, or that it is not fallacious, or that it relies on a good interpretation of the relevant data, or that it is not leaving out of sight some relevant moral or prudential consideration, or that it is a worthy aim. It simply means that it is cast in a certain way so as to appeal to 'public values expressed by a political conception of justice'.[76] Therefore, the assertion that policies whose aim cannot be justified in terms of Rawlsian public reason fail the legitimate

---

But then proportionality (a legal test, rather than a word) plays no role in the court's decision, not even that of allowing the court to engage in open-ended moral reasoning.

[72] Grégoire Webber, 'Rights and the Rule of Law in the Balance' (2013) 129 (Jul) LQR 399, 411.

[73] See *Challenging Critics* 725, and *Socratic* 159.

[74] For examples of rival positions see Michael Sandel, *Public Philosophy: Essays on Morality in Politics* (Harvard University Press 2005) Chapter 23, and Joseph Raz, *The Morality of Freedom* (Oxford University Press 1986) part II.

[75] See, for example, *Handyside v United Kingdom* (1979–80) 1 EHRR 737 para 52, and n 23 in Chapter 8.

[76] John Rawls, *Justice As Fairness: A Restatement* (Harvard University Press 2001) 91.

aim test does not provide much guidance. This certainly applies to Möller's examples of abortion and euthanasia. If – as Rawls believed in relation to the abortion debate[77] – those arguments favouring a ban can be and often are presented as arguments relating to the respect of the rights of others, without relying on comprehensive views on the good life, then they would be compatible with the idea of public reason. This does not mean, as Rawls also remarks, that those positions are more reasonable than other positions against them.[78] And the same can be said of arguments supporting liberalisation of euthanasia and abortion. The implications of this for our purposes is that even if antiperfectionism became part of the law, more precision would still be needed to guide judges in addressing complex moral and political debates.

Something similar occurs with the necessity and adequacy prongs. They do seem to direct to something more precise: to an assessment of whether a certain measure is in fact apt for achieving the legitimate aim, and whether there are other less intrusive means that could be used to attain the aim. Nevertheless, as Möller acutely observes with relation to the necessity prong, '[t]he traditional formulation of the necessity test [. . .] is simplistic. The problem is that often there exists an alternative policy which is indeed less restrictive but has some disadvantage',[79] like, for example, being less effective, more expensive, or imposing burdens on third parties.[80] The question is then 'whether the additional gain of the more restrictive policy [. . .] justifies the additional burden on the right holder'.[81] But to answer this question one needs to do more than establishing whether a certain mean will attain a particular end, or whether there are other less restrictive means that could equally attain the end. It requires a normative assessment of the kind that is performed at the balancing stage. And this is why, as Möller observes, it is clearer to assess this question at the balancing stage.[82] This does not mean that the necessity and adequacy stages cannot be interpreted as having a precise, technical meaning. But it greatly diminishes the importance of that assessment, since in all cases but the trivially easy ones, the relevant

---

[77] See Rawls' example of what he considers an argument 'clearly cast in the form of public reason' against 'a decision to grant a right to abortion' in John Rawls, *Political Liberalism* (Columbia University Press, paperback edn 2005) liv n 32.

[78] Ibid liv–lv.

[79] *Challenging Critics* 714.

[80] Ibid 714.

[81] *Global Model* 196.

[82] *Challenging Critics* 714; and *Global Model* 194–5.

question is not so much the one addressed by the necessity and adequacy test, but whether those adequate and necessary means are justified in the light of alternative policies that could realise other similar ends through other means.[83] This requires the kind of inquiry characteristic of the balancing stage, which, as has been established, provides no legal direction.

The relation between the structure of the proportionality test and its allowing for open-ended moral reasoning is best understood following some of the insights in Denise Réaume's work on proportionality. The first three tests (legitimate aim, adequacy, and necessity) can be seen as establishing a conflict between particular rights, values, principles, or interests. The legitimate aim test identifies the value that conflicts with the right infringed. This will require more or less open-ended moral reasoning in assessing whether an aim is legitimate or not, or part of a restricted aspect of the public good as specified by some limitation clause – for example, national security. The adequacy subtest requires determining the values or principles or interests that are in conflict: it requires assessing whether a particular 'objective is not in play in this situation'.[84] The necessity prong can, if interpreted strictly, show whether 'there is a real conflict'.[85] Up to this point, the most that the legitimate aim, adequacy, and necessity subtests can do is to clarify what are the values, interests, or principles in conflict. The crucial question of which of the conflicting values, interests, or principles at stake will have priority is resolved at the balancing stage, where the proportionality test requires unconstrained moral reasoning. Thus, we could say more precisely that the account of proportionality explained in this chapter is one that understands proportionality as allowing for unconstrained moral reasoning *in establishing what are the rights, principles, values, or interests involved, and particularly in deciding which of the conflicting rights, principles, values, or interests takes priority in the concrete case.*

In a reply to a much-summarised version of this argument,[86] Kai Möller argues that proportionality does provide guidance, and that this guidance

---

[83] See *Global Model* 196: 'The proper way to handle such a situation must be to assess all possible policies relative to each other'. Citation omitted.
[84] Denise Réaume, 'Limitations on Constitutional Rights: The Logic of Proportionality' (2009) 2009 26 Oxford Legal Research Paper Series 1, 10.
[85] Ibid 11.
[86] See Francisco Urbina, '"Balancing as Reasoning" and the Problems of Legally Unaided Adjudication: A Reply to Kai Möller' (2014) 12 Int'l J Const L 214.

is relevant, only that it is 'structural guidance', rather than 'substantive guidance'. He argues:

> [T]he doctrine of proportionality *does* provide judges with guidance; but this guidance is primarily at the level of *structure* and not *substance*. [. . .] Suppose a friend asks you for advice in a personal matter. Often, the adequate way to respond to such requests is not to tell your friend what to do with his life. Rather the best course of action may be to talk him through the problem in a structured way [...] Similarly, while proportionality does not tell the judge which outcome to reach, it nevertheless helps her identify the important questions which need to be considered in order to reach a decision on the merits: what are the candidate interests which this policy tries to protect? Are these interests the legitimate concern of the state? Does the policy as a matter of fact contribute to the protection of these interests? Would there have been different, less intrusive ways of achieving the same goal? Is the policy, despite there being no reasonable alternative, disproportionate? This *structural* guidance is important and helpful for judges.[87]

But this misses the point of the argument. The point is not that proportionality fails to provide 'substantive guidance'. My argument does not entail that only substantive guidance is helpful, while structural guidance is irrelevant. The problem is not only that the test asks questions while at the same time provides little guidance in answering them. If it asked precise questions, the test could provide enough legal direction. The point is that, on Möller's account, the proportionality test asks extremely broad questions, such as whether a measure is legitimate, or whether there are better reasons for favouring one position over the other, or whether there would be better (more just? more efficient?) policies that could be enacted instead of the one under review, while at the same time failing to provide direction as to how to answer them. The purpose of this section has been to show the little guidance that each part of the test provides.

Furthermore, Möller's distinction between 'substantive' and 'structural' guidance does not dissolve the tension between guidance and constraint. Structural guidance also constrains. And the more it guides, the more it constrains. Structural guidance provides more guidance when it points to more precise considerations, and when it comes closer to pointing to the full range of considerations necessary for deciding the issue: when it asks, for example, 'were the goods transported in a reasonable way?', rather than 'did the plaintiff act reasonably?'; and when the former is the controlling

---

87 Kai Möller, '"Balancing as Reasoning" and the Problems of Legally Unaided Adjudication: A Rejoinder to Francisco Urbina' (2014) 12 Int'l J Const L 222, 223 (emphasis in the original).

question (so that, if the plaintiff did act reasonably, then that settles the dispute). But the more precise the considerations that structural guidance points to, and the more sufficient it is for aptly deciding the issue, the more it will exclude other considerations. *This* is actually one of the main uses of guidance: in the face of a plurality of considerations, guidance is needed to highlight which are the considerations that actually matter.

For guidance not to exclude, it must be guidance of a very watered-down type, one for which using the word 'guidance' seems inappropriate. It must be the kind of guidance you have no especial reason to follow. But then how can we say it is 'guiding'? Suppose I need to decide which job to take. There are different factors bearing on the decision, say X, Y, Z, but I am not sure how to relate them, or if there are more factors at stake. A friend suggests that X is the most important factor. This friend is not particularly wise or smart, and he has no experience in these matters. I have no especial reason to follow his advice on this. The most I have a reason to is to bear in mind the possibility that X may be the most important consideration, just in case. Here, my friend's advice is not excluding anything (I have no reason to disregard other alternatives opposed to the one proposed by my friend), but at the price of also offering little help. I am not really guided by my friend's comment.[88] Whenever one is truly guided, be it by some advice, or by the law, there is some form of exclusion (at least some fading out) of alternatives – the alternatives to the actions or thoughts that one is guided to undertake.

This is particularly clear in the realm of advice: more authoritative advice offers more guidance than less authoritative advice. In some cases the type of guidance that is needed is authoritative guidance – the kind of guidance that excludes the considerations offered by other sources. We seek authoritative advice for many important matters. If my ears hurt and I want to know how to cure them, and my neighbour – who has no special medical competence – offers some thoughts on what he thinks might be causing the pain and how to diminish it, those thoughts are not especially helpful. They just add to the many potential explanations I may be

---

[88] The same is the case if my friend says something like: 'B is also an important consideration'. If I had contemplated this possibility before, then again the advice is not particularly helpful and hence it is not really guidance. If I had not contemplated that possibility before, the advice may be helpful, in that I may conclude that it is actually a relevant consideration that I was missing. But I need to establish that, and the fact that my friend says so is no reason for me to give any weight to that possibility. It is as if I had fallen down the stairs and landed on a big sign with the letter B on it, and then thought 'actually, I was forgetting about B'. It seems to me that in both cases there is no real 'guidance'.

entertaining on the issue. I still do not know how to act (and whether to adopt any of the explanations I came up with, or the one my neighbour offered, or the advice of my landlady, etc.). It is better if I receive advice I can treat as authoritative: advice that can reasonably exclude other proposals. If the doctor gives me a precise diagnosis and suggests a precise course of action to cure my ears, then that is better advice than that of my neighbour, not only on account of its precision (my neighbour's proposal may have been quite precise), but crucially because, by being authoritative, it can exclude other considerations (the possible diagnoses and cures I came up with, as well as those proposed by my neighbour), and therefore it is more sufficient in that it comes closer to providing conclusive reasons for what I should do. Authoritative guidance, *qua* authoritative, guides more, because it not only adds a consideration, but also relates it to other potential considerations offered by other sources, yielding an answer to the second order question of which source of considerations to follow. This, in any case, is the way the law works, by providing authoritative reasons for action.[89]

All this applies to structural guidance as much as it applies to substantive guidance. If my doctor is a Socratic doctor, and guides me to come to my own conclusion regarding my illness, then he will provide more guidance by being authoritative, and also he will provide more guidance the more precise and to the point his questions are. If he asks only 'where does it hurt?' and 'what kind of treatment would achieve your aims at the least possible cost', then I will think him to be a very bad doctor, but not for being Socratic and offering only structural guidance, but simply for being unhelpful. If, on the other hand, he asks questions such as 'do you grind your teeth at night?', 'do you feel your jaw tense because of the grinding?', or 'do your ears hurt more when you grind your teeth more?', I will start seeing a pattern, and those questions will bring me closer to a diagnosis of my illness, and put me on a path to finding the right treatment. But by presenting those questions as the relevant questions, other questions (such as 'have you heard laud noises lately?') are excluded from sight. My Socratic doctor might be eccentric, but if he asks questions that are precise and sufficient enough, he may provide me with enough guidance. But real guidance always implies some form of exclusion of alternative considerations.

If Möller's proposed understanding of proportionality provided considerable legal guidance, it would sacrifice its ability for allowing courts to engage in open-ended moral reasoning. This, Möller believes, is the

---

[89] I return to this point in the next chapter in Section 7.4.1.2.

problem with my proposal of replacing proportionality and balancing
with more precise legal guidance (see Chapters 7–9). He argues:

> [R]emoving 'balancing' from the set of tools available to a judge will result
> in removing his ability to realize justice. The *moral* guidance which Urbina
> wants to increase would become *immoral* guidance, that is, guidance that
> prevents judges from deciding the case before them according to what jus-
> tice and fundamental rights require.[90]

In the next chapter I explain at length how legal guidance, by constraining choice, can allow also for the exclusion of the relevant moral categories. The risk of immoral guidance is an ever-present one. But from the
fact that it is possible that legal categories provide immoral guidance does
not follow that legal guidance is always immoral. The question is whether
it is generally better for legal adjudication to be guided by the law or not.
This, I address in the next chapter. My point here is a different one. If legal
adjudication is to be guided, it will be constrained as well. That legal adjudication is constrained by legal categories is not peculiar to my proposal,
but it is the necessary consequence of legal guidance. If legal constraint is a
problem because it does not allow judges to engage directly with considerations of justice, then Möller's proposal does not have this problem. It does
not have this problem precisely because, and to the extent that, his account
of proportionality provides little and almost trivial legal guidance.[91]

6.5 Introducing the Objections

One important argument against vague legal methods is that they are
opposed to the ideal of the rule of law. The values associated with it – such
as certainty and predictability in human relations – are severely harmed,
if not sacrificed, when we make law through legal categories that are so

---

[90] Möller (n 87) (emphasis in the original).
[91] In any case, Möller in other parts of his work readily acknowledges the idea that proportionality provides little legal guidance. So, for example, as a rebuttal to the objection that
'proportionality is morally neutral and thus avoids the moral issues', he claims that '[t]he
application of the proportionality principle must also be moral reasoning'. After illustrating this claim with the *Odievre* case of the European Court of Human Rights, he says: 'One
might say that your job as a judge is to apply the Convention, not to develop free-standing
moral arguments. . . . *But it is one of the crucial features of the proportionality test that it
simply directs judges to assess the weights of the respective rights and interests without giving
them further instructions.*' Möller *Challenging Critics* 716–17 (emphasis added). The lack
of guidance provided by proportionality, and particularly by the balancing test, is also
acknowledged by Möller in his engagement with the objection that balancing is 'impressionistic'. Ibid 727–8. I return to this below in Section 8.2.

vague that they allow judges to reason morally on what is the best solution to the case, without any effective constraint imposed by the law. The law then becomes uncertain and unpredictable, and there is no guarantee that state power will be bound by clear and previously established legal rules, known by its subjects, and applied equally to those in the same situation. Grégoire Webber has already explored insightfully the abandonment of the ideal of the rule of law by certain doctrines of proportionality, as well as its costs, in a recent article. He argues that 'by appealing to general practical reasoning, the principle of proportionality offers too many channels and too many directions to guide the legal subject's and legal official's practical reasoning and so fails to satisfy the rule of law'.[92]

Holding those important costs in mind, one can feel tempted to think that there is a trade-off between, on the one hand, formal rule of law values (such as certainty and predictability), and, on the other, substantive values (such as justice and respect for people's dignity).[93] Furthermore, the defender of proportionality as unconstrained moral reasoning could say that, since that trade-off exists, the question is how to relate all those values in the best way in each case, which is precisely the task of the judge deciding a case applying 'proportionality as unconstrained moral reasoning'. Formal rule of law values should be also assessed, together with substantive values.

One possible reply to this defence is to question whether courts are more likely to assess those different values than other institutions, and thus, whether it makes sense that courts review the decisions of those institutions. Or to question whether courts are more able to issue the necessary kinds of directives, at the right time and in the right manner, than other institutions. These two possible replies concern the epistemic advantages and institutional capacities of courts as compared to those of the legislature or the executive.[94] Another potential reply is that the rule of law would suffer harm even if courts never decide to sacrifice it for the sake of substantive values – the mere fact that they can do so and are always prepared to abandon the rule of law when there is a greater gain on the side of the substantive values creates uncertainty. Though the risk of harm to the rule of law may be significantly reduced by a stable practice of courts of awarding a great weight to rule of law values.

---

[92] See Webber (n 72) 416.

[93] See ibid 400, 419.

[94] On an analysis of courts' epistemic advantages and disadvantages, see Adrian Vermeule, *Law and The Limits of Reason* (Oxford University Press 2008). On the problem of institutional capacities, see Cass Sunstein and Adrian Vermeule, 'Interpretation and Institutions' (2003) 101 Michigan LR 885.

I intend to provide an objection to proportionality as unconstrained moral reasoning that circumvents these issues by challenging the premise implied by them – that there is a trade-off between formal rule of law values, and substantive values such as justice in the particular case. When evaluating proportionality and contrasting it with other legal methods, one should not be distracted by the mere logical possibility of a case where, for example, there is a trade-off between predictability and justice. What matters is which institutions and legal methods make it more likely that justice and other relevant values at stake in adjudication will be served. My claim is that from this perspective, there is no trade-off in adjudication between rule of law-values, and substantive values. This is because legal direction in adjudication is not only required by the ideal of the rule of law, but also greatly increases the likelihood of arriving at the substantively most reasonable solution. Legally directed adjudication is better than unconstrained moral reasoning both for the rule of law, as well as for justice and other substantive values involved in the case.

The Need for Legal Direction in Adjudication

7.1 Introduction

As seen in the previous chapter, recent trends in human rights law seem to advocate for some form of legally unconstrained open-ended moral reasoning in human rights adjudication. Yet one of legal practice's most distinctive aspects is that it is largely constrained and informed by *authoritative legal categories*. By 'legal categories' I refer to all legal concepts that apply to different types of situations, determining the legal significance of the facts, and their legal consequence. Examples of legal categories are legal definitions, legal requirements, legal norms of different kinds (such as rules, principles, or standards), attributions of competence, etc. By legal categories being 'authoritative' I mean that legal categories make a claim to control the behaviour, reasoning, and decision of whoever is applying them, or is ruled by them.

There are good reasons for legal reasoning and adjudication to be informed and constrained by authoritative legal categories – to be *legally directed*. Adjudication achieves important benefits when it is legally directed. These benefits go beyond respect for rule of law values such as certainty and predictability (important as they are), but rather are intrinsically connected to the ability of legal adjudication to realise justice and other substantive values.

Legal direction is a complex practice. It affects how the law is produced, how it is applied, and generally the form, quantity, and organisation of all legal categories. Here I do not intend to exhaust this important topic.[1]

---

[1] An exhaustive account of legal direction in adjudication would require more than a chapter. As a consequence, a number of important and interesting issues will not be explored here. One important issue I do not address here is legal scepticism. The account of legal direction I offer below is compatible with some moderate scepticism of legal categories and their ability to guide (and to some extent, determine) adjudication. My account assumes that legal direction cannot be total and thus some degree of legal indeterminacy is to be expected (Sections 7.6. and 7.4.1.5), and concedes that legal categories can be unsound and

The purpose of this chapter is to provide an account of legal direction in adjudication that conveys the essential aspects of this practice, emphasising those aspects that are relevant for my critique of proportionality as unconstrained moral reasoning in Chapter 8, and for the alternative to proportionality that I sketch in Chapter 9. The chapter calls for a renewed appreciation of traditional modes of legal reasoning. This is especially pertinent in the area of human rights law, where, as we have seen in previous chapters, such modes are being challenged and replaced.

7.2 Legally Unconstrained Adjudication

It will be clearer to start our inquiry by asking about the alternative to the way things are under our current legal practice: why can legal adjudication not be unconstrained from legal categories? Wouldn't it be better if judges simply applied their sense of what is just and unjust, instead of focusing on legal technicalities? As seen in the previous chapter, recent trends in human rights law seem to advocate for legally unconstrained open-ended moral reasoning in human rights adjudication. The traditional conception of legal reasoning as constrained by positive sources (such as statutes and precedents) has been regarded as characteristic of a culture that values respect for authority. This is contrasted with the kind of legal reasoning that is more characteristic of a culture that places greater value on reason

---

thus give expression to immoral or even wicked beliefs and attitudes (Section 7.4.1.6). Yet I cannot here refute the radical sceptic who denies that the law can guide and constrain behaviour, or at least do so to a substantial degree. As Jacco Bomhoff notes, scepticism has flourished in America particularly with the Legal Realist movement, though it has not been especially relevant elsewhere. See Jacco Bomhoff, *Balancing Constitutional Rights: The Origins and Meanings of Postwar Legal Discourse* (Cambridge University Press 2013) 2–6. For a brief yet insightful account and critique of legal scepticism in American legal culture from the inside, see Lawrence B. Solum, 'The Supreme Court in Bondage: Constitutional Stare Decisis, Legal Formalism, and the Future of Unenumerated Rights' (2006) 9 U Pa J Const L 155, 166. Though note that the Legal Realists were opposing the excesses of what has been termed 'classical jurisprudence' – a view that is far bolder in its faith in the determinacy of law and legal adjudication than the one I present here. See Thomas C. Grey, 'Langdell's Orthodoxy' (1983) 45 U Pitt LR 1, 6–10. In any case, radical scepticism places oneself out of the debate with which this book is concerned. For the radical sceptic any debate about whether a legal test is sound or not must appear pointless, as adjudication is fully unconstrained, regardless of what tests are said to be part of the law that applies to the matter under consideration. And, with regard to proportionality, though the radical sceptic will not be persuaded by my argument, which relies on the capacity of legal categories to guide and constrain legal reasoning, by the same token he will see no advantage in proportionality as unconstrained moral reasoning, as legal reasoning is always unconstrained.

and justification. From this perspective, adherence to statutes, doctrine, or precedent is seen as little more than an obstacle to the realisation of substantive values.

This position is not without intuitive appeal. It is easy to imagine positive law and technical legal categories as detached or even opposed to what justice requires. The sometimes cryptic legal categories that only lawyers understand can seem (especially to the lay person) to be removed from actual questions of justice. This is why time and again there have been proposals for freeing legal adjudication from the constraints of the technical legal categories of lawyers, and allowing judges to engage directly with questions of justice. Part of the German 'free law' movement in legal theory advocated for legally unconstrained adjudication.[2] It was also commonly promoted by those that favoured the idea of the 'people's justice', as with those advocating for revolutionary understandings of legal adjudication, of which communist Cuba provides one of the most emblematic examples.[3] These are perhaps some of the more explicit versions of an idea that in more moderate form suggests simply leaving matters for judges to decide on a case-by-case basis with a great degree of discretion, or that judges engage directly with the values or principles that inspire the law that applies to the case. The exact proposals are not my concern here, but the general idea that grounds them.

[2] See Wolfgang Friedmann, *Legal Theory* (5th edn, Stevens & Sons 1967) 344.
[3] 'The tribunals embodied the notion that "men will be tried by their peers, that justice will be done by the people". The new order entrusted the common man with the administration of justice and the ability to reach the "right decision".' Paul Bernstein, 'Cuba: Last Look at an Alternative Legal System' (1993) 7 Temp Int'l & Comp LJ 191, 196 (quoting from Ian McColl Kennedy, 'Cuba's Ley Contra La Vagancia – The Law on Loafing' (1972) 20 UCLA LR 1177, 1186). There were many different motivations at work in socialist revolutionary reforms of legal systems. Only one of them was to better pursue justice by getting rid of legal 'formalism'. Other motivations commonly at work were the destruction of pre-revolutionary institutions, the incorporation of the working classes into roles of authority, the education of the citizenry in the values of the revolution, overcoming problems associated with the lack of legal professionals, and taking power away from a class (lawyers) associated with the ideas of the pre-revolutionary state. All these motivations were at work in the Cuban case. See Luis Salas, 'The Emergence and Decline of the Cuban Popular Tribunals' (1983) Law & Soc Rev 587, 597. Here it is particularly interesting to note that eventually, in the 1970s, reforms were implemented to make legal adjudication again formal, legalistic, and applied by lawyers. See ibid 607–9, and Bernstein (n 3) 197. A similar process occurred in China, with proposals for overcoming legal adjudication's legalism under Mao, and a subsequent return to more legalistic forms of legal adjudication after his death. See Shao-Chuan Leng, 'The Role of Law in the People's Republic of China as Reflecting Mao Tse-Tung's Influence' (1977) 68 J Crim L & Criminology 356.

This idea is a particular view of legal reasoning and of the role of doctrinal legal categories in adjudication that is implied in some academic accounts of legal reasoning, and, I believe, is consistent with widely shared views of legal practice in society at large. It consists of three elements. The first element is an understanding of reasoning according to the law and of moral reasoning as largely independent. This understanding accepts that on occasion moral reasoning can fill gaps in the law, and that law can specify what is morally underdetermined, but it nonetheless conceives of legal and moral reasoning as different and separated forms of practical reasoning, which can yield different outcomes for the case.[4] The second element is a view of legal rules and doctrines (of legal categories in general) that conceives them as obstacles in the path of moral reasoning towards justice and substantive values. Legal categories are seen as curbing moral reasoning. In principle judges could reason about the morally best solution to the case, but they face the constraint of legal rules, which can foreclose what would otherwise seem the more just or reasonable decision.[5] And the third element is attributing different values to each form of reasoning. Moral reasoning about the right outcome to the case is oriented to realising justice and other substantive values. Reasoning according to doctrinal legal categories, on the other hand, is necessary for the realisation of formal, rule of law-like values, such as 'definability of interpersonal issues and determinability of human disputes'.[6] Thus, for this view, there is a trade-off: the more legal reasoning is informed and constrained by legal categories, the less it is about the morally best decision for the case; in turn, the more adjudication is about moral reasoning, the less it will realise formal rule of law values, such as determinacy and predictability.

If one accepts this picture of legal adjudication, one has reasons to propose to free adjudication from the constraints of rules and other legal categories, so as to allow judges to better engage with moral considerations on

---

[4] This is implied in Shapiro's distinction between 'legal reasoning' and 'judicial decision making', or in Raz's distinction between 'reasoning about the law' (or, more recently 'formal legal reasoning') and 'reasoning according to the law'. See Scott Shapiro, *Legality* (Harvard University Press 2011) 248; Joseph Raz, *Ethics in the Public Domain* (Oxford University Press 1996) 326; and Joseph Raz, *Between Authority and Interpretation: On the Theory of Law and Practical Reason* (Oxford University Press 2009) 321. David Lyons draws this distinction explicitly in 'Justification and Judicial Responsibility' (1984) 72 Cal LR 178. For Lyons, it is the duty of the judge to perform both kinds of reasoning, and, if the legal outcome is not morally acceptable, then it should be discarded – thus, there are no easy cases, since legally easy cases still need to be assessed from the perspective of morality.
[5] See below Section 7.7.
[6] Neil MacCormick, *Rhetoric and the Rule of Law* (Oxford University Press 2009) 151.

how to realise justice and other values in the cases they decide – to propose that legal adjudication turns 'from interpretation to public reason oriented justification'.[7] Or, if those legal categories were indispensable (because they realise some important other value, like certainty), to create and interpret legal categories in a way that allows as much room as possible for open-ended moral reasoning about the right solution to the case.

I believe that this is a distorted view of the role that legal categories play in legal adjudication, and the specific contribution they make. It overlooks the ways in which legal categories can aid judges in arriving at substantially reasonable decisions in the circumstances of real-world adjudication. Legal adjudication does not face the dilemma of following authoritative legal materials and realising rule of law values, or engaging in unconstrained moral reasoning and realising the substantial values at stake in the case. Legal practice is equipped with a complex technique – what I here call legal direction – for realising both kinds of values in legal adjudication.

7.3   Berta the Judge

There are reasons for adjudication to be legally directed. These reasons consist of benefits that adjudication can achieve when it is legally directed. These benefits greatly increase the likelihood of legal adjudication (as it takes place in the circumstances of real cases) arriving at a just result, while at the same time realising some other values at stake in the practice of adjudication.

These benefits can be understood as remedies to deficiencies that adjudication would have if it were not legally directed. Thus, I will start by explaining these deficiencies. I will do this through an allegory of a judge who has to decide cases without any guidance of law or doctrinal categories.[8] The allegory tells the story of a community of survivors of a shipwreck who settle on a desert island. When the first conflicts arise, they realise that they need someone to decide them. They choose Berta. Berta has no knowledge of law, but she is chosen as the judge of this community on account of her known honesty, thoughtfulness, and patience. But Berta will encounter several problems in performing her task.

---

[7] *Socratic* 142.

[8] The purpose of the allegory is to show some obstacles that adjudication is likely to face were it not legally directed. To illustrate this point with maximum clarity, we need a situation where adjudication takes place with no direction from legal categories. I do not know real examples of this kind of situation, and therefore, I offer to the reader an invented story that narrates the travails of a judge who finds herself in the very artificial situation of having to adjudicate completely unaided by legal categories – the story of judge Berta.

One day Jill and Ted come to Berta with the following complaints. Jill claims that Ted has not been a good neighbour. He said he was going to give Jill a big seashell: now it has been six months since he promised. Ted quickly interjects that the agreement was that he would give Jill a seashell if she gave him ten bananas on Sunday, but instead she gave them to him on Saturday. Ted found this unacceptable and returned the bananas. But Jill's allegations continue. Ted has been generally impolite, and furthermore, he should be punished since the reason she wants a new seashell is because the one that she had was destroyed when Ted leaned his boat against Jill's wall, causing the wall to collapse and destroy Jill's beautiful seashell. Jill also wants to complain that Ted has not delivered a Jane Austen novel that he saved from the shipwreck, which he had promised long ago to give to Jill. Instead, he gave it to Stacey. Ted pays too much attention to Stacey, neglecting his poor dog, which walks around all dirty and hungry.

If you are a lawyer, you have a sense of how to order this confused account of facts. You know what this conflict is about (while reading the paragraph above you probably intuitively think: 'this is a tort', 'this is about contracts', 'here the question is whether there has been a punishable offence', etc.), and what it is not about (it is not about 'who is a good neighbour', or 'who is nice', or whether Stacey is a bad influence on Ted). You also have a sense of the different considerations that are relevant to address the different issues (you would apply different tests to establish whether there was an obligation in tort to compensate for destroying the seashell, than you would to establish whether Jill or Ted breached a contractual obligation, or whether Ted needs to be punished for an offence) and what further questions would need to be asked to know other relevant facts that, while not mentioned by the parties, are crucial for deciding the case.

Each one of these issues has a complexity of its own. Take, for example, the question of whether Ted must compensate Jill on the grounds of him destroying Jill's seashell. This depends on a number of considerations, which have been systematised by legal doctrine in different legal systems. Though the way these considerations are expressed and ordered by legal doctrine varies from jurisdiction to jurisdiction, developed legal systems attempt to give expression to similar considerations. Legal learning provides you with knowledge of these considerations. In the example, the first question is whether Ted committed a wrong against Jill (if Ted's making Jill worse-off was not the product of him wronging her, then he shouldn't have to compensate her). To establish this we need to first answer the question of whether Ted owed Jill a duty of care – a duty to contemplate that he could cause harm to Jill or her property by leaning his boat against Jill's wall, and take reasonable measures to avoid that. This in turn depends on a number of factors: could Ted have foreseen that his actions would cause the wall to collapse and destroy Jill's seashell? Yes he could, since Jill's is a weak wooden wall that collapses easily. Was it reasonable for him to lean the boat on the wall? No it was not, since there was no reason for leaning the boat there instead of somewhere else. Did Ted make Jill worse-off, or simply omit an action that would have made her better-off? Clearly the former. Was the harm serious, or did he merely cause some distress? Yes it was serious, affecting Jill's property. If it is decided that Ted owed a duty of care to Jill, would this expose Ted to having to bear responsibility for damages disproportionate to his guilt? There is no reason to think that. He would just have to compensate for the seashell, which he actually destroyed. Would deciding that Ted owed a duty of care to Jill weaken the sense of responsibility of the people under Berta's jurisdiction; would it affect negatively the general interest of people living in the island? Not at all.

Once it is established that Ted owed Jill a duty to take care not to lean his boat against Jill's wall, we should establish whether Ted breached that duty. In the case it is clear he did. So, it becomes clear that Ted committed a wrong in relation to Jill. Then, it must be established whether Jill suffered some kind of loss as a result of Ted's wrong, which she clearly did. Thus, Ted should compensate Jill for her loss of the seashell.

Further questions might be raised in relation to how this compensation should be made, and in relation to all the other issues involved in the case. All this shows the complexity of the case that Berta has to decide. But since Berta does not possess any legal learning, she does not know the doctrinal categories that would help her make sense of these complex issues. Furthermore, Berta does not have the additional benefit of the issue being presented by lawyers. In a typical court case the lawyers present the facts already organised in a logical order in accordance with the legal categories that apply to the case, and the decision is expected to turn on the application of those categories. But Berta cannot count on that either.

Thus, the first problem she meets is an epistemic one. The facts and the claims of the parties are disorganised and complex, and she has to find out what is morally relevant and irrelevant in the case, and how to relate the morally relevant considerations. This might not be a problem for Dworkin's Hercules,[9] but it is for Berta. She is a conscientious judge, but

---

[9] See Ronald Dworkin, *Taking Rights Seriously* (Harvard University Press 1978) 105 [hereinafter *TRS*]. See also Ronald Dworkin, *Law's Empire* (Harvard University Press 1986) 239 [hereinafter *LE*].

not a moral genius, and she is under severe time and resources constraints. Thus, we should expect Berta to be confused when trying to decide cases, failing to understand which are the relevant considerations, including irrelevant ones, and giving poor reasons for her decisions. In this story she is confused. She wonders whether it should make a difference that Jill delivered the bananas one day late and whether that justifies Ted not giving her a new seashell. But, and this Berta is sure of, impoliteness is always a bad thing. Perhaps the general impoliteness of Ted should be a reason to find that Jill is right and make Ted give her a new seashell. Furthermore, he should have given the Jane Austen novel to Jill, who is a much better girl than Stacey, who has already a couple of books she saved from the shipwreck. Perhaps all that bad news about Ted amounts to an intuition: that Jill is right and Ted is wrong. But Berta would have a hard time explaining precisely the reasons why she is deciding in favour of Jill, or clearly establishing the exact extent of Ted's responsibility.

Perhaps other persons in Berta's position could make a better job at responding to the morally relevant aspects of the case.[10] But there is no

---

[10] Though we should not be very optimistic. An illustration of lay judges adjudicating without knowledge of the law (when not with direct contempt for it) is the series of stories that the *New York Times* published in 2006 on New York's town and village courts ('justice courts'), where, it reported, abuse and injustice was widespread. What is remarkable for our purposes is the vivid connection in the stories between abuses and injustices, and that adjudication in these courts was largely not directed by the law, due to the fact that the judges were lay people with almost no legal training, and also due to some judges thinking that enforcing their own views on justice would be better than following the law. Thus, for example, one of the judges, 'who cursed at defendants and jailed them without bail or a trial', among other abuses, is reported as saying: 'I just follow my own common sense. And the hell with the law.' The story reports that '[l]ike many small-town justices, he said many of his decisions were down-to-earth solutions'. Another judge, 'in what the Commission on Judicial Conduct called "a shocking abuse of judicial power", [...] single-handedly went after a man he decided was violating local codes on the keeping of livestock [...] The judge interviewed witnesses out of court, tipped off the code-enforcement officer, lobbied the town board to deny the man approval to run a trailer park, then jailed him for 10 days without bail – or even a chance to defend himself.' The judge said 'the commission seemed to be chasing legal technicalities rather than real justice'. Many judges seem to have requested more legal training. One of them, 'a meat cutter who routinely jailed defendants in Tupper Lake to coerce them into pleading guilty, neatly summed up his insecurities in one closed hearing: "I'm almost like a pilot flying by the seat of my pants."' Basic procedural rights were denied as well: A judge, 'fretted that she did not "really have the time to puzzle this out" when a criminal defendant argued that evidence had been seized illegally. So she had the prosecutor write her decision, the commission said.' Another decided in favour of a defendant who had not even formally appeared before the court, after, on his own initiative, the judge went to personally interview the defendant and witnesses, and told the defendant he would throw out the case. The judge 'told the

reason to think that they will, if they are not legally trained. They do not need to know when a contract is considered unfulfilled, and what are the possible responses to that situation; nor do they need to know the conditions under which one has a duty to compensate someone for making them worse-off; nor do they need to know the conditions for a promise to be binding, etc. If you do not know these legal categories, there is no reason to assume that you will be able to give order to the facts and understand the different considerations at stake, and the proper response to them. What is likely, then, is that Berta – or any other person that does not know the law enough – is confused when faced with the case, or, worst, that a less conscientious judge greatly simplifies the issues at stake and hands down an unreasonable or unfounded decision. I call this the 'problem of the confused judge'.

Berta faces another problem. She is not sure about what would be a just outcome to this case, but she has a sense that at least Ted is not obliged to give the Jane Austen novel for free. But this is an important issue for Jill. And Jill is a very well-respected member of the community. Many people have approached Berta to tell her they think Jill is completely right, and that that mean fellow Ted deserves to be punished severely. Berta is not sure whether Ted deserves any punishment, or whether Jill is right about anything at all. What she is sure of is that many people in the community will be enraged with her if she does not decide in favour of Jill. And Ted has friends too, who will feel angry with her if she decides against him. She feels under more pressure to make a decision in favour of Jill though, or, and this seems the perfect solution, promote an agreement between the two, lest she have to bear the burden of an unpopular decision. Perhaps Jill will be willing to give another ten bananas, and, if so, perhaps Ted will be willing to repair the wall? This may not be just. But it might maximise

---

commission that he had never heard of the elementary legal rule that bars a judge, except in the most extraordinary circumstances, from secret contact with one side of a case. "It's not even explained in my manual," he said'. The same judge displays the underestimation of the law characteristic of some of the judges in this story, affirming that his interest in the law 'does not include a fascination with the technicalities that occupy lawyers. "If you look at the laws, it's all common sense" he said'. See 'Broken Bench – In Tiny Courts of NY, Abuses of Law and Power', NY Times, 25 September 2006, available in http://www.nytimes.com/2006/09/25/nyregion/25courts.html?pagewanted=all&_r=0, and 'Broken Bench - Small Town Justice. With Trial and Error', NY Times, 26 September 2006, available in http://www.nytimes.com/2006/09/26/nyregion/26courts.html. Waldron refers to this series of stories in Jeremy Waldron, 'Lucky in Your Judge' (2008) 9 Theoretical Inq L 185, 188–9.

the preferences of the parties, and thus reduce dissatisfaction with the decision. I shall call this 'the problem of the unduly influenced judge'.

Berta is thoughtful and cares for justice. But, like everybody, she has passions that can cloud her good judgement. Good passions, since Berta is a good person. For example, she cares very much about animals, and feels very mad when people mistreat animals. These are generally good feelings that arise out of compassion and a sense of responsibility. But her anger affects her evaluation of this case. Ted has neglected his dog – the poor animal. Berta feels more than willing to give a lesson to Ted. Perhaps he should deliver a seashell, and something extra for the nuisance, and also give Jill the Jane Austen book, plus any other book that he has. That will teach him a lesson not to neglect his dog and be more careful. This, I call 'the problem of the passionate judge'.

From the perspective of Ted there is another problem. He is subject to another person: Berta – perhaps to her whims, or perhaps to her more rational opinions. He remembers that in the place where he grew up people would say that they were ruled by laws and not by men. But Ted is ruled by another person. Even if everybody agreed on Berta being the judge of the village, and even if it is true that Berta is generally a thoughtful and honest judge, it remains true that Ted is subject to the unbound will of Berta. Which is a problem in itself, since it departs from a valuable ideal, but also has negative systemic consequences. These consequences become clear if we imagine that the town of shipwreck survivors has grown and now they have appointed three more judges, besides Berta, and have sent them to different places of the island to do justice. Since each of these judges is deciding cases independent of the others there is no reason to expect consistency between the different rulings of the different judges. So, Ted is not so happy with his ruling once Berta decides that he should give Jill a new seashell. He knows that last week judge Guadalupe did not make James pay for anything when he accidentally broke a plate that belonged to Carmen. And judge Albert has a completely different style of addressing these cases, promoting compromise between the parties. So Ted thinks it is unfair that he has to compensate Jill, while others in similar circumstances do not have to. This I shall call 'the problem of the subdued party'.

A related problem has to do with Ted not acknowledging Berta's authority. Why would he? Why would he acknowledge Berta's superior standing on these matters? What is so special about her after all? He does not see reason to attend the trial nor obey Berta's rulings. Others in the community feel the same. This I call 'the problem of legitimacy'.

Now, Robert the entrepreneur has an idea. He knows that many people want to read the Jane Austen novel. He wants to buy it from whoever has a right over the book, and make some copies of it to sell them to the public. At the same time Orson the philanthropist wants to buy some copies of the book and give them to the school, so that children can benefit from the few books that were rescued from the shipwreck. They would like to enter into an agreement right away (and with Orson's money, Robert could go ahead and order some pens and paper to be made, for the copyists he will hire). But they do not know what Berta will decide in relation to the book. For all they know, Berta could even decide to destroy the book – the source of conflict. Orson also does not know what Berta would decide if Robert kept the money and failed to provide the copies of the book. Thus, they decide to wait until Berta decides about the book, and then, perhaps, Orson will be willing to take the chance of paying Robert in advance so that he can buy the materials and get started with producing the book. This I call 'the problem of uncertainty and unpredictability'.

Under these circumstances it is unlikely that Berta will be able to adjudicate well. She is faced with obstacles that, if she does not possess talent, character, and charisma to an outstanding degree, will make it very unlikely that she will be able to hand down a good decision and provide the appropriate reasons for it. And even if she did, some of the problems – like the problem of the subdued party, or the problem of uncertainty – will remain.

7.4   The Benefits of Legally Directed Adjudication

The story of Berta illustrates some of the obstacles that adjudication is likely to encounter. These challenges are not specific to a particular case, court, or parties, but rather arise from the circumstances in which adjudication typically takes place (for example, the parties can be expected to care deeply about the outcome of the case; the issue typically involves some exercise of authority that is unwelcome to one of the parties) and from the nature of adjudication (deciding about the fate of persons and property, etc.).

In what follows I will further explain the obstacles that adjudication must face. I will also explain what means can be deployed to overcome them. We can expect of judges that they be conscientious and honest, but we cannot expect them to be geniuses, heroes, or charismatic leaders. Those are qualities difficult to find, and few persons possess them. If we want to increase the likelihood of adjudication succeeding in overcoming the obstacles I identified, we cannot put our hopes in looking for better people to adjudicate. We need institutions and practices that can increase the likelihood of the judge adjudicating well. Legal direction is one such practice.[11]

By adjudication being legally directed I mean that it is based on reasoning that is constrained by positive sources (such as precedent and statutes), and articulated and guided by *technical doctrinal legal categories* – which can be gathered from positive sources or from traditions of legal thought and practice. Aided by legal direction, adjudication is well equipped to face the obstacles that I presented through Berta's example.

There are two kinds of obstacles or problems. The first is that of 'outcome-related' problems. They make it less likely that the conscientious judge can arrive at a reasonable or correct solution. The second kind is composed of problems that are not outcome related. They point to deficiencies generated by the way the issue is decided, whatever the outcome, and I call them 'intrinsic problems'. The benefits of legally directed adjudication consist of its potential to be a remedy to these problems.

I will explain at greater length the first benefit of legally directed adjudication, which is related to 'the problem of the confused judge'. I will do so because this benefit has been generally missed by prevailing accounts of legal reasoning and rule-following (see Section 7.7), and because a proper account of this benefit is crucial for understanding the need for a body of law to be composed of diverse and precise legal categories – which is an important premise in my critique of proportionality as unconstrained moral reasoning, and especially in the positive account of legal human rights that I sketch in Chapter 9. On the other hand, the explanation I will provide of the other benefits of legally directed adjudication will be relatively brief, since they are not controversial and have been addressed by others. I also focus almost exclusively on the benefits of legal direction *for legal adjudication*, which is the issue at stake in debates on the use of the proportionality test in human rights law. This does not mean that what I say on legal direction does not bear on the application of law more generally, outside the courtroom. But I do not explore that here.

---

[11] There can be others. For example, rules that guard against partiality on behalf of the judges, prohibiting them from deciding a case where they or someone close to them has an interest. Or the institutions that express the rule of law idea that the office is to be distinguished from the person that on a particular occasion holds it.

OUTCOME-RELATED PROBLEMS

7.4.1   The Problem of the Confused Judge

7.4.1.1   Complexity and Legal Knowledge

Berta does not have something that judges typically have: knowledge of legal categories. These categories are learned through a legal education that comprises not only statutes and court decisions as positive sources, but also doctrine and generally a tradition of thought about legal problems and institutions. Legal categories can guide the judge through the complexity of concrete cases, expressing what is relevant from the perspective of practical reason for a given type of case.

Legal categories are sometimes complex because the problems they address are complex. They provide guidance because there is a need for guidance. This accounts for the sense of perplexity when one confronts a new case without the conceptual tools to understand it, as the allegory of Berta portrays. This is so because even ordinary legal problems are not trivially easy.[12] They are composed of a more or less complex array of facts, and when presented for solution they raise countless potentially relevant considerations. To solve the problem correctly,[13] one has to give order to those facts and select which are the relevant facts and considerations. If this task can be difficult for the average judge, it can be perplexing for the lay-person. What are we to do with the two men who agreed one to sell and the other one to buy 'Babieca', one thinking this was a horse and the other one an ox? Or with the parents who dispute custody of the child, one basing her claim on her ability for better providing for the child's needs, and the

---

[12] Weber held that the complexity of cases increased with the advent of modern capitalism (which, in turn, increased the need for a more technical, rational formal law). Max Weber, *Economy and Society* (Guenther Roth and Claus Wittich eds, Ephraim Fishoff and others trs, University of California Press 1978) [1956] 977. But this does not imply that cases in less complex societies are so simple that the problem of the confused judge does not arise. Weber himself notes that, for example, in primitive societies there is no distinction between civil redress and criminal punishment (even if, we could add, this distinction is morally relevant). Ibid at 647. This inability to differentiate properly is to be expected in societies where legal learning has not developed enough to serve as an effective guide to the judge and the community, or in societies where the judge is to decide according to his own moral judgement (what Weber calls 'Kadi-justice'), or according to some kind of concrete revelation (Weber's 'charismatic justice'). Ibid 976.

[13] This is, to give a reasonable solution to the case. What I have to say on the benefits of legally directed adjudication does not depend on (nor do I see it as being in tension with) any of the contesting views on the debate on whether there is normally one right answer to hard cases.

other on the fact that he has devoted much more time and effort to the care of the child? Or with the board of directors of a company that is being sued for an illegal transaction made, without the board of directors' knowledge, by an employee of the corporation? And, finally, with the man who killed a burglar who, he thought, posed a threat to his family?

In all these cases, we seek a practically reasonable solution.[14] If you are a lawyer you will instinctively think of the legal categories that apply to these cases (you will think of common mistake; of the principle that the best interest of the child is paramount; of the board's duty of monitoring; and of the conditions for pleading legitimate defence). This is, you already know to some extent – sometimes completely – what is relevant: to what kind of things you should pay attention, and to what you should not. Legal categories point to what 'you should pay attention to'. And, at least in developed legal systems, what the law tells you to pay attention to is not arbitrary. It tries to express what practical reason demands in that particular problem, what justice, morality, economic efficiency, and other considerations that could bear on the problem demand. If the law is successful in doing this, knowledge of the law is a relevant practical knowledge for solving the kind of conflicts brought before judges. Because legal cases are complex, and because courts work under time and resources constraints, this guidance provided by legal categories is an important aid for legal adjudication.

In this respect, law is similar to medicine.[15] You have an annoying symptom (say, earache). You do not know very well why or how to cure it, though you might have some hypothesis. You go to the doctor and start talking about your problem. You may say a number of things that are not really relevant, though you think they are, or have doubts whether they could be (e.g. I caught a cold last week, and then I got the earache). The doctor, on the contrary, knows what is relevant. He knows what to discard of your explanation, and what questions to ask (e.g. while you sleep, is there any grinding of your teeth?). Because he has the relevant knowledge he is more likely to understand and solve the problem correctly (e.g. your

---

[14] We could say that in all these cases we want to achieve a 'just' solution, 'to do justice according to law'. But I think we want more than that. Other considerations might be relevant as well. For example, if decision X does justice to the parties, but it would create uncertainty in the markets on the limits of certain responsibilities, thus increasing the cost of business enterprises, and decision Y also does justice to the parties, but at the same time it crafts a more precise ruling that would not have as a result the increase of costs for business, then we would like judges to hold these considerations in mind and decide Y.

[15] The analogy is suggested by Aristotle in his enumeration of forensic arguments in *Rhetoric* (W. Rhys Roberts tr, Dover 2004) [c. 350 B.C.E.] at 1375b.

earache is caused by something that is swollen because of your grinding your teeth at night. The solution is not related to your cold; what you need to solve is the bruxism problem – use a dental guard). And we have good reasons to submit to his authority on health matters and do as he says, precisely because he has that particular knowledge that makes it more likely that he will get it right, and thus, by following his dictates, I have more chance of recovering from my illness.[16] Of course, a non-physician of infinite medical talent and with infinite time and resources at his disposal to conduct research and experiments might also reach the right answer. But since we do not know such people, and anyway the nature of the problem does not allow for infinite time, medical knowledge is crucial.

But in the legal context, the complexity of the problem and difficulties it implies for a normal person who is not a legal expert tend to go unnoticed. They are obscured precisely because when lawyers start to reflect about the kinds of conflicts they have to deal with they have already been introduced to the problem through certain conceptual categories present in the law. We learn the law, and learning the law we come to think about the problem the law is dealing with. And sometimes we deal with a new problem, of course, but we already have a repository of concepts there, available to make sense of it. And if none of the categories available seems appropriate to deal with a new problem, then we deem it to be of an extraordinary complexity and difficulty. Well, imagine we had no legal categories: would not all problems seem difficult[17,18] This complexity of legal issues is

[16] I take this way of presenting the problem of authority from Joseph Raz, *The Morality of Freedom* (Oxford University Press 1986) Chapter 3 ('normal justification thesis').

[17] I avoid at this point talking of 'hard' and 'easy' cases, since in the literature those terms are associated with whether the decision 'flows almost inexorably from a relatively straightforward application of plainly applicable and identifiable legal rules contained in easily located pre-existing legal materials'. Frederick Schauer, 'Easy Cases' (1985) 58 S Cal LR 399, 410. See *TRS* 81, and *LE* 55–6. I also avoid the terms 'clear' and 'problematic' to avoid implications with MacCormick's pragmatic way of distinguishing them – a case is problematic if it is 'a case in which a problem has been raised'. See MacCormick (n 6) 51. I prefer to use non-technical terms like 'complex' ('not easy to analyse or understand; complicated or intricate') and 'difficult' ('needing much effort or skill to accomplish, deal with, or understand', according to the Oxford English Dictionary).

[18] It could be objected that there are some very simple cases nevertheless, which do not give rise to the problem of the confused judge, such as standard assaults, unpaid debts and murder. Even if this were true, the problem of the confused judge would reach a large number of cases. But I think that the standard cases hide a complexity of their own as well, as the story of Berta shows. For example, murder might seem uncontroversially wrong, and deserving of punishment. But, what counts as murder? If I kill in self-defence? If someone dies as a result of my conduct, but without me willing his death? If I did not kill the person,

a problem for which a solution is needed. The solution is legally directed adjudication.

7.4.1.2   What Lawyers Know

Legal direction is a way of overcoming the problem of the confused judge. This is the specific advantage of lawyers. They know the law and how to reason with legal categories, and thus they know how to adjudicate according to the law.[19] For legal learning to help judges overcome the problem of the confused judge it must not only provide guidance, but it must provide morally relevant guidance. The question here is, what kind of morally relevant knowledge is conveyed by legal categories? There are three types of knowledge conveyed by legal categories.

I. The first kind of knowledge we can see in the law is one that derives directly from moral reflection. There are things that moral reasoning identifies as right or wrong, as violating a duty or a right, as demanding the intervention of some person or organ, or as legitimising use of force. The law has to consider these reflections that are the product of deduction from basic moral principles and its logical application to concrete cases ruled by law. It uses this knowledge to create the

---

but paid someone else to do it? How can we answer these questions in a principled way that allows for consistency in the reasons that justify our punishing different offences through time? The complex body of legal categories of the criminal law that apply to murder show the complexity of the considerations that we need to assess in order to aptly decide whether someone deserves punishment for murdering someone else, and the magnitude of the punishment. Or take the relatively simple example concerning an unpaid debt. By framing the issue as 'concerning the payment of a debt' over the background of our legal culture, we are already presupposing a set of considerations that will be relevant for deciding the issue and others that will be irrelevant. For example, on a very basic level, we tend to treat this kind of problem as involving an issue of justice, and not as being concerned with the bad character of the person who did not pay the debt – which is irrelevant for answering the question of whether the debt should be paid. Moreover, the law informs the response that is to be given to such a situation – excluding, for example, some measures, like imprisonment, thus giving expression to other requirements of practical reasoning. All this is to say that legal direction is at work in a non-trivial way even in these cases, that are easy precisely because they are 'standard', that is, they fully fall into the type of cases for which the law has provided clear direction on how to act. But this direction is not morally obvious, and the fact that older or current less developed legal systems treat it differently (in ways that we would not approve for our own) attests to that.

[19] This point (on the specific knowledge that lawyers possess) has been stressed by Charles Fried, 'Artificial Reason of the Law or: What Lawyers Know' (1981) 60 Tex LR 35, though I believe the issue is obscured when presented as one concerning the distinctiveness of the intellectual discipline of law as compared to, for example, the discipline of moral philosophy or economics.

technical legal categories that will express the relevant moral considerations that bear on a given issue, and thus secure or at least make
more likely that they will be given due consideration in the reasoning
and decision of the case. An example of this is *mens rea*. It is unjust to
punish someone without attending to what she actually chose, that
is, to the structure of means and ends she considered and intended.
Criminal law has to consider this moral demand and express it in its
categories.[20] Moreover, there are choices that are more wrong and thus
deserve more punishment than others: choosing directly to harm
another person is worse than choosing a course of action hoping that
others will not be hurt but without taking due precautions that this
will not happen. Criminal law also has to consider these distinctions
because they are morally relevant. And it typically does in developed
legal systems – though criminal lawyers from different jurisdictions
might find different categories to express these moral distinctions in a
coherent and complete form.[21]

II. Not everything in the law derives in this more direct form from practical reflection. Some issues are left underdetermined by practical
reason. Some alternatives might be excluded as unreasonable, but
there remain many reasonable alternatives all of which are equally
acceptable. There might be a need, though, for choosing one option.
This need is commonly the need for coordinating collective action.
Reasons of fairness can also compel us to have a general norm that

---

[20] Though the relevance of intention has been at times contested or forgotten. For an account
of the moral relevance of intention, see Sherif Girgis, 'The Mens Rea of Accomplice
Liability: Supporting Intentions' (2013) 123 Yale LJ 460; and John Finnis, *Intention and
Identity, Collected Essays* II (Oxford University Press 2011) 173.

[21] It is not disputed that in some occasions legal categories can fail to express the relevant
moral requirements that should bear on the case. Jeremy Waldron has illustrated this with
the US Supreme Court decisions on abortion, where the court, according to Waldron,
engaged in a detailed discussion on the previous case-law and other related positive
sources, all of which left untouched the two crucial issues in the debate: the moral personality of the unborn and whether the woman has a right to autonomy such that could
ground a claim to perform an abortion. Jeremy Waldron, 'The Core of the Case Against
Judicial Review' (2005) 115 Yale LJ 1346, 1382. I think that this case should be seen as a
departure from the norm; as a pathology. What I am trying to provide is an account of
what such cases are a pathology of, and of why, despite the all too evident risks of crafting
categories deficiently, there are reasons to pursue this task. (See below Section 7.4.1.6.)
Furthermore, in Waldron's example what might have impelled the court to stretch certain
categories beyond their proper ranges of application is precisely the attempt to overcome
one of the problems of legally unaided adjudication, namely, the problem of legitimacy.
See below text accompanying footnote 59.

decides the issue for all similar cases. Here the pertinent authority has to settle for one (or perhaps more, but a definitive list) of the reasonable alternatives. This decision is usually made through a legal norm. Once the decision of the authority has been made the problem ceases to be reasonably underdetermined, since the decision made by the authority is grounded on a collective need, and thus there are reasons for respecting it.[22] Knowing the relevant authoritative determinations that bear on the case is also part of the relevant practical knowledge that those who know the law possess. Examples of this kind of considerations are countless: traffic regulations provide many examples (what should be the exact speed limit?); settling the exact amount of a compensation or a fee is another such rule that embodies not only knowledge of the reasonable frame, but, crucially, of the relevant authoritative choice.

III. Knowledge of the law is also the knowledge of what experience has shown as to the application of moral principles to the circumstances of society. One such knowledge is knowledge of how things can go wrong. There are typical ways in which people can fail to comply with the moral requirements set in the law. The law can foresee this, and can alert to those possible breaches, and establish a proper response. So, for example, in bankruptcy, we can expect that one of the creditors might try to get his payment independently of the process of bankruptcy (probably trying to enter into an agreement with the insolvent debtor before it is manifest that the latter is insolvent). This would be unfair to the other creditors, and so bankruptcy laws commonly refer to this possibility and establish some legal response: for example, one can request that that payment be declared void.

A special and very relevant kind of knowledge is that of authoritative decisions made by a competent body when that competent body has epistemic advantages over courts. This is relevant for the setting up of complex schemes of social cooperation. Given the fact that an important role of the law is to solve complex coordination problems,[23] and that many times those schemes of cooperation are set up by a competent body that has epistemic advantages over courts, it is worth elaborating on this. Knowledge of the reasonable and complex enactments of authority, which the court would not have been able to make, or was less apt

---

[22] On *determinatio* see *NLNR* 284.
[23] Ibid 276.

to make, is part of the relevant knowledge present in the law. This is not only knowledge of the second kind (knowledge of *determinationes* made by the competent authority on what reason leaves underdetermined) but also knowledge of the first kind (knowledge of what is determined by reason) and of the third kind (of probable injustices and breaches). It is knowledge of the second kind insofar as it is knowledge of valuable authoritative determinations. It is knowledge of the first kind insofar as it is knowledge of what would be a reasonable content for such complex authoritative enactments – and this knowledge is particularly relevant when the body that issues the enactment has superior epistemic capacities. By following the enactments of a competent authority courts can benefit from the epistemic advantages of that authority. An example can be provided by the general taxation scheme. In every society there is a need for a general, coherent, efficient, efficacious and fair taxation scheme sanctioned by authority. In designing that scheme, the authority needs to take into account a complex array of considerations of justice, economic policy, expediency, etc. A court could not set up such a scheme. Not only because of the kind of norms courts can create, which lack the generality required by a taxation scheme; and not only because of the constraints courts face in relation to the timing of their decisions (since they can only decide an issue when a case that gives rise to that issue is presented to them). An important reason why a court would not be able to set up a good taxation scheme is because it does not have the epistemic resources to properly assess many of the considerations that are relevant for setting up such a scheme, such as policy considerations.[24] The legislator is typically better suited for engaging with those considerations aptly. Nevertheless, once the scheme is set up, by knowing the legal framework that rules the tax scheme, courts can decide, for example, whether an action contradicts that scheme. In doing so, the court is helping to preserve the scheme by contributing to its efficacy. But in order to do so the court does not need to fully understand the reasons behind each of the rules that constitute the legal framework of the tax scheme. It is enough that it knows those rules and the general principles of the system. This is, that it understands primarily what these rules require of each person, and, roughly how the system works, so as to better apply

---

[24] On courts' limited ability to assess complex policy considerations, particularly in the form of empirical research and statistical analysis, see Paul Yowell, 'Empirical Research in Rights Based Judicial Review' in Peter Huber and Katja Ziegler (eds), *Current Problems in the Protection of Human Rights: Perspectives from Germany and the UK* (Hart 2013) 155, 155.

those rules. And in applying those rules it is solving a particular case in accordance with a reasonable scheme of cooperation, and thus providing a reasonable solution to a concrete case – a solution that, because it is consistent with the scheme of cooperation, is more sensible to the requirements of practical reason (which require the existence of a reasonable tax scheme of certain characteristics) than it would be had the court been left without the guidance of the authoritative decisions that realise those requirements by setting up the tax scheme. Knowledge of the law is also knowledge of what constitutes a concrete reasonable scheme of cooperation and of how to act in accordance with that scheme.

This is particularly relevant in the circumstances of legal adjudication, where it is too easy for the judge to see only the interests and claims of the parties, without considering adequately the general impact of the ruling in the interests and claims of other persons. Knowledge of reasonable schemes of cooperation and of what actions are consistent with them helps courts to adjudicate in a way that is more responsive to the interests and claims of all the relevant persons – because these interests have been considered in establishing a particular scheme of social cooperation – and avoid over-focusing on the interests and claims of the parties.

Legal doctrinal categories attempt to express all these sorts of considerations, and relate them in a coherent and clear way. In this sense, the knowledge conveyed by the law is moral knowledge. It is knowledge relevant for deciding conflicts justly, and for regulating a particular situation according to justice and the common good. From the perspective of adjudication, all this knowledge we can find in the law is indispensable, because of the problem of the confused judge. The complexity of the problems that courts have dealt with over centuries is matched by knowledge of doctrine and institutions that are the product of reflection – not only by courts, and not necessarily only in the context of adjudication – on moral and prudential considerations that bear on those same problems.

Thus, the law can be seen as a source of knowledge that can aid non-Herculean judges, with limited time and resources, in solving complex moral problems by clarifying what are the relevant practical considerations that are at stake in the case through technical categories that allow judges to know which precise questions they need to answer to decide a case reasonably. The technical categories of the law will normally allow the judge to 'break' the complex problem into more discrete and manageable relevant questions, thus making it more probable that the judge will address the issue and decide it in a way that is responsive to all the relevant demands of practical reason that should bear on the case.

If the law expresses what is relevant in the concrete case, it also has a way of expressing what is irrelevant. One of the main features of legal reasoning is the exclusion of a number of considerations.[25] Legal reasoning is a special kind of practical reasoning that is characteristically constrained by legal sources and categories.[26] This is the constrained aspect characteristic of legal reasoning. Constraint is the flipside of guidance; the law can guide as to which are the relevant considerations that should bear on the case only if it can single them out, if it can draw a contrast between what matters and what does not. This is done through the legal technique of crafting legal categories. Legal adjudication can then be seen as concerning the faithful application of those legal categories through legal reasoning, this is, a form of reasoning that is articulated through these legal technical categories. Thus the law excludes from sight what is not expressed in legal categories, which in turn provides a valuable service for the judge when (and legal practice and scholarship devote enormous amounts of time and energy to this) legal categories are well crafted so as to express what is relevant in the case.[27]

7.4.1.3   When the Law Does Not Guide

Difficult cases will remain, to be sure. But even in difficult cases, the question is usually narrower than it would have been without the guidance provided by the law. As John Finnis has remarked: "'[E]asy legal reasoning" is a very important element in the structure of almost all hard cases: the "hard" issue in such cases is usually quite distinguishable from many other, more or less easy issues which are present in the case.'[28]

Furthermore, in cases where the law resorts to vague terms, such as 'reasonable', 'fair', or 'due care' it is not necessarily opening a gap of complete discretion. Lon Fuller noted that those terms can provide much guidance in certain contexts. Fuller's example is commercial practice, where such

---

[25] Honoré refers to a 'canon of unacceptable arguments', the existence of which constitutes 'the essence of the Roman gift to modern Western civilization'. Anthony M. Honoré, 'Legal Reasoning in Rome and Today' (1973) 4 Cambrian LR 58, 64.

[26] See Robert Alexy, *A Theory of Legal Argumentation: The Theory of Rational Discourse as Theory of Legal Justification* (Ruth Adler and Neil MacCormick trs, Oxford University Press 1989) 212.

[27] What is said here on the knowledge conveyed by the law should not be confused with a particular stance on the question of the grounds of authority. Epistemic advantages are only one of the reasons that can justify that a particular body is granted authority over a particular domain.

[28] John Finnis, *Philosophy of Law, Collected Essays* IV (Oxford University Press 2011) 372.

terms 'can take a definiteness of meaning from a body of commercial practice and from the principles of conduct shared by a community of economic traders'.[29] The term 'reasonable', for example, can provide much guidance if it is used in relation to a practice where it is relatively clear what is reasonable and what is not (e.g. 'the reasonable care that carriers typically employ in transporting fragile goods'). The same is true for other such terms.

It should also be noted that these seemingly open-ended terms are often used to point to one discrete element in the issue, one particular fact-sensitive question where the law leaves the judge unguided. There is a difference between a norm that says to the judge 'when X, decide what is reasonable', and a norm that says 'when X, the person who was obliged to transport the agreed items will have to redress the owner if he did not act with *reasonable* care in transporting the items'.

This shows that the presence of vague legal standards is not a sign of complete lack of legal direction. The standard could be used in a context where it does afford relatively precise guidance. It could also be the case that it does not provide any guidance, and thus affords the judge full discretion, but only in relation to one discrete aspect of the decision. Thus, the issue here is not whether it is preferable that some area of law uses rules or standards. Depending on the circumstances, both rules and standards can be used to provide enough legal direction in some type of case.

Knowledge of the law is still of assistance in cases where the law that applies to the case leaves some issue underdetermined. An illustrative example is the UK case of *Mitchell and Anor v Buckingham International plc.*[30] The details of this insolvency case need not worry us. It concerned an application by judgement creditors to be given precedence over other creditors. The case required the application of two remarkably vague sections of the Insolvency Act 1986 – one, s 168(5), allowing the court to reverse or modify a decision by the liquidator 'as it thinks just', and the other, s 183(2)(c), providing that 'the right conferred on the liquidator may be set aside by the court in favour of the creditor to such extent [. . .] as the court thinks fit'. Counsel characterised the powers given to the court as those of a 'Cadi sitting under a palm tree', and Harman J noted, referring to s 183(2)(c), that the 'wholly undirected width of the whole sub-section does seem to me unhelpful'.[31] What is interesting for us are the resources with which the

---

[29] Lon Fuller, *The Morality of Law* (rev edn, Yale University Press 1969) 64.
[30] [1998] BCC 943 Ch (Eng).
[31] Ibid 951.

judge filled the gap. He acknowledged that the applicants had been 'very badly treated' by Buckingham International, but that 'the conduct which frustrated their entitlement was not the conduct of the unsecured creditors, or any of them'.[32] The general rule must apply, then. '[T]he statutory scheme of pari passu distribution amongst all creditors of the same class at the date of liquidation was the overriding principle.'[33] No precedent provided an exception for this rule.[34]

It is interesting for our purposes how even in cases where there is some lack of guidance in the law that applies to the issue, the general legal categories in that department of law can provide assistance to solve the conflict. Harman J is in a much better situation than Berta. He knows the general institutions of insolvency law, and understands the idea of fairness embodied in the scheme of *pari passu* distribution among creditors. Furthermore, he has the resources to frame the issue not as one concerning the applicants and the company that wronged them, but as one concerning the applicants and the other creditors of that company – who are not responsible for the company's actions and who would see their interests harmed by any preference given to the credit of the applicants. Legal guidance can be more or less direct, but even when the norms that apply more directly to the case provide little guidance, other legal categories that apply generally to the same area of human affairs can help the judge in dealing with the complexity of the case.

7.4.1.4   Departments of the Law

What has been previously said of the epistemic benefits of legal direction can help us provide an explanation of the practice of dividing law into departments. This relates to the important issue of the need for highly differentiated legal categories – an issue that is crucial for thinking about alternatives to the proportionality test in human rights law, as I will argue in the following chapters.

Ronald Dworkin provides an account of compartmentalisation. This is relevant for his theory since Hercules' interpretation must try to 'fit' the materials that are closest to the case, as defined by the areas or departments of the law to which the categories that apply to the case belong, which gives 'some kind of local priority' to such departments.[35]

---

[32]   Ibid 952.
[33]   Ibid 953.
[34]   Ibid.
[35]   *LE* 250.

His explanation for the practice of dividing law into departments starts from the premise that 'the boundaries between departments usually match popular opinion'. So, for example, 'many people think [. . .] that the state needs a very different kind of justification to declare someone guilty of a crime than it needs to require him to pay compensation for damage he has caused'.[36] The reason for dividing the law in different departments is that:

> to match that sort of opinion promotes predictability and guards against sudden official reinterpretations that uproot large areas of law, and it does this in a way that promotes a deeper aim of law as integrity. If legal compartments make sense to people at large, they encourage the protestant attitude integrity favors, because they allow ordinary people as well as hard-pressed judges to interpret law within practical boundaries that seem natural and intuitive.[37]

It is far from obvious that lay people have such knowledge of the different departments of the law. This probably depends largely on whether we are talking about people in a more legally informed culture or in one that is less so. The fact that in pre-modern legal cultures some of the very distinctions that Dworkin mentions (between punishment and compensation) are blurred[38] suggests that the distinction is not immediately obvious for people with independence of their knowledge of the law. But even in places where most people are largely ignorant about the law, law is still taught and organised in departments. Should the division of the law in departments be abandoned in these places?

There is surely value in the law being clear, and for that it can help if the law expresses widely shared moral convictions and does not depart too much from them.[39] But people have moral judgements and intuitions about the substance of the law, about its particular requirements, but not necessarily about how the law is organised in different departments. And in any case, the benefits of clarity are achieved when the law orders its subjects to do something that they can understand and be guided by (which occurs more naturally when the requirements of the law are consistent with moral judgements and intuitions),[40] not by the division into departments.

---

[36] Ibid 252.
[37] Ibid.
[38] See Weber (n 12) 647.
[39] Though of course this does not provide a conclusive reason for expressing those widely shared moral convictions in the law.
[40] See the discussion on 'moral clarity' in John Gardner, 'Rationality and the Rule of Law in Offences against the Person' (1994) 53 Cambridge LJ 502, 513.

Furthermore, we should expect that some divisions would be better known than others by the population at large, when, for example, the departments at issue are well known in that particular culture, and they address issues that are different enough for the lay person to see a clear difference between them (e.g. contract and criminal law). But some of the departmental divisions will be completely ignored by the lay person, even in countries with a strong legal culture, as those that relate to more technical areas of the law (e.g. conflicts of laws), or those areas that are new (e.g. elder law, biotechnology law). Then how can the need to track popular conviction explain the existence of departments, when some come to existence before public opinion can be aware of them, and others, because of their highly technical nature, are expected to be known only by lawyers, and there seems to be no deficiency in this?

I propose a different explanation and justification for the compartmentalisation of the law. Different moral and practical considerations apply to different kinds of conflicts and social affairs. It is not only that '*many people think* [...] that the state needs a very different kind of justification to declare someone guilty of a crime than it needs to require him to pay compensation for damage he has caused'.[41] The state *does* need a different kind of justification in both cases. The moral principles that apply to questions of compensation are different from those that apply to the question of punishing wrongs. And these are different as well from the principles and other considerations that apply to issues regarding voluntary exchanges and agreements, or to the collective administration of a business owned by many different persons, etc.

If technical legal categories attempt to give expression and concretion to these moral and prudential considerations, then it is only expected that there will be very different legal categories for different kinds of issues. Only at the highest level of abstraction can we find common principles ('do not harm'). But not much guidance can be given at such level of abstraction. Furthermore, there is no reason to expect that all the relevant considerations that bear on all the different issues that the law regulates can be reduced to a simple set of abstract principles to be specified in each area of the law. If we need to craft legal categories that are able to guide judges by expressing the different relevant moral and prudential requirements that bear on the different kinds of cases, we will need to express through the law the specific way in which the abstract principles bear and apply to the

---

[41] *LE* 252 (emphasis added).

different kinds of cases, as well as the rest of the relevant considerations that are more specific to the issue. There is a need for the law to be differentiated enough, providing different legal categories for different kinds of problems. 'One size fits all' legal categories (legal categories that apply equally to different kinds of problems that give rise to different kinds of moral and practical issues) are not enough. 'One size fits all' legal categories can only 'fit all', if at all, by being very abstract, and thus, cannot offer much guidance.

So, we will have different legal categories aimed at expressing the relevant moral and prudential considerations that apply to different areas of social life. Sets of categories will give shape to one particular institution (e.g. bankruptcy), and this in turn will relate to some other institutions and categories in trying to regulate one relatively distinctive area of social affairs. Because legal categories that apply to the same area often interrelate, and because there is a need to know what is the law in a determinate area, legal doctrine attempts to systematise legal categories by organising them into departments, bringing together and ordering the different technical legal categories that apply to a similar type of issue.[42]

7.4.1.5   The Burkean Paradox

It could be argued that a difficulty for the view defended here is Adrian Vermeule's 'Burkean paradox':

> The paradox is that if many participants in the line of precedent or tradition followed the precedent or tradition [. . .], then the informational value of the line of precedent or tradition is lower to that extent; there are fewer independent minds contributing to the collective wisdom. [. . .] The sting in the problem is that a strategy that is individually rational for judges at any given time – following precedent – is harmful to all if followed by all, because it drains precedent or tradition of any epistemic value.[43]

According to the Burkean paradox, then, if a judge follows received legal categories (as, below, I argue they should so as to achieve the benefits of legally directed adjudication: see Section 7.5), she is not improving the law, and thus, if all judges do the same, the law would not develop, and thus it would be unable to guide judges and help them overcome the problem of the confused judge.[44] On the contrary, if judges improve on the law, they

---

[42] Dworkin hints at this explanation in ibid 406.
[43] Adrian Vermeule, *Law and the Limits of Reason* (Oxford University Press 2008) 76.
[44] Though if there already exists a relatively sophisticated tradition of legal knowledge, then judges and lawyers can benefit from it even if they have done nothing to contribute

do so at the expense of not being guided by the law, and thus not benefiting from legal direction. Is this a problem for the view defended here?

It is not. It must first be noted that those developing the tradition need not be the same as those applying it. The 'Burkean paradox' has little sting outside the common law tradition. In the civil law tradition there is a greater (though, granted, porous) divide between those that apply legal categories (courts) and those that develop them (legislatures, and also commentators). Vermeule proposed the Burkean paradox as part of his argument against what he calls 'epistemic legalism': the view that 'the limits of reason support judicial lawmaking over lawmaking by other institutions – legislatures, executive officials, and administrative agencies'.[45] My argument is agnostic about that debate. If some argument, based on the Burkean paradox or on something else, was successful at establishing that courts are not well suited to both apply legal categories and develop them, this would not affect my argument here, which aims at establishing that adjudication needs to have legal direction, and thus there is a need for courts to apply legal categories that are prior to the case. Both arguments would be complementary, one establishing the need for legal direction, and the other establishing who is better suited for crafting the legal categories that should guide courts.

In any case, the Burkean paradox does not provide a reason for courts to abandon the task of crafting legal categories. Judges do not face the dilemma of whether only to apply received legal categories, or only to contribute through their inventiveness to the stream of precedent. In between those alternatives lies a common phenomenon: development of and within a tradition. The judge can frame the issue and evaluate the claims of the parties in the way it is dictated by received legal categories, but once the issue has been framed, some question might still remain unanswered, or there might be some need to make a particular legal category more discriminating and precise, or of simply abandoning it if, for example, it is giving expression to illegitimate considerations. Judges can do this while benefiting from legal direction. Though of course, the more they depart

---

to it – it is not necessarily a 'bring and share' party. Medieval judges and lawyers had at their disposal the legal tradition of Roman law, from which they could benefit, and would have been able to do so even if they had not contributed at all to its development. Though of course if no one contributes to the tradition, then it is likely that it will be unable to improve, and to address new situations. In that case we could say that lack of contribution to the tradition 'drains' tradition of epistemic value, because it becomes less helpful to address conflicts occurring in society.

[45] Ibid 2.

from received legal categories, the less they are benefiting from them. But benefit from legal direction is usually considerable even in landmark cases.

And this should not come up as a surprise. A comparison might help clarify the issue. It is possible to improve on something that has already been made, as, for example, it is possible to fix a door in a house. And, as in the example of a house, it is typically easier to improve on something than to build it from scratch, and thus, one still benefits from the building even if one changes it a little. But one can truly improve it. Furthermore, many people are able to improve their houses little by little. Very few could build their houses from scratch. The same applies to law and legal development. Courts can apply the bulk of received legal categories to a case, and still find some small (in relation to the rest of the legal categories that are not challenged) aspect of the law that needs improvement. In those cases the court can both contribute to legal tradition and benefit from it.

We do not need to go further into this discussion. My argument does not challenge Vermeule's basic position – that legislation has better epistemic credentials than judge-made law for the purposes of deciding constitutional matters. My point is at a more basic level: there is a need for adjudication to be legally directed, and this explains why an important part of legal practice is related to crafting legal categories that can direct adjudication aptly. In relation to judge-made law, the Burkean paradox does provide a valuable lesson. United with an awareness of the problems of adjudication that is not legally directed, it gives a powerful reason for courts to develop the law slowly, timidly, improving bits and pieces one at a time.[46]

---

[46] An important aspect of legal development not addressed in Vermeule's insightful book is the role played by epistemic leaders. Law does not work democratically, so to say. The law has never been about merely collecting the thoughts of 'many minds'. Discriminating between better and worse qualified minds has always been crucial. Since Roman times an important aspect of legal practice is identifying the people or bodies that are better able to understand the relevant moral considerations that bear on cases and craft the required legal categories that can help judges make sense of the cases. The law develops largely through the work of these identified authorities. Different legal systems use and institutionalise in different ways the work of epistemic leaders. A typical way of doing so is by appointing people qualified to serve as epistemic leaders (or people who already are, as influential scholars) as judges of upper courts. This could provide reasons for judges from upper courts to be less constrained by received legal categories than judges from lower courts – though they should also remember the important problems for which legally directed adjudication is a solution, and avoid overestimating their intellectual and moral powers. Here I am not concerned with explaining the concrete mechanisms through which legal categories are created so as to contain the relevant knowledge that can give judges an epistemic advantage. Therefore I do not examine this issue further.

7.4.1.6   Bad Legal Categories

There is such a thing as bad legal categories – legal categories that fail to fulfil their task of expressing the requirements of practical reason that apply to the situation, and that perhaps obscure those requirements, or even express a principle that is plainly immoral. Bad legal categories can do great harm precisely because of the trust we put in them. Take a simple illustration: a judicial decision espouses, without giving much argument, a legal principle that is based on the wrong considerations, and which thus modifies existing legal categories for the worse – for example, that certain acts that should be considered torture will not be considered torture and sanctioned accordingly. At that point you have legal doctrine: a legal category (a bad legal definition of torture) that will guide further decisions. Because legal direction unburdens judges from revising what has been already established,[47] further decisions dealing with the issue can rely on that precedent without opening for debate whether the legal categories applied are reasonable ones. The decision can be arrived at through technical legal reasoning, and thus the immorality or other imperfections of the legal categories applied may not be assessed.

Above I have shown how legal categories can be an important aid to proper legal adjudication. Now I show how legal categories can go wrong and become an important obstacle for proper legal adjudication. Are these latter remarks a good reason for abandoning legally directed adjudication and replacing it for unconstrained moral reasoning, where there is no risk of bad legal categories distorting the reasoning of the judge?

At the outset it must be pointed out that some of the benefits of legally directed adjudication would still apply even with respect to bad legal categories. Of course, it is not clear what legal adjudication wins when judges can deflect the pressure exerted by the parties or public opinion by attributing the decision to the law, if the law directs them to a morally wrong decision. But some benefits of legally directed adjudication will still fully apply, as for example the benefits related to certainty and predictability.

But the main points are two. First: legal categories are, at least in the legal systems of developed democracies, for the most part successful in aiding adjudication. By 'successful' I do not mean perfect. I mean that they can increase the likelihood of adjudication realising justice and other relevant values in the concrete case. This I presuppose here. To fully prove this, one would have to engage in the Herculean task of assessing one by one

---

[47] See Cass Sunstein, *Legal Reasoning and Political Conflict* (Oxford University Press 1998) 42.

all legal categories in a given legal system (or at least a substantial portion of them – perhaps the most widely used?) and analyse what considerations they express, how successful they are in doing so, and whether these considerations are in fact morally and prudentially sound or not.[48] Yet for the purposes of the point I am assessing here I can provide an indirect reason for the aptness of the bulk of legal categories. Legal categories have the potential to confuse legal reasoning precisely because we (judges and the legal community) trust them. The more unclear, imprecise, contradictory, or simply wrong legal categories are, the more pressure there is for resort to extra-legal considerations – typically in the form of more ambitious forms of interpreting the sources where, instead of being guided and 'taught' by the law on what is of relevance in the case, the judge is guided by his own moral reasoning, which is dominant over the sources. Were legal categories systematically wrong there would be no reason for trusting them, and judges would feel a moral need to revise those categories over and over again. The fact that they can deflect the reasoning of a conscientious judge suggests that legal practice assumes that legal categories are generally sound and thus relying on them is generally safe.

Second: regardless of the value of current legal categories, the remarks on the problems of adjudication that is not legally directed show that there is a need for legal categories guiding adjudication. The fact that there is a need does not prove that there is a remedy for that need, or that the remedy works. Hunger is not bread. But it does show that leaving adjudication unguided is not an option. Therefore, it is right for the legal community to have engaged for millennia in the task of crafting legal categories, devoting substantial knowledge and energy to evaluating received categories,

---

[48] The problem here is not lack of 'empirical' evidence. As it often happens in human affairs, whether legal categories can and do play the role I assign to them here in overcoming the problem of the confused judge cannot be established through empirical studies. It requires a moral assessment of the correctness of legal categories, and of the complexity of human conflicts. As said above, fully establishing this is a Herculean task. Here I offer an indirect argument for the soundness of legal categories. I grant that this can only suggest, but not fully establish, that legal categories are largely sound and able to help courts overcome the problem of the confused judge. An additional reason in favour of the account I offer here is it being consistent with the general shape that the law has in developed legal systems (appearing as a complex body of highly differentiated and precise legal categories, structured into several departments), and with some characteristic features of legal adjudication (as its appearing to be largely informed and constrained by legal categories), and legal education (which is mostly concerned with legal categories and their application). This, I think, is a strength of this account, at least when compared with the quick dismissal of legal authorities by authors defending the idea of proportionality as unconstrained moral reasoning.

thinking of ways of improving them, and crafting new ones. The real pos-sibility of bad legal categories is not a reason for unconstrained moral rea-soning in adjudication. It is a reason for having practices and institutions for correcting bad legal categories promptly and efficiently.

7.4.2 The Problem of the Unduly Influenced Judge

In legal cases there is commonly pressure on the judge to decide the case in one way or the other. The pressure can come from the parties, some other person (including other state authorities, business interests, parties, etc.), or public opinion, and it can be considerable. The legal system has ways of dealing with illicit forms of pressure. For example, one cannot threaten or bribe a judge. But some degree of pressure from the parties or sometimes from society at large is unavoidable. Legally directed adjudication helps judges to divert some of that pressure, by imputing the decision of the case to the law and not to the judge's own legally unaided evaluation of the merits of the case.

Without the direction of the law that allows for the judge to impute the decision to it, the judge would have to bear the whole responsibility for the decision. In a world where not everybody is a hero, this would affect legal adjudication. It puts a strong incentive for judges to change the criteria by which they decide cases, from seeking to do justice, to trying to accommo-date the will of the parties and other stakeholders, promoting some sort of bargained compromise among those involved. In this sort of bargain-ing we should expect the more powerful party to have a great advantage. Legally directed adjudication, on the contrary, allows the judge to divert the pressure by imputing the decision to the law. When there is enough legal direction, the judge does not need to be a hero.

7.4.3 The Problem of the Passionate Judge

In dealing constantly with different forms of human misery and injustice, the pressure against reasonable decision-making comes not only from external sources, but also 'from within', so to speak. The passions of the individual human judge can also play a role against proper adjudication.[49] Criminal law provides countless examples of cases where the alleged deeds of the accused would infuriate or scare any normal person, and make her

---

[49] See Finnis (n 28) 127.

prone to punish the accused in a vindictive way. Adjudicating based on previously settled rules also helps remedy this feature. In cases like those mentioned, the judge ideally should not have to decide how to punish the guilty, but apply the punishment that the law establishes for the deed (or decide within a restricted frame that typically not only sets bounds on the quantity of the punishment, but also on the kind of punishment).

INTRINSIC PROBLEMS

7.4.4   *The Problem of the Subdued Party*

An important aspect of the ideal of the rule of law is being ruled by laws and not by other persons. Endicott refers to this as the 'best feature of a concern for the rule of law: the determination not to subject parties and the community to the arbitrary will of an official'.[50] One would not depend on the whims of others, and hopefully not as well on other preferences that, even though more rational, are not pertinent to the issue nor in some way embodied in the impartial and publicly available standards of legal norms.[51] Legal direction reduces judicial discretion, thus increasing the area of affairs where the parties can trust that they will be given a decision based on a previously settled general standard.

This enhances the legitimacy of adjudication (see next subsection), and it protects the freedom of citizens subject to the power of judicial authorities. According to Weber, 'formal justice [adjudicating based on pre established abstract rules][52] is thus repugnant to all authoritarian powers [. . .], because it diminishes the dependency of the individual upon the grace and power of the authorities'.[53] The underlying thought is that power that is not exercised in accordance with general rules is an absolute power the exercise of which depends only on the will of the person who wields it.[54] Restraining absolute power in society requires legally directed adjudication.

---

[50] Timothy Endicott, 'Legal Interpretation' in Andrei Marmor (ed), *The Routledge Companion to Philosophy of Law* (Routledge 2012) 109, 110.

[51] The law must provide 'public standards for the resolution of disputes'. See Solum (n 1) 181–2.

[52] Weber (n 12) 657.

[53] Ibid 812 (reference omitted).

[54] See John Locke, *Two Treatises of Government* (Peter Laslett ed, Cambridge University Press 1988) [1689] II sec. 137.

Subjecting the parties to the rule of another person, and not of the law, creates further problems, which are related to the need for coordination between *different* courts, and over time. When judicial decisions are unconstrained by the law, then it is expected that different individuals or groups of individuals will decide similar cases differently. If the decision is dependent only on the subjectivity of the judge, then we should expect that different judges decide differently, even when confronted with similar cases. This is to be expected because different people have different values and sensibilities, but also because of the outcome-related problems mentioned above. If legal problems were easy, then there should be a salient alternative so that it would be obvious what to decide for every judge, and thus we would have a reason to expect that – if there are no strong pressures on the judge or other distortive elements – different judges would decide similarly. Because legal problems are not usually easy, but rather, as seen above, they are difficult and complex, there is no reason to expect that different judges will coordinate and deal with cases in a similar way. The force and direction of the pressure exerted by the parties or other persons will typically depend on the contingent interests of those involved. The same happens with the passions of the judge that could distort her judgement of the case. All this suggests that different judges will not deal with cases in a similar way. This has at least three moral deficiencies: first, it is unfair that people in the same situation (e.g. having committed the same crime, or being bound by a similar contract) receive a substantially different judicial treatment only because a different judge or group of judges decides the case; second, it is arbitrary 'if the best explanation of an individual's suffering a certain adverse legal outcome is that a particular standard happened randomly to be applied to his case',[55] as is the case with the judge that decides the case, which depends largely on chance; and third, it does not allow for certainty and predictability (see below Section 7.4.6).[56] Since the contrary would be desirable, a coordination problem arises: how can we coordinate different courts, over time, to decide similar cases similarly?

Legal direction addresses this coordination problem. By providing guidance for all the different courts as to how to address different kinds of cases, legal direction greatly increases the likelihood of different courts over time arriving at a similar result in similar cases, since the same law is directing them all. Here we need to be cautious. Because legal direction is a matter of degree, and it can never be total (offering complete guidance

---

[55] Jeremy Waldron, 'Lucky in Your Judge' (2008) 9 Theoretical Inq L 185, 191.
[56] I take the three moral deficiencies from ibid 190–1.

for addressing all cases), some disparity between the decisions of different courts is to be expected. But an excessively sceptical view would also misrepresent the reality of adjudication. Take the straightforward example of determining sentences for offences. Jeremy Waldron exemplifies the problems of different judges dealing with cases differently with the example of two judges deciding criminal sentences, who are 'given discretion to decide between a sentence of zero years in prison and a life sentence and absent any posited "sentencing guidelines"'.[57] In this example we should expect great disparity in the decision of the judges. But in real-life adjudication the law does provide limits as to the different sentences that correspond to different types of offences, and also provides sentencing guidelines to determine the precise sentence for a concrete offence, within the limits of the law. This substantially constrains the decision of the judge and allows for similarity in the decisions of similar cases by different courts. Here we have an illustration of the potential of the law for guiding adjudication and remedying the deficiencies mentioned in this subsection.

Furthermore, this ability of legal direction to coordinate different instances of legal adjudication is crucial for legal change. We want the legal system to be able to adapt to new circumstances and improve upon legal categories. For this we need to allow for the possibility of change in the legal categories. Legal change does not occur when some individual court changes the way it decides a certain matter, leaving unaffected the way other courts and legal officials deal with the same matter. Legal change is always *coordinated change*: a change in the way the legal system, through its different officials, generally deals with a certain matter. Only this kind of change counts as a change in the law. For this coordination around change to be possible, legal direction is essential, even when legal change requires that some court departs to some extent from legal direction[58] – as it occurs when the change is produced by a court's decision, rather than, say, by legislation.

7.4.5   The Problem of Legitimacy

There is a legitimacy in law; in norms that we have consented to (like contracts and democratically approved legislation), and, arguably, in shared authorities (even epistemic) that we acknowledge as such. Legally directed

---

[57]   Ibid 208.

[58]   As said above, it is possible that a court departs to some extent from legal direction, and still benefits from it. See Section 7.4.1.5.

adjudication benefits from these sources of legitimacy. Adjudication that is not legally directed is not necessarily illegitimate, but it can give rise to issues of legitimacy, particularly in connection with the ideal of the rule of law and the previously mentioned problem: if I am to be ruled by laws and not men, and in our society legitimacy of state authorities is achieved through law, why would it be legitimate for this person to decide my case when he decides it according to his own judgement?

It could be said that the mere holding of the office is enough to grant legitimacy. I do not intend to establish on a normative level under what conditions a judicial decision is legitimate. Rather, I will make two points, one normative and one more pragmatic. The normative one is that given the legitimacy of the law, a judicial decision can increase its legitimacy by partaking of the legitimacy of the law through legally directed adjudication. The pragmatic one explains why this would be relevant. Legitimacy is easy to challenge, particularly in the face of undesired decisions. Therefore, courts may need and often benefit from the added legitimacy that the law brings to judicial decisions, even when no one disputes that the judge is (as is the case with Berta) the person appointed by the community for making that sort of decision, and the moral importance of her mission. As Jeremy Waldron notes: 'Courts are concerned about the legitimacy of their decision-making, and so they focus their "reason-giving" on facts that tend to show that they are legally authorised – by constitution, statute, or precedent – to make the decision they are proposing to make.'[59]

7.4.6   The Problem of Uncertainty and Unpredictability

Legal direction gives certainty and predictability as to what the decision in particular conflicts will be. It also allows for greater social coordination, which otherwise would be unlikely. Certainty and predictability sound less morally appealing than justice or other values that could be at stake in adjudication. But it is crucial for people being able to participate in values that are important to their own lives. It allows for citizens to be able to order their lives according to the plans and long-term projects they have themselves adopted. Therefore, '[a]n important element of most theories of the Rule of Law is that those who make and administer state policy should do what they can to diminish its unpredictability and provide a solid and reliable basis for calculation by ordinary citizens.'[60]

---

[59] See Waldron (n 21) 1383–4.
[60] Waldron (n 55) 191.

Justice is fragile. It can only blossom under particular circumstances. It is difficult to know what it requires, and, once known, it is difficult to realise. Legal direction helps address these difficulties, increasing the likelihood of justice being done. Thus, the task traditionally imposed on judges of doing 'justice according to law' is a good description of the legal practice of adjudication, which captures both its aim and the technical legal direction that improves substantially the odds of that aim being attained, and of other moral requirements that bear on adjudication being realised.

Legal direction in adjudication is a matter of degree, and thus the benefits that arise from it (or the deficiencies that are not remedied when there is not enough legal direction) are also a matter of degree. How much is enough is something that cannot be said in the abstract. But we can assert a link between legal direction and certain important benefits on which good adjudication largely depends in the circumstances of the real world.

7.5 Achieving the Benefits of Legally Directed Adjudication

Legal direction is a matter of degree, and so is the enjoyment of the benefits derived from it. They will be enjoyed more when the law is able to guide more, and when the judge adjudicating the case allows himself to be guided by it. The degree to which the legal system benefits from legally directed adjudication thus depends on how the law is made and on how it is applied.

The practice of the law is not only about applying the law and bringing about justice, but also about crafting good law – thus, increasing the likelihood of justice being brought about by the application of the law. And thus, in the same way that we need an understanding of how to interpret and apply the law well, we need an understanding of how to craft the law well. The idea of legally directed adjudication is a crucial part of the latter. Those who craft the law (particularly, though not exclusively, legislators and judges) and those who influence that practice (such as commentators) need to be aware of the relevance and purpose of the technical enterprise of crafting legal categories so that they can provide appropriate guidance, and see it as a crucial part of the task of law-making. By 'appropriate guidance' I mean that the body of legal categories should fulfil two standards, one quantitative and one qualitative: it needs to provide a *substantial* amount of guidance (enough to be an important aid for judges in overcoming the problems of legally unaided adjudication),[61] and it needs to

---

[61] Though total guidance is neither possible nor desirable. See below Section 7.6.

provide generally[62] *good* guidance, that is, it needs to guide in the right direction, expressing the moral and prudential requirements that bear on the issues to which the legal categories apply, and excluding irrelevant or illegitimate considerations. A body of legal categories that fulfils these standards will have two distinctive features. First, it will contain *precise* legal categories. Legal categories will not provide only abstract guidance (such as the guidance provided by general legal principles, such as Ulpian's 'do no harm', 'live honestly', 'give to each his or her own'),[63] but also more specific guidance as to how to address the details of particular cases, so as to meet the standard of providing substantial guidance. Therefore, the law provides precise definitions, tests, requirements, rules, etc., that are aptly tailored to address concrete cases. Second, it will be a body of *differentiated* legal categories. This is a natural consequence of the first feature, and of the fact that what is of moral and prudential relevance is different in different types of cases. Only at a very abstract level can one say that a moral consideration applies to many different types of cases equally, and therefore, if we want to express it in a legal category, that legal category would apply equally across a wide range of different cases. For example, principles such as 'do no harm' would apply to cases of tort, criminal offences, contracts, family law, etc. But these abstract principles do not provide enough guidance, and therefore precise legal categories are needed. But since the moral and prudential requirements that are relevant in different cases are different, then the legal categories that express those requirements must be different as well. What is relevant in establishing the responsibilities of a board of directors for a fraud committed by the CEO of the company is not the same as what is relevant in establishing whether a particular action constitutes murder or manslaughter. Therefore, different legal categories are needed. As said above (Section 7.4.1.4) this justifies the usefulness of organising legal categories into different departments. The need for diversity and precision in legal categories plays a key role in the account of legal human rights and their delimitation that I sketch in Chapter 9.

---

[62] Again, it is expected that there will be some error in the body legal categories – some deficiency in capturing what is morally relevant in a particular situation to which they apply. Therefore, the standard is not that the body of legal categories provides always good guidance, but that it provides generally good guidance. The ideal that informs the practice of crafting legal categories is, of course, that it provides always for good guidance, and, therefore, all deviations from this ideal are seen as deficiencies to be corrected. But full conformity with this ideal is not to be expected.

[63] *Digest* 1.1.10 (Ulpian).

In relation to this, we also need an account of what institutions should craft what aspects of the law, so as to better bring about its benefits. This cannot be fully established in the abstract, since it depends on the particular aspect of the law at stake, and on the particular circumstances of different societies, including institutional considerations. In developed legal systems crafting legal categories is a common enterprise in which legislatures and courts, as well as other actors, play a role. I do not here explore this question. Just one caveat is in order: what was said about the epistemic benefits that legal direction has in relation to the problem of the confused judge does not tilt the balance in favour of judge-made law, as crafted through precedent. It is true that promoters of judge-made law, as opposed to parliamentary legislation, often rely on the idea of tradition in the field of law.[64] But I agree with Adrian Vermeule that there are generally no greater epistemic benefits in judge-made law as such than there are in parliamentary legislation.[65] A legislative body can benefit from legal learning as much as a court. Codification in civil law jurisdictions is a good example of this. Civil codes were not created from scratch. Not even those that were drafted by very few experts – or even only one expert. Perhaps the more extreme case is that of the Chilean Civil Code. Written in the nineteenth century, it has been used since then by many countries throughout Latin America up until this day. It is the work of the genius of one man, Andrés Bello, who drafted the code that was later, with few emendations, enacted by parliament. Nevertheless, even in this extreme case, legislation benefited from received legal knowledge, drawing from sources in Roman law, German law, medieval Spanish law, colonial law, and French civil law, among others.[66] Codification was a matter of selection, emendation, and formulation of these categories – many of which were valid law before the code was enacted – into an ordered and coherent body. There is no reason to think that legislatures are of necessity unable to gather and use competently the relevant legal knowledge; they have done so on many occasions, and in many places they clearly possess the institutional capacities to do so well.

But achieving the benefits of legally directed adjudication is not only a matter of crafting good law, but also of adjudicating in a way that allows the court to benefit from legal direction. There is no need to add here

---

[64] Vermeule (n 43) Chapter 2.
[65] Ibid.
[66] Alejandro Guzmán Brito, *Andrés Bello Codificador. Historia de la Fijación y Codificación del Derecho Civil en Chile* (Ediciones Universidad de Chile 1982) 407.

one more theory of interpretation to legal scholarship. It will suffice to make a general distinction between two modes of adjudication: adjudicating according to legal categories, and adjudicating without direction from legal categories. The distinction lies in the way judges see their task, and, particularly, in the way they relate to legal categories – whether they understand their task as one that is ordered mainly to the correct application of legal categories to the case at hand, or whether they think their task is not informed in that way by legal categories. (The distinction does not lie, as it might seem, on the relative vagueness of the norms that apply to the case.) When judges adjudicate according to legal categories, they are primarily concerned with establishing which legal categories apply to the case, and how these legal categories should be interpreted. This is not necessarily a mechanical exercise. Sometimes a great deal of interpretation is needed to understand a particular legal category. In those cases, the judge might do a number of things: she can resort to legislative history, or see whether there is some analogous institution that solves the case. She might also try to see that legal category in its best light, trying to understand what is its purpose and thus get an insight on how it should bear on a difficult case. The idea of adjudicating according to legal categories cuts across different theories of interpretation. For example, both textualist and purposivist[67] judges can adjudicate according to legal categories, as long as they understand legal interpretation as ordered to the competent application of legal categories.

This view – which conceives of the primary task of the judge in adjudication as one of making sense of the applicable received legal categories so as to do 'justice according to law' – is consistent with what legal reasoning should be so as to achieve the benefits of legally directed adjudication. At the core of this view of adjudication is the particular way in which the judge relates to legal materials, to received legal categories. But this is not the only way in which one can understand the relation of the judge and the legal categories that apply to the case. A rival alternative is to adjudicate without the direction of legal categories. This form of adjudicating includes obviously the kind of fully unconstrained adjudication of a judge who has no legal categories at his disposal, and has to decide the case according only to his or her sense of justice (Weber's 'Kadi-justice').[68] But it also includes other more subtle ways in which adjudication can be

---

[67] For a survey of these different positions, see John Manning, 'What Divides Textualists from Purposivists?' (2006) 106 Colum LR 70.

[68] See Weber (n 12) 976.

actually unconstrained from legal categories, as, for example, a form of adjudication in which the judge does not see her reasoning and decision of the case as constrained and informed by legal categories, but merely as inspired by them. An example of such a form of relating to legal categories is what I call 'adjudicating according to values'. This view sees the task of the judge as one of realising values to the greatest extent possible. The question the judge asks herself when adjudicating is a different one from the traditional view in which the judge does 'justice according to law'. Here, the primary question is how certain values that are at stake can be realised through adjudication. The relation with the sources is therefore different. To the extent that there are legal sources that apply to the case, these sources are seen as trying to give expression to a value. The task of the judge is to uncover the value behind the sources, and then use her own powers of reasoning to figure out how that value should be instantiated in the case under her consideration.

Adjudication according to values might seem the best way to realise substantive values in society. But this is wrong. Adjudication has greater chances of arriving at morally reasonable decisions if it is legally directed. Therefore, adjudication must follow the first model. It is only thus that the benefits of legally directed adjudication can be brought about.

7.6 Gaps in Law and Legally Directed Adjudication

My argument for legally directed adjudication does not imply that legal categories completely determine the outcome to every case. Sometimes legal direction will be substantial, but not complete, thereby still performing a valuable service for legal adjudication (see Section 7.4.1.3). In other cases, such as those dealing with new problems and questions, the only available legal categories may be remote from the issue, such as general legal principles providing very abstract (and perhaps trivial) guidance. Legal direction cannot be complete for every possible case, given the limitations of our language. Legal prescriptions will always have what Hart called an 'open texture', that is, they will always be formulated in terms that will be in some ways vague, leaving some issues indeterminate.[69] It is impossible to express everything that matters in every possible case, so as to determine completely the outcome of every possible legal question. To be sure, lack of full legal determinacy and guidance

---

[69] See HLA Hart, *The Concept of Law* (3rd edn, Oxford University Press 2012) 128.

is not always a deficiency: it can allow legal officials to accommodate new facts that the lawmaker might not be able to foresee, or some other valuable aims that were not considered when the rule was adopted.[70] Relatively vague and general language might also be necessary for the law to guide effectively (since too detailed a regulation might be difficult, if not impossible, to apprehend and apply by those subject to it).[71] In the real world, therefore, lack of complete legal determination (and therefore, guidance) for every possible case is desirable. The attempt to determine future legal issues beyond what can be reasonably known and aptly expressed and applied would render legal categories useless and prejudicial for many cases. Therefore, there will be 'gaps of legal guidance': relevant legal questions for which legal categories do not provide an answer, or at least a complete answer. Lawyers and judges experience these gaps frequently.

The existence of gaps of legal guidance holds regardless of whether it is the case that (1) there is always (or almost always) some law that applies to any issue for which legal determination is required, or that (2) there are gaps in the law, so that sometimes there is no applicable law for addressing a certain issue, and thus discretion is granted to whoever needs to decide it.[72] The idea of gaps of legal guidance is obviously not in contradiction with the latter position. It is also not in contradiction with the former one, since the proposition that for any case there is applicable binding law does not imply that there will be legal direction capable of guiding completely as to how to decide every case. Suppose that there can be no gaps in the law, and the reason is that there are general legal principles that apply

---

[70] See ibid 128–9.

[71] See Timothy Endicott, *Vagueness in Law* (Oxford University Press 2000) 190. Though this last consideration about the limits of the ability of those applying the law for handling complexity should be assessed bearing in mind that in modern societies, where labour is divided and functions differentiated, most of the application of the law is mediated by legal experts, precisely so that the necessary legal complexity can be dealt with appropriately. This allows for the law to be applied competently even when it is of great complexity. Thus, though there is such a thing as excessively complicated (even if sound) law, the legal system can handle a high degree of complexity.

[72] These are the two positions in the famous debate in legal philosophy between HLA Hart and Ronald Dworkin. See Hart (n 69) 272–6; and *TRS* Chapter 4, *LE* 37–9 (these are the two texts Hart engages with). Dworkin stated his position more explicitly in a later essay, claiming that 'there [are] no gaps, or very rarely gaps in the law'. Ronald Dworkin, 'On Gaps in the Law' in Paul Amselek and Neil MacCormick (eds), *Controversies About Law's Ontology* (Edinburgh University Press 1991) 84, 89. He explains how and in what sense it is possible that there is a gap in the law in ibid 88–90.

to every legal issue.[73] It is still possible that legal direction will be incomplete (or even almost absent) if nothing but abstract principles apply to the matter. There are gaps of legal guidance in determining how those principles are specified in the concrete case.[74]

What has been said here on legally directed adjudication does not deny that there are gaps of legal guidance My point has not been a conceptual one about necessary features of the law, but a normative one about certain benefits of a specific legal practice: the practice of crafting precise legal categories capable of providing substantial guidance to judges, and of adjudicating according to those categories. One can hold that there are gaps of legal guidance, and also hold that legal guidance provides important benefits, and that an important degree of guidance is crucial for avoiding the problems of legally unaided adjudication.

Three final remarks can further clarify the relations between the benefits of legally directed adjudication and the gaps of legal guidance. The first is that the problems of legally undirected adjudication do not arise whenever there is a gap of legal guidance. As discussed above (Section 7.4.1.3), legal direction may provide much guidance in addressing a legal case, running out only with respect to some discrete aspect of it. When this happens, lack of legal direction in that respect may not be a real problem. Some of the problems of adjudication that is not legally directed may not arise – or not rise to the level where they make it unlikely that adjudication will succeed in realising justice and other values – depending on the amount of guidance provided and on the nature of the issue to be decided. For example, the problem of the confused judge does not arise if there is enough legal direction to aid judges and lawyers in understanding the different

---

[73] A different argument for why there are no gaps in the law is that 'it is always logically possible, although sometimes inadequate, to apply the legal order existing at the moment of the judicial decision'. Hans Kelsen, *General Theory of Law and State* (Anders Wedberg tr, Transaction Publishers 2005) [1949] 149. There are no gaps in the law because when there seems to be no legal rule that applies to the matter, then the issue is simply not regulated and thus there are no legal rights and obligations in that respect. Talk of gaps in the law would signal situations where the application of the current law would have an 'unsatisfactory result'. A new norm is needed, which can create a distinction for the particular case so that the result is satisfactory. The fiction of gaps in the law would serve to restrict 'the authorisation of the judge to act as legislator' in correcting the law. Ibid 148–9. Even if this is true, there will still be gaps of legal guidance in establishing when the result of applying the applicable legal categories is unacceptable, and what norm would be necessary to enact so that the result could be acceptable.

[74] '[I]ndividual principles do not determine results [. . .] they incline a decision one way, though not conclusively'. *TRS* 35.

considerations at stake in a given issue, with legal direction running out with regard only to some easier or simpler aspect of the issue. Here the problem of the confused judge does not arise, not even to a proportionate small degree. Ingesting a whole whale may kill someone, but eating a little chunk of it does not need to kill or harm anyone 'a little'. Depending on how much legal guidance is provided with respect to an issue, and on some characteristics of the specific problems for which there is no guidance (their difficulty, how controversial the topic is, whether it is likely to arise the passions of the judge, etc.) the different problems of adjudication that is not legally directed will each be present to a smaller degree, and some perhaps not at all, even when there is no legal direction with respect to some aspect of an issue. But, again, if trivial or no guidance is provided, then adjudication will face all those problems.

The second remark is that the question of legal direction is different from the question of whether a particular issue should be decided or reviewed by a court or not. Even when there is no legal direction with regard to a particular issue, there may still be good reasons for having a court decide a particular matter. Such reasons may relate to concrete circumstances of the issue to be decided or of the society where the issue arises: if in that society judges are less corrupt, or more diligent than other potential decision-makers, that would be a reason for them to decide those kinds of issues, even if they do not possess the advantages that legal direction would provide. In defining the competence of the courts one should be aware of the benefits legal direction provides and that without it courts will lack some of the institutional advantages they otherwise possess. But bearing that important cost in mind, we may still prefer that in a particular society courts decide a certain type of issue, even without legal direction.

The third remark is that we should not be complacent about the problems of legally unaided adjudication, even in those situations where it is preferable to other institutional alternatives. These problems still need to be overcome where possible. Therefore, there are reasons for attempting to produce a body of legal categories that applies to those different situations, so as to provide the needed legal direction – at least to the degree that it is reasonable to do so, considering the limitations of our ability to craft legal categories mentioned above in this section. These reasons are connected to the benefits of legally directed adjudication. The practice of crafting precise legal categories and of adjudicating according to them, the practice for which I have been arguing in this chapter, should be pursued when initially there are no legal categories that apply to the issue.

7.7   Legal Categories and Legal Reasoning

Above (Section 7.2) I said that the idea that grounds proposals for uncon-strained moral reasoning in legal adjudication has three main elements. The first element is the idea that reasoning according to the law, and moral reasoning about the more just or reasonable solution to the case, are largely independent. The second element is an understanding of legal rules, and of legal categories in general, that conceives them as curbing moral rea-soning, at times foreclosing what would otherwise seem the more just or reasonable decision. The third element was assigning different values to each of these different forms of reasoning: justice and the realisation of other substantive values would be realised by moral reasoning; and cer-tainty and predictability, or other similar rule of law values, would be real-ised by reasoning according to legal categories.

Though there is some truth to these elements, the picture they convey of legal reasoning and of the role of legal categories is a distorted one.

Take the second element. Frederick Schauer has insisted that rules '[screen] off from a decisionmaker factors that a sensitive decisionmaker would otherwise take into account'.[75] Rules 'gain their ruleness by cut-ting off access to factors that might lead to the best resolution in a par-ticular case', and they 'function as impediments to optimally sensitive decisionmaking'.[76] To be sure, Schauer's statement is correct insofar as it captures the *force* of rules: they are binding even if one thinks that an alter-native course of action would be more reasonable than doing what the rule requires one to do. And it is also true that because rules are couched in general terms, a legal rule can apply to cases unforeseen by the drafters of the rule, where the rule may yield an unjust or inefficient outcome.[77] But to focus solely on the force of rules leaves something important out of the picture: the *purpose* of having rules, and, more generally, of authoritative doctrinal legal categories. What a legal system aims for is that legal rules and other legal categories capture the reasons relevant in a particular situ-ation, and leave out the irrelevant ones; that they establish requirements

---

[75] Frederick Schauer, 'Formalism' (1988) 97 Yale LJ 509, 510.

[76] Ibid 539; see also ibid 537, and Frederick Schauer, *Playing by the Rules: A Philosophical Examination of Rule-Based Decision-Making in Law and in Life* (Oxford University Press 1991) 1. Though Schauer also explains that a decision *procedure* according to rules may be optimal, even if it cannot be optimal in all cases. See ibid 101–2.

[77] See Paul Yowell, 'Legislation, Common Law, and the Virtue of Clarity' in Richard Ekins (ed), *Modern Challenges to the Rule of Law* (LexisNexis 2011) 101, 102. See also, Larry Alexander and Emily Sherwin, *The Rule of Rules: Morality, Rules, and the Dilemmas of Law* (Duke University Press 2001) 53–4.

that increase the likelihood of the subjects of the law (including those that apply it) conforming to those relevant reasons. That is what we aim for when designing legal categories. When we realise that something relevant was not captured, we think that that is a good reason for modifying or replacing that legal category. Much of legal practice (be it at the legislative level, or through legal adjudication, or in academic doctrinal commentary) is devoted to this enterprise of better adapting the legal categories that apply to a type of situation to the moral or prudential considerations that bear on that kind of situation. While it is true that, given the limitations of our foresight and language, it is not possible that rules will always succeed in capturing all the relevant reasons and exclude irrelevant considerations for all cases, it is an important aim of legal practice that they do so as much as possible, at least to a substantial degree and for a substantial number of cases. It is not a necessary feature of a legal rule to curb moral reasoning, if by necessary we mean that it is a feature that it is always present in any application of the rule. The point and purpose of legal categories is realised when this is not the case, and, instead, legal categories discipline practical reasoning according to the relevant moral and prudential considerations that bear on the case. Jurisprudential accounts of the role of rules in legal reasoning and adjudication must also consider this, if they want to fully understand the purpose of rule-constrained and guided adjudication, and evaluate well proposals on the role that rules and rule-following should have in legal adjudication.

The third element, the idea that technical legal reasoning about legal categories and moral reasoning realise different values, is unfounded. When the benefits of legally directed adjudication are considered, particularly the outcome-related ones, one can see that legal reasoning structured through legal categories greatly improves the likelihood of securing justice and realising other substantive values through adjudication by making it more likely that the relevant moral and prudential considerations are featured in the decision of the case, and by helping judges overcome undue pressure and their own sub-rational motives that could run against a reasoned decision aimed at doing justice and realising other values at stake in the case. But it is not only more likely that the full range of moral values that bears in adjudication will be better realised through legally directed adjudication. It is also the case that ideal adjudication – adjudication that fully realises all the relevant moral values at stake – is not even possible if adjudication is not legally directed. This is because the intrinsic benefits of legally directed adjudication (those associated with the rule of law, with legitimacy, and with certainty and predictability) are not available to adjudication that is not legally directed.[78]

What I have said in this section suggests a particular phenomenology of judging, which relates to the first element. Judges do not necessarily think first of a reasonable way to decide the case and of good reasons to justify that decision, and *then*, in a separate mental process, reason about how legal categories bear on the case, allowing legal categories to curb their initial moral reasoning. If, as argued above, it is true that legal issues are generally difficult and complex; and if legal categories generally provide guidance as to how to deal with the difficulty and complexity of cases – a guidance that is needed by judges of limited talent and resources; then, it is likely that the phenomenology of legal reasoning is a different one: lawyers and judges typically see themselves confronted with a complex array of facts, and they resort to their knowledge of legal categories to find a way of making sense of those facts, and to think about the problem in an ordered fashion that allows the relevant considerations to be properly assessed. Surely sometimes they might realise that a particular legal category runs counter to what morality requires. Much has been made in discussions on law and morality about this possibility. But in the bulk of cases (and even with respect to most of what constitutes a hard case)[79] the relation of the moral reasoning of the judge to legal doctrinal categories is not one where the latter curbs the former, but one where the latter guides the former – not only with respect of 'how to think about this problem within the boundaries of the artificial system of the law' but also on how to aptly assess all the relevant moral considerations at stake. The phenomenology of legal adjudication that I propose here is one that acknowledges that in many cases the judge's and the lawyer's reasoning about the morally best decision to the case, and their legal reasoning about the application of legal categories, are commonly instantiated in *one reasoning* about the best decision to the case, which is guided by legal categories. When this happens moral reasoning and legal reasoning can still be distinguished for analytical purposes. But there are no reasons to think that this distinction occurs necessarily, or even usually, in reality.

---

[78] It does not follow from this that always the best response to a conflict is legally directed adjudication. As said above, it is possible that the legal categories available are so deficient or wicked that legally unaided adjudication would be preferable. It is also possible that there are no legal categories that apply to the case, and therefore legally unaided adjudication is the only possibility.

[79] See Finnis (n 28).

7.8   Conclusion

Given the nature of adjudication and the circumstances in which adjudication occurs, it is likely to face several obstacles. These obstacles make it unlikely that adjudication will succeed in delivering a decision that is just, reasonably argued, and able to realise other important values at stake in the case. They ground the need for adjudication to be legally directed.

From what has been said above we can derive the following conclusions on (good) law-making and legal adjudication.

First: there is a need for adjudication to be directed by legal categories able to express the relevant considerations that bear on the case, show how these considerations should relate to each other, and do all this *with enough precision and detail* so as to guide the judge effectively to a reasonable decision to the case.

Second: since the relevant considerations are different for different types of cases, and are generally complex, there is a need for legal categories to be complex and differentiated as well (i.e. there is a need for different bodies of different legal categories that apply to different types of problems).

Third: there is also need for these legal categories (or the bulk of them) to be backed by some form of authority – be it positive law or established doctrine, which makes the judge's decision a decision supported by those authorities.

A body of authoritative legal categories can provide direction as to how to decide a particular type of case, and this legal direction allows judges to overcome the obstacles that threaten adjudication. It makes likely that average judges will be able to adjudicate well. For judges to benefit from legal direction, they must comply with the following standard:

Fourth: the legal practice of adjudication needs to relate to the authoritative legal categories in a certain way. It needs to allow itself to be constrained and guided by legal categories.

If we craft and apply the law in this way, we will have a legal practice that is not different from the one we have now in most areas of the law, and which we have had for centuries. There will be different departments of law, each of them composed of different authoritative legal categories that are relevant for different types of situations, and which are applied by judges who see their task as that of doing justice through the application of those authoritative legal categories. What I have presented here is an explanation of the reasons for this aspect of legal practice. Understanding these reasons should lead us to a renewed appreciation for characteristic technical modes of legal reasoning and the sources that should guide it – an appreciation that is much needed in the field of human rights.

8

Proportionality and the Problems of Legally Unaided Adjudication

8.1 The Objection to Proportionality as Unconstrained Moral Reasoning

The main problem of proportionality as unconstrained moral reasoning is that it dissipates the benefits of legally directed adjudication. The conclusion of the previous chapter set standards for law-making and legal adjudication. In relation to law-making, the standards point to the desirability of having legal categories that are (1) precise, in that they provide specific guidance in relation to what is to be done or decided in the situations to which they are applied; (2) differentiated, since what is morally and prudentially relevant is different in different situations, and, if the legal categories are to express what is relevant in those situations, they need to reflect this difference; and (3) authoritative, in that they need to be backed by legitimate authority binding on the judge and the community. If legal categories that fulfil these standards are available, then legal adjudication must also meet a standard: (4) it must adjudicate according to these legal categories. If these standards are met, legal adjudication benefits from legal direction, which, as shown in the previous chapter, is crucial not only to realise rule of law values such as certainty and predictability, but also to realise justice and other substantive values at stake in adjudication.

Proportionality as unconstrained moral reasoning does not meet these standards. It realises them to the almost lowest degree possible. As said above (Section 6.4), on this account, the proportionality test and the human rights it applies provide almost no guidance. Thus, as legal categories they fall below standard (1). As a consequence, they also fall below standard (2). Only very abstract guidance can apply to such a broad range of situations as those regarding limitations with broadly conceived human rights under the proportionality approach. Different moral and prudential requirements will be at stake in these situations, and thus only abstract, trivial guidance – such as 'act proportionally', strike a 'fair balance' between the considerations at stake, or decide on an overall 'balance of reasons' – can apply to all these situations. More precise guidance would require differentiation. As for the third standard, it must be noted that even though authors defending proportionality as allowing for unconstrained moral reasoning elaborate on some abstract moral requirements that should be taken into account in human rights cases (see Section 6.4), these elaborations (or the moral theories that inspire them) are not authoritative, in the sense that they are not backed by legitimate authority binding on the community. It is not even proposed to turn said abstract moral requirements into precise, differentiated authoritative legal categories that can provide guidance to judges. The abstract moral requirements are left in the domain of moral theory, from where they may (or may not) inspire judges in their open-ended moral assessment of the reasons presented in favour of and against a measure limiting a right. Furthermore, proposals for understanding proportionality as unconstrained moral reasoning also rely on a view of adjudication that downplays the role of text, precedent, and of legal authorities in general, favouring instead an understanding of adjudication as concerned primarily with moral reasoning about the realisation of values (see Section 6.1).[1]

A doctrinal legal category that allows for and requires unconstrained open-ended moral reasoning is law badly crafted, which deprives judges of the aid that substantive law is supposed to give them. Proportionality conceived in this way comes at the price of forgoing the benefits of legally directed adjudication. In adopting the account of proportionality as unconstrained moral reasoning, adherents to proportionality sacrifice the ability of proportionality to bring more rationality to the political process and generally to adjudication, leaving human rights adjudication exposed to the problems of adjudication that is not legally directed. As we have seen, these are important obstacles that make it unlikely that justice, the rule of law, and other important values be realised through legal adjudication. Law can do much better.

8.2   Negative Effects

How would the problems of legally unaided adjudication manifest themselves in proportionality cases? It has been suggested that to sustain claims that proportionality grants courts 'too wide a discretion' one would have to show 'that the use of this seemingly too wide a discretion leads to negative effects. This kind of proof was not given and it is unlikely that it exists.'[2]

---

[1] See Grégoire Webber, 'Rights and the Rule of Law in the Balance' (2013) 129 (Jul) LQR 399, 400, arguing that 'standards of proportionality and balancing [. . .] exacerbate rather than attenuate the weak guidance offered by bills of rights'.

[2] *Proportionality* 487.

The problem I am trying to show is not exactly that there is too much discretion. Discretion is a consequence of the problem, which is lack of legal direction in adjudication. Now, before concluding whether lack of legal direction in proportionality has negative effects or not, one needs to know what kinds of negative effects to expect. Some negative effects will not be manifested in the outcome of the decision, but in some other intrinsic problem with the way the outcome is reached, as is the case with the intrinsic problems of legally unaided adjudication mentioned in the previous section: the problem of the subdued party, the problem of legitimacy, and the problem of uncertainty. We should also expect judges to encounter the outcome-related problems mentioned above: to encounter pressure and to find it harder not to yield to it – though it will be difficult to gather from the decision whether the outcome is influenced by pressure. More visibly perhaps, we should expect judges to have problems dealing with the complexity of particular cases, leaving out important moral considerations, including irrelevant ones, over-simplifying the issue, and failing to provide a clear explanation of the reasoning that leads to their conclusion, among other ways in which one can fail to assess correctly the moral complexity of a particular case.

These last negative effects related to the complexity of cases are addressed in Tsakyrakis' critique of proportionality (Section 5.1). He devotes substantial effort to showing the lack of moral sophistication in the courts' analysis when dealing with human rights cases as if they concerned only unspecified interests, without discriminating which of them are actually legitimate as public aims, which of them are protected by a right; and what the special normative force of such a right would require. This lack of sophistication in analysis is precisely what we should expect of individual judges dealing with complex moral problems under constraints of time and resources. A related vice that illustrates this particular 'negative effect' is the 'black box' phenomenon that some authors detect in proportionality. Tsakyrakis says that in proportionality cases we find a 'characteristically impressionistic assessment of the relative weights of competing considerations, which does not lend itself to a rational reconstruction of the argumentative path that has led to a particular decision.'[3] He is not alone in this. Both critics and defenders of proportionality have noted that proportionality decisions tend to be opaque and 'impressionistic'.[4] Timothy Endicott has tackled this particular

---

[3] Stavros Tsakyrakis, 'Proportionality: An Assault on Human Rights?' (2009) 7 3 Int'l J Const L 468, 482.

[4] Finnis notes the European Court of Human Rights' notable lack of sophistication in dealing with the governmental aims in the *Hirst* case. John Finnis, *Human Rights and the Common Good, Collected Essays* III (Oxford University Press 2011) 44–5. Elsewhere, in relation to the English *Begum* case he remarks: 'The conceptual slackness of human

issue more directly, in response to scholars who claim that proportionality is a structured form of inquiry and who present this as one of its characteristic advantages. Endicott observes that

> [T]he crunch point is the final, crucial node in the structure, where the judge decides whether the impact on the claimant is *too much*. The attractive structure of the judicial role crumbles at that point into an unstructured, opaque choice, when the task involves 'balancing' the unbalanceable.[5]

Leaving aside the problems with incommensurability that Endicott raises at the end of the quoted passage, he is correct in that at this crucial point of the inquiry, proportionality is devoid of any structure and consequently of any of the putative advantages that structure would bring to legal reasoning. Other parts of the test also provide little guidance (see Section 6.4).

Proponents of proportionality as unconstrained moral reasoning acknowledge this, at least with respect to the crucial 'balancing' subtest. Thus, Kai Möller affirms that

> the principle of proportionality does not provide a substantive test as to how to conduct the balancing: rather, it directs judges to 'balance' all the relevant considerations in order to decide whether the policy in question is proportionate or not.[6]

---

rights law in action is impressive.' 'Endorsing Discrimination Between Faiths: A Case of Extreme Speech?' in I Hare and J Weinstein (eds), *Extreme Speech and Democracy* (Oxford University Press 2009), 430, 433. For a similar claim, see JD Heydon, 'Are Bills of Rights Necessary in Common Law Systems?' (2014) 130 LQR 392, 407. Letsas, in his defence of proportionality, acknowledges that the reasoning of courts 'under the heading of proportionality is often scant and conclusory, as is typical in civil law jurisdictions'. George Letsas, 'Rescuing Proportionality' in Rowan Cruft, S Matthew Liao, and Massimo Renzo (eds), *Philosophical Foundations of Human Rights* (Oxford University Press 2015) 318 (though I believe that the association between 'scant' and 'conclusory' legal reasoning and civil law jurisdictions is unfounded; after all, these same defects in proportionality reasoning have been found by authors commenting on decisions of common law courts, as Finnis does in the second text mentioned in this footnote, and Endicott in his article cited in the next). Lord Reid, in an opinion that applies the proportionality test, notes that proportionality is 'a concept applied by the ECtHR', though it usually approaches the matter of balancing the demands of the general interest and the requirements of the protection of the individual's fundamental rights in 'a relatively broad brush way'. *Bank Mellat v HM Treasury* [2013] UKSC 39, [2014] 1 AC 700 [70] (Lord Reed). See also text attached to footnotes 6–7.

[5] Timothy Endicott, 'Proportionality and Incommensurability' in Grant Huscroft, Bradley Miller and Grégoire Webber (eds), *Proportionality and the Rule of Law: Rights, Justification, Reasoning* (Cambridge University Press 2014) 328.

[6] *Challenging Critics* 727.

In 'balancing' the relevant considerations, judges are not guided by the law or other relevant sources:

> As a matter of moral reasoning, it is often not evident why the balance between two values in a given case ought to go one way or the other. A comprehensive argument about this would require a general, substantive moral theory of balancing, that provides guidance about how to conduct a balancing operation correctly; however, such a theory does not, to my knowledge, exist yet.[7]

I interject: up until this point, Möller is simply acknowledging the lack of legal direction provided by proportionality, and the epistemic problem that it generates – what I called 'the problem of the confused judge' (Section 7.4.1). To overcome the problem, though, more is needed than a 'theory of proportionality'. Instead, what we need are authoritative legal categories that express the requirements of practical reasoning (articulated perhaps by a moral theory) that bear on the issues to which they apply. But let us continue with Möller:

> As long as this remains the case, all of us, including judges, have no choice but to rely to some extent on our intuitions when striking a balance between a right and a competing value.[8]

Möller's explanation for the impressionistic character of balancing is that 'the issues are complex, in fact, too complex to be resolved in a theoretically satisfactory way at the moment when we have to decide the case'.[9] We can now see that Möller's reply to the objection that balancing is impressionistic is not a reply. It is simply an explanation of how some of the 'crucial features of the proportionality test' – the way it 'simply directs judges to assess the weights of the respective rights and interests without giving them further instructions'[10] – produces the defect that the objection of impressionism points to. This, if anything, reinforces the objection. It shows how the problem of the confused judge can manifest itself in applying the proportionality test, thus explaining the 'impressionistic' and 'opaque' character of proportionality decisions.

---

[7] Ibid 728.
[8] Ibid.
[9] Ibid 729.
[10] Ibid 717.

Möller seems to believe that the epistemic 'problem of the confused judge' is somehow mitigated in proportionality cases by the help we could receive from our intuitions. He says:

> Fortunately, however, in many cases we have moral intuitions to which we are sufficiently strongly committed to feel confident in saying that the balance between the two values should go one way or the other.[11]

I believe this is an overly optimistic view. There is no reason to think that human rights cases are easy, and that intuitions can guide us through their complexity – particularly if human rights are interpreted in the generous way Möller interprets them, as embodying a general right to autonomy and therefore to anything that the agent believes is in his interest. Furthermore, people have different intuitions regarding these cases: the fact that there is often (heated) disagreement on human rights cases attests to this. Remove the optimism, and what this view ultimately amounts to is that the complexity of human rights cases is such that courts, unguided by legal categories, are expected to fail to reason their way towards a sound decision to those cases, 'hav[ing] no alternative but to rely on [. . .] intuitions'. This also relates to our fourth problem of legally undirected adjudication – the problem of the subdued party – in that we expect to be a community ruled by law, and not by some person's intuitions.[12]

This is not the place for an exhaustive study of how proportionality cases can display some or more of these negative effects. Any such study would run into the difficulty that proportionality is understood in different ways, and, this book argues, these ways of understanding proportionality have

---

[11] Ibid 729.

[12] All this is in tension with Möller's assertion that, because proportionality is a form of review of the reasonableness of a measure (rather than a method for making the best or the correct decision in a given situation), requiring from judges 'to ask questions, press the state for justifications for its actions, and assess the plausibility of the reasons given', it is 'something which a capable judge will most likely be comparatively good at'. Kai Möller, '"Balancing as Reasoning" and the Problems of Legally Unaided Adjudication: A Rejoinder to Francisco Urbina' (2014) 12 Int'l J Const L 222, 224–5. If courts cannot be expected to provide enough reasons for their decisions in a type of case, then they are not well suited to address cases of that type. In thinking about courts' capacities, one should bear in mind that legal direction is an important institutional advantage of courts. Remove legal guidance, and courts cannot be expected to remain as capable of dealing with the complexity of the issues brought before them as if they had the advantage of adequate legal direction. As Möller concedes, human rights cases are complex, even if in those cases courts only have to review the conformity of a measure with human rights, rather than make an all things considered judgement as to the best possible decision. Because human rights cases are complex, legal direction is relevant for overcoming the problem of the confused judge.

different vices. Moreover, a defect in a legal decision can be the product of the shortcomings of either account of proportionality. For example, one defect of a legal decision may be that it does not acknowledge that a particular interest falls within the domain protected by a right, and thus fails to acknowledge the priority of that interest in relation to other considerations. This defect can be the product both of a method (as the maximisation account of proportionality) that is blind to considerations of rights, or of the confusion to be expected when there is no legal direction (as in the account of proportionality as unconstrained moral reasoning). At this point my aim is to illustrate what kinds of negative effects we should expect to see in legal decisions if proportionality were the kind of test proposed by the defenders of the idea of proportionality as unconstrained moral reasoning. I do not claim that proportionality is today the kind of test that Möller, Kumm, and others claim it is, or should be. My argument is at a conceptual level, and a normative one: if proportionality is understood as allowing for unconstrained moral reasoning, it would have some important deficiencies. These deficiencies – which are inherent to an important understanding of the proportionality test – would explain some of the defects that the above-mentioned commentators and others have found in proportionality decisions.

This brings us back to the way proportionality as unconstrained moral reasoning was thought to avoid the objections made against proportionality. I said that some defences of proportionality rely on a distinction between objections to proportionality as such and objections against the deficiencies of a particular application of the proportionality test (see Section 6.3). Examples of the former are the ones made in the first part of this book against the maximisation account of proportionality: the incommensurability objection, and the idea that the method fails to capture what morally matters in human rights cases, particularly considerations regarding the pre-eminence of human rights. These objections and other similar ones do not apply to proportionality as unconstrained moral reasoning, since it can allow for all the relevant reasons to be assessed by the court.

The second kind of objection points to deficiencies in some application of the proportionality test. Examples of these deficiencies are that proportionality conceals the moral reasoning of judges with technical parlance, that proportionality reasoning is opaque or impressionistic, and that proportionality analysis gets the moral questions wrong. It would be easy to dismiss these objections (or some version of them) as a problem of a particular judicial decision that applied proportionality wrongly, and thus, as not relevant for assessing the merits of proportionality as such. This would be a mistake. We can now establish a closer connection between these kinds of deficiencies and the idea of proportionality as unconstrained moral reasoning. The point here is this: the deficiencies that those objections refer to are the likely consequence of adjudication that is not legally directed enough. If proportionality is conceived as allowing for a form of adjudication that is not legally directed, then it is likely that the decision of a court applying it will have these deficiencies.

Take the objection that proportionality conceals the judge's moral reasoning. We should expect courts to take refuge in technical parlance, because of the heavy costs associated with acknowledging that they perform their own moral analysis of the case. These costs can be associated with all the intrinsic problems of adjudication that is not legally directed (lack of legitimacy, lack of respect for the ideal of being governed by law and not by men, and lack of certainty), but also with outcome-related problems. Because these cases are morally difficult, the judge might be uncertain about the outcome and the reasons that justify it, which creates incentives for adopting a technical parlance under which one can hide the moral complexity of the case. Even a genius judge able to deal with the moral complexity of the case might realise that her moral views are not shared by everybody in society, and that they perhaps touch on issues that are intensely debated.[13] This creates costs for overtly engaging in moral reasoning in the decision, costs that relate to the possibility of criticism and to challenges to the judge's legitimacy. Hence, judges have good reasons for adopting technical parlance. These reasons do not need to relate only to the judge's self-interest – in her not being criticised, in her reputation, etc. A conscientious judge could realise as well that adjudication that is not legally directed leaves her open to pressures from the parties and society: a way to divert this pressure, so as to make it easier to judge impartially, would be to indicate that the decision is driven by technical reasoning, and thus it is objective and the judge has little discretion.

Or take the objection that proportionality is opaque, that when judges apply it they don't make clear their reasons. The cause of this could relate to the kinds of incentive structures that I mentioned in the previous paragraph. Or, as previously explained, it could simply be a function of the complexity of the cases. It can be extremely difficult to make clear your reasons for solving a complex problem. Legal academics can devote many months, if not years, to provide a clear argument for one precise problem – and we

---

[13] See Larry Alexander and Frederick Schauer, 'Law's Limited Domain Confronts Morality's Universal Empire' (2006) 48 Wm & Mary LR 1579, 1583 ff.

do not always succeed. In a situation where the problems and their variety are multiplied, and where there are more severe time constraints, clarity in argument becomes less probable. The same principle applies to the objection that proportionality gets the moral questions wrong. It is difficult to consider comprehensively the complex array of interests[14] and moral considerations that are at stake. It is improbable that an average, and even competent person, under time and resource constraints, will be able to consider all these interests and moral considerations, let alone put them in the most reasonable relationship, without some guidance.

What needs to be placed in the forefront of the analysis is the idea that the problems arising from lack of attention to the moral complexity of cases and opaqueness in reasoning (as well as others less apparent in judicial decisions) are not exotic. They are precisely what we should expect of non-Herculean judges dealing with complex moral and political conflicts. What is artificial is the clarity and guidance that the law typically provides in adjudication. Remove that guidance, and we should expect obscurity and reductionism to be the rule, when not bargaining and unprincipled compromise.

Without legal direction, legal adjudication loses many of the advantages that would make it an appropriate institution for demanding justification of almost every conceivable act of political authority, as Möller, Kumm, Cohen-Eliya, and Porat propose. Unconstrained moral reasoning on behalf of judges has costs. These costs will manifest themselves with greater strength in the more complex cases, in the cases where there is more pressure, and in the cases where the judge has a particular personal opinion or interest in the outcome.

8.3   Justification and the Problems of Legally Unaided Adjudication

As seen in Chapter 6, the proportionality test is often associated with an ideal of justification. This ideal, at its most basic, requires that government authorities provide good reasons for their actions. Is proportionality really able to promote this ideal? Mattias Kumm has argued that judicial review and proportionality – in his understanding of the test as allowing

---

[14] Aleinikoff notes that courts applying balancing tests often purport to be assessing all the relevant interests, but they seldom do, leaving out of their reasoning the interests of one or more persons. Alexander Aleinikoff, 'Constitutional Law in the Age of Balancing' (1986) 96 Yale LJ 943, 977.

for unconstrained moral reasoning – serve a healthy practice of demanding justification for authorities' acts, evaluating whether they can be justified in terms of public reason. This practice of demanding justifications
he calls 'Socratic contestation', which he characterises as an activity that,
first, 'forces a certain type of enquiry onto others',[15] an enquiry that, in
the case of courts engaging in judicial review, Kumm describes as one of
'compel[ing] public authorities into a process of reasoned engagement'.
Second, the role of the court is not the construction of theories or the
elaboration of answers, but mainly the 'examination of reasons' – 'asking
questions [. . .] and assessing the coherence of the answers' and their plausibility. And third, the process is independent from ordinary politics.[16]

But a practice of demanding justification through courts does not have
much value if it is asking for the *wrong* reasons. It risks striking down
relevant pieces of legislation or policies for failing to provide arguments
related to considerations that were not morally relevant or decisive in that
case. Surely a culture of healthy scepticism towards state authority cannot
harm – bearing in mind that judicial authorities are also state authorities.
But the ideal that public authorities must provide justifications for their
acts needs an institutional counterpart that asks what kinds of institutions
should realise this practice of justification, how should they do this, and,
more specifically, whether it is courts that should perform this function
through legal adjudication. Then we need to think as well of what technical legal categories would better direct judges to reasonable outcomes
and increase the likelihood of the relevant practical considerations being
correctly assessed. We need to consider whether this particular institution, applying these particular doctrinal categories and judicial methods,
is likely to be able to discharge this function that moral reflection identifies as valuable in a democracy. In this respect, the benefits that arise from
legally directed adjudication have to be considered, since without them it
will be less likely that courts will be able to fulfil their role properly.

And in this respect, there is a tension between the ideal of justification,
and the conception of proportionality as unconstrained moral reasoning.
If proportionality is to allow for unconstrained moral reasoning, it will
have deficiencies that will reduce the likelihood that methods for demanding and assessing justification, such as Socratic contestation in the form of
proportionality review, will be able to further this ideal.

---

[15] *Socratic* 154.
[16] Ibid 154–5.

Take Kumm's theory of Socratic contestation. Kumm claims that Socratic contestation can help remedy four pathologies of political decisions, namely:

- The inclusion in the decision-making process of reasons that are not legitimate and thus cannot ground a legitimate decision by an authority (like those based on prejudice, or simply in 'convention, tradition, preference' not supported by reasons).[17]
- The inclusion of reasons 'relating to what it means to live a good, authentic life' (such as reasons based on religious beliefs or other 'comprehensive conceptions of the good'), which 'may not qualify as the kind of reasons that can be invoked in a liberal democracy to justify rights infringements'.[18]
- 'Lack of serious engagement [on behalf of the authorities] with the realities to which the law [or the decision of some political authority] applies'.[19] Instances of this pathology can range 'from government hyperbole to ideological radicalization'.[20]
- '[T]he capture of the democratic process by rent-seeking interest groups.'[21]

The first three are referred to as 'forms of thoughtlessness',[22] and all four of them point to deficits of rationality in the authorities' decisions (though it is highly contested whether the second one is a pathology at all – a point not addressed or defended by Kumm).[23] By demanding justification from the authority that made the decision, Socratic contestation would

---

[17] Ibid 158.
[18] Ibid 159–60.
[19] Ibid 160.
[20] Ibid 161.
[21] Ibid 163.
[22] Ibid 160, 163.
[23] For examples of rival positions, see Michael Sandel, *Public Philosophy: Essays on Morality in Politics* (Harvard University Press 2005) Chapter 23, and Joseph Raz, *The Morality of Freedom* (Oxford University Press 1986) II. Particularly in some cases where the law requires considering the well-being of children, it seems somehow unavoidable for legal reasoning to include some understanding of what constitutes a good life. See, for example, *Re G (Children)* [2012] EWCA Civ 1233. 'Very recently, Herring and Foster have argued persuasively [. . .] that behind a judicial determination of welfare there lies an essentially Aristotelian notion of the "good life". What then constitutes a "good life"? There is no need to pursue here that age-old question. I merely emphasise that happiness, in the sense in which I have used the word, is not pure hedonism. It can include such things as the cultivation of virtues and the achievement of worthwhile goals, and all the other aims which parents routinely seek to inculcate in their children' [29] (Munby LJ). Perhaps awareness of this unsettled debate explains Kumm's remarkably hesitant characterisation of this 'pathology' as consisting of reasons that '*may* not qualify' as acceptable reasons (emphasis added).

increase rationality by ensuring that the authorities' decision only survives if supported by appropriate reasons. But the deficiencies of legally unaided adjudication will creep into these putative remedies as well.

The first two 'pathologies' would be remedied by proportionality's ability to exclude inappropriate reasons. 'One important function of proportionality analysis is to function as a filter device that helps to determine whether illegitimate reasons might have skewed the democratic process against the case of the rights-claim.'[24] In an earlier article Kumm had noted that the idea of 'excluded reasons' is a 'relatively pervasive feature of moral reasoning'.[25] But it must be noted that, as seen above (Section 7.4.1.2), it is a pervasive feature of legal reasoning as well. It is good that the law works in this way; it brings about the benefits of legally directed adjudication that I mentioned above. There is nothing remarkable in proportionality if it purports to exclude some reasons, since the law commonly does this. The constraints that the law imposes on legal reasoning have precisely that function: to exclude. The question from the technical perspective is how successful a given legal doctrine is in excluding reasons that should be excluded, and in including reasons that should be included, putting them in a correct relation to each other, and in doing all this with precision and clarity. Here the problems of adjudication that is not legally directed become relevant. If proportionality allows for unconstrained moral reasoning, then it does not exclude anything. It is for the judge then to do all the 'excluding', and to discriminate by herself between what counts as a good reason for that particular case and what does not – a task the moral complexity of which should not be underestimated, as explained above in relation to the 'problem of the confused judge' (Section 7.4.1.1). Proportionality offers no help in this task of excluding reasons.

The third pathology relates to lack of serious assessment of the facts because of hyperbole or ideological radicalisation. This points to the heart of a real political problem, which is pervasive in almost every political context. Politics is a realm of intense feelings, disagreements, debates, pressures, and expectations. It is decisive that the political process can manage this intensity. This is why Max Weber said that one of the three 'pre-eminent qualities' of the (good) politician was 'a sense of proportion', which he distinguished from the other two (passion and a feeling

---

[24] *Socratic* 160.

[25] Mattias Kumm, 'Political Liberalism and the Structure of Rights: On the Place and Limits of the Proportionality Requirement' in George Pavlakos (ed), *Law, Rights and Discourse: The Legal Philosophy of Robert Alexy* (Hart 2007) 165.

of responsibility) by calling it 'the decisive psychological quality of the politician'.[26] And to achieve a sense of proportion, detachment from the situation is crucial. Thus, '[l]ack of distance *per se* is one of the deadly sins of every politician'.[27] Detachment and a consequent sense of proportion and perspective are thus important for proper political action grounded on an adequate assessment of reasons – against which the realities of politics that pull towards hyperbole and ideological radicalisation conspire.

However, Kumm does not tell us how proportionality-based judicial review can be an effective remedy against this pathology. He moves from briefly characterising the pathology, to conceding that 'courts might not be particularly good at analysing complicated means–ends relationships or striking balances between competing goods', followed immediately by the assertion: 'But there are sufficiently common instances of pathologies ranging from hyperbole to ideological radicalization that judicial intervention is reasonably good at detecting.'[28]

Kumm does give us a brief exposition of an example of courts undertaking this role in relation to the US government counterterrorism measures after 9/11. But an example is not an argument. Not because more examples are needed (it could be a representative example), but because the fact that a court remedied that pathology in one case or in a set of cases does not show that courts are apt to do so. An argument should explain why they are generally apt to do so – why the example should be seen as the rule and not the exception. It should explain what is it about a court that makes it resist better than political bodies the allure of ideological radicalisation or hyperbole or other similar vices in a given situation. An argument is needed because, after all, courts are composed of human beings as well, living in societies, and thus are exposed to the same ideologies, passions, and fanatic doctrines as the rest of their fellow citizens.

There is actually one characteristically legal way through which courts achieve the necessary detachment from the situation so as to avoid being caught in the impulsive or radical feelings that lead to lack of careful consideration of the reasons at stake. This is legally directed adjudication, which consists precisely of having general norms that control (at least to a considerable extent) the outcome, and which have been established *before* the actual case the judge is facing. In this way, crucial aspects of the final decision of

---

[26] Max Weber, 'Politics as a Vocation' in HH Gerth and C Wright Mills (eds), *From Max Weber: Essays in Sociology* (Routledge 2009) 115.

[27] Ibid.

[28] *Socratic* 161.

the case were adopted by a process that is 'detached' of the contingent pressures and passions aroused by the concrete case, because previous to it.

But if proportionality is understood as requiring unconstrained moral reasoning, that particular benefit of legally directed adjudication is lost, and with it is lost the characteristic feature of legal adjudication that would allow it to resist Kumm's third pathology.

Something similar happens with relation to the fourth and last pathology, related to the 'capture of the democratic process by rent-seeking interest groups'.[29] In this case there is a reason for thinking that courts are in a better comparative position to deal with this pathology than democratically elected representatives, since the former have less of a dependency on interests groups for preserving their position of authority than the latter. Courts do not typically have constituencies or need access to money or the media to be able to stay in office.

This deserves three caveats: Firstly, I said courts have 'less of a dependency', because judges in many jurisdictions are promoted through a system that to some degree depends on the decisions made by political authorities, and thus the pressure that interest groups can put on politicians can indirectly be placed on judges. Secondly, if courts are to have a greater role in making decisions that affect interests groups (an inevitable consequence of the expanded role Kumm and other proportionality defenders attribute to courts in a culture of justification), those interest groups will have stronger incentives to seek to pressure the judiciary, either directly or indirectly through politicians that appoint them. Thirdly, the more discretion judges have, the more we should expect them to be the object of pressure, since, after all, they can make the decisions that interest groups want. As mentioned above (Section 7.4.2), legally directed adjudication aids judges in resisting external pressures. When the decision of the case is largely controlled by previously settled law and doctrine, external pressure can only play a diminished role, since courts have less discretion anyway, and they can attribute the decision to the law. But again, legally unrestrained adjudication cannot receive this aid from the law, and thus, it has less ability to deal with this particular pathology.

8.4   Conclusion

Proportionality as characterised by Kumm, Möller, and others is an appealing idea. It can achieve the most perfect justice, precisely because of its unrestrained character. But the same freedom that allows for the most

---

[29] Ibid 163.

perfect justice can allow for the gravest injustice. We should pay more attention to a different question: does proportionality make it more likely in the circumstances of the real world that justice and other relevant values will be realised through legal adjudication? The technical perspective bears on this question, given the potential of technical legal categories to help achieve justice in adjudication. This potential is realised to a great degree by legally directed adjudication. This chapter and Chapter 7 were aimed at showing the price it is paid when adjudication is not legally directed.

With this concludes the main, critical, part of this book. There are different ways of understanding what the four-part proportionality test described in Chapter 1 requires. There are two main accounts of this test. So far I have criticised these main accounts of the proportionality test: the maximisation account of proportionality (in part I) and the idea of proportionality as unconstrained moral reasoning (in part II). In the course of arguing against these accounts, I have made a number of positive claims regarding human rights and legal adjudication. These claims, when put together, ground a more ambitious conclusion: not only are there good reasons for abandoning the main accounts of the proportionality test, but also no account of the test can be offered that is not open to objections of the kind I have raised against the two main accounts of proportionality. Furthermore, there can be no other alternative single method able to replace proportionality that is not itself open to similar objections.

The objections raised here against the maximisation account of proportionality show that human rights cases are morally complex. It is misleading to imagine these cases as only or primarily involving some sort of quantitative comparison, as the metaphors of 'scales' and 'balancing' suggest. They involve careful consideration of the different interests at stake, discriminating between legitimate and illegitimate interests, assessing the different potential realisations of incommensurable values, establishing the different relationships of justice that hold between the people whose interests are involved in a case, and assessing the particular normative force that the rights and duties that constitute those relationships have, among other considerations. This moral complexity is not properly captured by the maximisation account.

Legal systems have a specific way of dealing with the problems that moral complexity poses to adjudication, by providing judges, officials, and generally the subjects of the law with legal direction. This legal direction is provided by a precise and differentiated body of authoritative legal categories that attempt to express the relevant moral considerations that bear in different situations. Proportionality as unconstrained moral reasoning does not provide, and cannot take advantage of, legal direction. It is thus open to all the problems of legally unaided adjudication, which severely affect the likelihood of justice and other relevant values being realised through adjudication.

The two accounts of proportionality have important flaws that make them unsuitable as a general doctrinal test for deciding cases on the limitation of human rights. So, where to go from here?

The main aim of this book is critical. Nevertheless, I think that the argument made in the previous chapters can illuminate the kind of alternative that is needed. The temptation is to think that the next step should be to provide a better account of proportionality – or, if this is not possible, to replace proportionality with some other test. The new understanding of proportionality, or the new test proposed, would have to serve as a general doctrinal test for deciding cases on the limitation of human rights, and do so fulfilling two conditions, so as to avoid the deficiencies of the main accounts of proportionality. First, it would have to provide enough legal guidance. And secondly, it would have to do so through legal categories that can capture what is morally relevant in the kinds of cases to which it will be applied.

This is impossible. There is no test or understanding of proportionality that could perform the function assigned to proportionality, and at the same time fulfil the two conditions just mentioned.

The reason for this is the same reason why we do not have one single test to decide whether a person should be punished or not and how, or whether a person should pay compensation – and if so, how much – for making someone worse-off. The function we want the test to perform requires that it be applied to a great variety of cases – particularly considering the ever expanding domain of current human rights law – which give rise to different moral and prudential considerations. To fulfil the conditions posed above, the new test or understanding of proportionality would have to provide enough legal guidance for addressing these different cases. This can be done through legal categories that capture the relevant considerations that bear on those cases. But if the relevant considerations are different in the different cases, a variety of legal categories are needed. No one test, be it proportionality or something else, will suffice. What is needed is many different tests, definitions of rights' subject matter, rules that establish their priority, standards for public authorities, among other legal categories – not an abstract and comprehensive legal category, but many precise and differentiated legal categories. What is needed, then, in place of proportionality, is not a new test, but – and there should be nothing original or unexpected about this – a *body of law*.

PART III

9

Legal Human Rights

9.1 Introduction

In the previous chapters of this book I have argued against the proportionality test as a method for deciding about limitations of human rights. I further argued, in the conclusion of the previous chapter, that my argument entails that there can be no alternative understanding of proportionality that can overcome the deficiencies of the currently dominant conceptions of the test. So, where to go from here? If not proportionality, what?

I have argued that there can be no other single test that can replace proportionality as the default method for deciding human rights cases. Instead, what is needed is what I called a *body of law*, by which I mean several precise and differentiated legal categories. Not just one test is needed, but several legal categories. This is so because the moral and prudential requirements at stake in human rights cases are of a great variety. It is not the case that the same moral and prudential considerations are relevant in each human rights case. The moral and prudential considerations that bear on different cases involving different human rights – and even different aspects of the same human right – are usually different. If law is to provide enough guidance for each of these cases, and this guidance is to be sensitive to the relevant moral and prudential considerations at stake, then the law needs to match the diversity of the moral and prudential considerations potentially at stake with a complex set of differentiated and precise legal categories. Different legal categories give expression to different moral and prudential considerations, and are tailored to apply to different types of cases. Only highly abstract legal categories apply to a great variety of situations: for example, the legal principles that command that 'dignity shall be respected', and that one should 'do no injustice to others', apply to most situations that are the law's concern. But legal categories of this abstraction provide little guidance as to what one should do or decide in a given situation. It is necessary that legal categories provide sufficient legal direction to legal officials and all legal subjects more generally. This, as was said above (see Chapter 7), is not only desirable for reasons connected to the rule of law, but it is also essential for legal adjudication to succeed in realising justice and other related values. To provide the required legal guidance, legal categories need to be relatively precise, and as legal categories descend from abstraction to approach cases more closely they need to be differentiated, as the relevant moral and prudential considerations are different for different types of cases.

There is nothing remarkable in this alternative. As I said in Chapter 7, most of the law works in this way. We do not have a single test to decide whether we imprison someone, or if someone needs to compensate for damages, or for deciding whether one has a contractual obligation. All these issues are legally addressed by different bodies of differentiated and precise legal categories that apply to each of these issues.

In this chapter I attempt to provide a general outline of my alternative to the proportionality model that I criticise in the previous chapters. Since I am not proposing just another test, but instead arguing for a body of differentiated and precise legal categories, I cannot provide a full account of the alternative I favour – I cannot here offer such body of legal categories, or even provide a detailed description of it. The main aim of this book is to criticise a widespread form of reasoning about human rights, not to propose an alternative to such form of reasoning. Nevertheless, my critique does entail a number of positive criteria that can give shape to a better understanding of human rights and their limitations, and it seems to me that the critique itself is better understood when one has a sense of the alternative.

The aim of this chapter is to convey such a sense of the alternative, leaving a full account of it for some other occasion. The proposal, in short, is to specify human rights into a body of legal categories capable of providing legal guidance, and to apply such body of legal categories to the solution of human rights cases. In a way this is not an extremely original proposal. As I said, this is the default way in which other areas of law work. In the context of human rights others have emphasised the need for specification and delimitation of rights. Grégoire Webber's proposal is a prominent example of such a theory, presented specifically in the context of discussions on proportionality.[1] My account, though, introduces a new perspective. It adds to these valuable proposals an understanding of human rights specification within the context of a more general view of human rights as specifically legal categories. Crucially, it highlights the artificial nature

---

[1] See *Negotiable Constitution*. Specification plays an important feature in Finnis' account of human rights. See *NLNR* 8.5.

of legal human rights and the need for legal categorisation, focusing on the specific technical devices that allow legal categories to express some important features of human rights.

Here I first offer some general suggestions on legal and moral thinking about human rights. I claim that legal categories and the moral considerations that they serve are different, and one should not expect a necessary correspondence between the two. When this insight is taken into human rights law, it liberates us from having to assume that human rights are 'monolithic': that each legal human right must correspond completely to one single moral entity, such as a value, or an interest, or a principle, or a requirement to realise any of the former. Legal human rights can entail a plurality of different requirements. A systematic effort at specification and categorisation in human rights law would yield a complex body of human rights legal categories. The proposal entails, in some sense, to make human rights law more like the rest of the law. Nevertheless, there is also something distinctive about human rights, and a body of legal categories of human rights should be sensitive to it.

Secondly, I provide an account of the general shape that this body of legal categories of human rights should have by way of providing an account of what is distinctive of human rights for the law. I focus on two characteristic features of human rights in both legal and moral discourse: their special priority and their extensive reach. I believe these features must be at the core of a general account of legal human rights on grounds of their great power for illuminating issues relating to the force and content of such rights. Relying on an analysis of these features, I will outline an account of rights that stresses both their legal force and their diversity. This account rescues the best and most characteristic aspects of the legal and political discourse on human rights, while at the same time stands in sharp contrast to recent developments in human rights law.

Thirdly, I will suggest what this account of human rights as specified in a body of legal categories entails for legal adjudication. Courts should apply such a body of legal categories in addressing human rights cases, instead of proportionality. They also have a role to play in the elaboration and preservation of such legal categories. This form of adjudication based on legal categories is said to be prevalent in the United States, while proportionality is said to be dominant in Europe. These are rough characterisations, though, and I will cast some doubt on them. Be that as it may, my exploration of these issues will suggest how courts should address questions regarding limitations of rights from the perspective of the ideas on the specification and categorisation of human rights addressed in this chapter.

9.2   Thinking About Legal Human Rights

In thinking about rights it is useful to distinguish three levels. First, there is the level of the legal system. Here we find legal human rights given canonical formulation in legal sources, and applied as positive law by courts and officials. Legal human rights are artificial creatures. They are a human creation, in that they owe their existence to human enactment in positive law – be it legislation, treatise, or judicial decision – which determines its content.

Second, there is the level of moral discourse. Here human rights are viewed as moral rights. Human rights in this level are also the product of human making, but in a different sense: they are the way some person, or some community, has given expression to a certain moral reality.

And third, there is the moral level. This level is, I assume, objective. It exists regardless of whether someone makes it an object of inquiry and attempts to explain or describe it. At its most basic, it comprises reasons for acting or not acting in one way or another. These reasons are diverse: besides differences in content, some reasons are more general than others, some more stringent than others, some have supremacy and exclude others, etc.

Ideally, the second level should be dependent on the third, and the first on the second and the third. So: moral discourse is aimed at expressing the different reasons for actions that we have, how they relate to each other, and its different force or quality. It should try to understand which of these reasons should be imposed on others and should have pre-eminence over other considerations. Once one has established that certain moral requirements should be enforced by some authority in the community, we need to start thinking in legal terms. We think of what is the best way in which we can express those moral requirements through technical legal categories, so as to increase the likelihood of compliance with them. Then we craft legal categories such as legal human rights, to enforce a particular set of moral requirements, and under the conviction that this legal–technical scheme (legal human rights and the institutions associated with their enforcement) is apt for realising those moral requirements.

This understanding of legal human rights draws attention to the divide between the moral requirements associated with human rights (the third level, and its expression at the second level) and a specific technique for creating an artificial order of meaning that attempts to further said moral requirements: the law of human rights (the first order). As with all law, there is a moral and a technical dimension to it. On the one hand, there are some moral requirements at stake in a given situation. On the other, there are legal categories construed to attempt to give apt expression in the law to those moral requirements, so that the law can aid in the fulfilment of these requirements. Legal categories, as a human construct, can be imperfect; they can have specifically technical deficiencies, deficiencies that will render them less apt for giving expression in the law to the moral considerations – and to the prudential considerations at the service of moral considerations – they are attempting to realise. Legal categories can be over- or under-inclusive, excessively vague or ambiguous, or otherwise unhelpful. Of course, they can have the more basic deficiency of being inspired in a flawed and perhaps perverse understanding of the relevant moral and prudential considerations that bear on a given situation (see Section 7.4.1.6).

Thus, legal categories of the kind we are familiar with in contemporary legal systems should not be naturalised: they are a human creation that attempts to reflect moral and prudential considerations, but they are not those considerations themselves. And thus they should not be thought of as necessarily 'monolithic': they should not be identified or taken to correspond necessarily to one single moral value or requirement. A legal category can simply be a part of a complex scheme that attempts to give expression to one or a set of moral and prudential reasons; and a single legal category can attempt to capture a range of moral and prudential requirements. There is no reason to think that there must be a one-to-one correspondence between a legal category and something in morality.

This applies to legal human rights as well as to any other legal category. One should not assume that each human right has this one-to-one correspondence with something in morality.[2] But much of contemporary legal and academic discourse on human rights seems to entail precisely this. It is easy to see how thinking about human rights can be led astray, if the distinction between the moral and the technical dimensions of human rights law is obscured. If one starts with the practice of legal human rights, and begins thinking about the moral reality that lies behind them, it is easy to assume that there are a group of things in morality that possess a common quality that is characteristic of them (as legal human rights have common *legal* qualities that are characteristic of them), and that those things correspond to the sort of loose requirements that legal practice identifies as human rights.

---

[2] There is no reason for thinking that legal human rights are monolithic. That legal human rights should ultimately be understood as non-monolithic follows from the account I offer below of the general shape that a body of legal categories for human rights should have based on the specific legal qualities of human rights.

Thus, a human right is understood, for example, as 'a' (note the singular) value, interest, or principle. It is seen as consisting in one moral consideration that extends to the whole scope of the right: as one and the same value, interest, or principle that is at stake whenever the right is engaged. Thus, legal human rights are often reduced to their convenient two-term formulation ('right to life', 'right to freedom of speech', 'right to freedom of thought', etc.), and understood as standing for one single value, interest, or principle which extends as far as the semantic reach of the given formulation of the human right that stands for them. Thus, for example, a right to freedom of speech is about a value of free speech, which extends as far as 'free speech' extends. When human rights are thought about in this way, they are thought about as if they were monolithic.

This bears on how cases regarding limitations of human rights are understood. These cases typically involve some other human right, or some constitutionally protected public good (such as public order, national security, the protection of morals, and other rights), which stands in opposition to the human right the limitation of which is being evaluated. Limitation, in this context, becomes a question of comparing the two monoliths, two magnitudes. If this is what cases regarding human rights are about, then methods such as proportionality and balancing – which are ultimately oriented towards a comparison of this type – seem appropriate to address them. When most or all human rights cases are seen as involving this type of comparison, then most or all human rights cases are seen as depending ultimately on the same set of questions, and thus, the same legal methods (namely, proportionality and balancing) can be used across the board for human rights disputes. It is still necessary to express the results of this method – the boundaries drawn between human rights and other public goods – into legal categories so as to provide legal direction, and because the boundaries of different human rights when confronted with other human rights or with public goods will be different, the legal categories that express (with enough precision so as to provide enough legal direction) this complex set of different boundaries should be diverse.

But if human rights were not monolithic, and, rather, they involved a bundle of different considerations, then human rights cases would be about specifying the precise considerations at stake and their normative force, and about expressing these considerations in precise legal form for the decision of cases and the ordering of the actions of those subject to human rights in accordance with these rights. Human rights cases then become mainly about defining an order of diverse and relatively precise right relations between different persons through law, and less about comparing values or interests. By abandoning the idea that rights are monolithic, one frees oneself from the expectation that the right must grant some form of uniform protection to everything within the reach of its subject matter. Below I argue that legal human rights are best understood as involving specific high-priority requirements, and thus though their force is great, their scope is narrow and in a sense plural – because the same human right can and typically does consist of more than one high-priority requirement. If this is true, then human rights are not monolithic. Furthermore, if human rights cases are then about specification and categorisation (to be made or improved, or in the matter at hand already made authoritatively and only left to be applied), then there can be no single method for addressing human rights cases, as there is no single method for specifying the different considerations at stake in different rights, and how these considerations should be expressed in different legal categories into a complex body of human rights law. This is for the same reason that legal categories are very diverse in law in general (see Sections 7.4.1.4, 7.5, and 7.8): the diversity of moral and prudential considerations relevant in different situations where human rights can be at stake. But these ideas will be best understood as they are developed in the following sections.

9.3   Specification and Categorisation

Here specification and categorisation mean two different things, and loosely correspond to the two different dimensions of human rights law that I refer to as the moral and the technical. *Specification* relates to the moral dimension. It is the operation of practical reason oriented towards determining the specific requirements involved in a broadly formulated prescription and their normative force.

It has been noted that human rights receive two canonical formulations in bills of rights, human rights treatises, and other such documents.[3] Perhaps the more common, not only in legal texts but also in legal and political discourse, is one that expresses a 'two-term' relation of the following form: 'Everyone has a right to X'. This formulation asserts a relation between a class of persons ('every person' as is usually the case with human rights) and a subject matter ('free speech', 'freedom of thought', 'privacy', etc.). This formulation is conspicuously silent as to how anyone must order his or her actions so as to conform to the right. It is necessary to further determine what the right requires, of whom it requires it, and in relation

---

[3] See *NLNR* 211.

to whom it requires it, for the right to be operative in the law. It is necessary to *specify* this right into precise requirements. Thus, for example, in an unspecified right to 'freedom of religion' one can find an absolute requirement that no one coerces anyone to accept, change, or continue to hold a religious belief; a requirement that the government does not ban or impose limitations on acts of worship as such; in some places, a requirement that the state adopt no official religion, etc. Below I elaborate on this example. For now, this quick illustration will do. Similar specifications can be undertaken for different human rights.

Specification is also necessary even when the right is formulated in more detailed fashion, conveying at least some requirements that follow from it. For example, the second common formulation of rights is this: 'no one shall be . . . ("subjected to torture", "held in slavery or servitude", etc.)'. This formulation can convey a requirement of enough specificity to guide action: for example, a requirement for every person not to torture any person. Nevertheless, it leaves questions open as to the full scope of the right: is someone (who?) required to punish acts of torture? To take reasonable measures to avoid the commission of torture where there is risk of its commission? To refrain from using evidence gained by torture in criminal trials? If a right not to be subject to torture includes something more than a requirement for everyone not to torture anyone, then these further requirements are not conveyed by the austere formulation of the right, even if it takes the second, more informative, canonical formulation. Which additional requirements actually follow from it need to be determined through specification of the right.

Categorisation, on the other hand, relates to the technical dimension of law. It has two related meanings. On the first meaning, categorisation consists of expressing certain moral and prudential requirements in legal categories so as to render them operative in the legal system. It is a technical enterprise, as it consists in creating an artificial order – an artificial order at the service of a moral order.[4] As explained in Chapter 7, the legal direction that these categories can provide is a great benefit for legal officials (particularly those tasked with adjudicating cases) and generally for those seeking to order their activity in accordance with the law. Categorisation is pertinent when a set of moral and prudential requirements should be given expression in the law. On the second, related, meaning, categorisation is a form of addressing a legal case or question by applying to it the relevant legal categories. Categorisation on the first meaning and categorisation on

---

[4] See John Finnis, 'Natural Law and Legal Reasoning' (1990) 38 Clev St LR 1, 6.

the second meaning typically occur at different moments (the first before the second). But they can take place in the same legal decision, as when a court elaborates a legal category (categorisation in the first sense) for the purposes of illuminating the issues in a particular case, to which the legal category is immediately applied for deciding it.

The moral and prudential requirements that are expressed through legal categories can be arrived at by specification or by some other method, but they need to be of enough precision so that the categories that express them are precise enough to be able to guide action and aid legal decision-making. Specification, as understood here, lends itself well for categorisation in the first sense, as its results are precise enough to be turned into legal categories that are able to provide real guidance to those bound by them. Achieving clarity as to the moral requirements at stake, and expressing those requirements in legal categories, are two different operations. But they do not necessarily occur at different moments, one before the other, in the mind of the jurist thinking about, say, a particular legal right. Very commonly the jurist thinks about the moral and prudential requirements at stake in a type of case when contemplating the legal categories that apply to such type of case, pondering how better to understand and apply them (categorisation in the second sense), or evaluating whether there is need for refining or more generally modifying something in them (categorisation in the first sense), so that that they better correspond to the specific requirements the jurist thinks implied in a broadly formulated legal prescription (specification). Thus, in practice, moral reflection can start from legal categories, and return to them once clarity as to the moral and prudential requirements at stake is achieved, in order to judge the category in terms of its aptness for expressing said requirements. Specification in human rights law typically starts from (unspecified) legal categories available (a human right expressed in abstract form in, say, a bill of rights or in received legal doctrine), and ends in a richer understanding of the diversity of requirements at stake. Categorisation starts from such an understanding and the need to express those requirements in legal categories, and to decide cases by applying those legal categories.

9.4   The Priority and Reach of Human Rights

Specification and categorisation in human rights law should give shape to a body of legal categories that have some distinctive features. The claim I will present in this and the following sections, in succinct form, is this: legal human rights have two specific features. The first is a special priority over other legal requirements; the second is an extensive reach, applying to the whole legal system. The priority of human rights is typically expressed in terms of higher hierarchy in the legal system. This legal priority is justified on account of the content of human rights. There is thus a correspondence between the content of rights and their priority: this correspondence needs to be such that the content of the right justifies its priority. When there is no such correspondence, either too little or too much is given priority as a human right. When too much is given priority, priority becomes unfounded and less significant. For a body of legal categories to provide apt expression to the kind of moral and prudential requirements involved in human rights issues, it is crucial that this right relation between content and priority of human rights is respected. Human rights consist in requirements that deserve this strict priority, and these requirements need to be acknowledged as such by human rights law. Furthermore, these requirements bear on all areas of law, and thus the second feature of legal human rights is justified with respect to these requirements as well. Thus understood, legal categories can express the content and the special normative force of the moral requirements associated with human rights.

At the level of doctrinal analysis, it is evident that human rights are given a specific legal pre-eminence in the legal systems of practically all developed democracies. They are typically enshrined in some norm that enjoys the highest priority over other norms of the legal system. Such a priority of one type of norm over another type of norm is commonly represented in legal thought as 'hierarchy': norms are imagined in a hierarchical order, with the higher norms enjoying some kind of *strict* priority over the lower norms. This priority entails that in case of conflict, the higher norm rules. This operates in different ways in different legal systems, but it commonly entails that when there is a conflict, the legal status of the lower norm is immediately compromised (for example, it is null and void). Besides this strict priority, there is a *loose* priority. A norm has loose priority over another norm when in a case of conflict the legal system provides means and incentives for officials to change the latter norm so that it conforms to the former norm, but the legal status of the latter norm is not immediately compromised and the former norm may not rule in that case. But in both cases of priority the expectation fostered by the legal system is that all norms conform to those norms that enjoy priority; the difference is in how aggressively the legal system seeks this conformity. Judicial review of legislation in its different forms is a common means of securing the supremacy of the higher norm by entrusting to a court the assessment of compatibility with it of lower norms. A second common feature of all norms enjoying priority is that *their* status *cannot* be compromised by lower norms, such that when a new incompatible lower norm is enacted this is not taken to derogate the norm that enjoys priority or to constitute an exception to it, but it is taken to constitute a legal anomaly – for which more or less aggressive remedies may be provided by the legal system.

Human rights are commonly enshrined in norms of the highest legal hierarchy, as in a written constitution or in a norm of constitutional status. As such they enjoy a specifically legal priority over most other requirements imposed by the legal system, and this priority is commonly *strict*. Different jurisdictions have different ways of ensuring that this kind of priority is respected in the day-to-day operation of the legal system. Some legal systems are more aggressive in their methods for ensuring that this priority is respected, some are less.

The legal priority of human rights exists even when these rights are not incorporated in a written constitution, but adopted in ordinary legislation, as is the case with the Human Rights Act 1998 in the United Kingdom. It is worth pausing over this example. The Act gives legal effect in UK law to the rights established in the European Convention on Human Rights. According to section 3 of the Act, legislation must be 'read and given effect' in a way that makes it compatible with human rights, 'so far as it is possible to do so'. According to section 4, if a piece of legislation is found incompatible with the human rights incorporated by the Act, some UK courts can issue a declaration of incompatibility. Then it is up to Parliament to decide whether to change that piece of legislation to make it compatible with rights, and section 6 provides a fast-track procedure for the discussion and passing of such legislative changes triggered by a declaration of incompatibility. Though the Human Rights Act 1998 is a piece of ordinary legislation, the human rights protected by it still enjoy a special legal priority. The UK legal system has in the Act a series of legal means that promote the conformity of all legal system to such rights. If, say, a later law is clearly incompatible with the rights protected by the Act, then it is not the case that this later law is taken to derogate the Act, or to establish an exception to the demands imposed by Convention rights. The rights protected by the Human Rights Act 1998, unlike ordinary legal rights and obligations established in the law, are not taken to be modified by later incompatible legislation; the legal regime imposed by the Human Rights Act 1998 is one that is intended to promote the compatibility of all legislation (prior and posterior to the Act) with the human rights protected by the Act. And so it is applied and understood by the UK legal community.[5] The legal human rights protected by the convention enjoy a specific legal priority under UK law, even if this priority is of the 'loose' kind I described above.

The example of the Human Rights Act 1998 illustrates a distinction between priority and entrenchment. Human rights may not be entrenched, yet they can still enjoy legal priority over other legal categories. Entrenchment concerns the process of legal change: it makes change harder.[6] If legal human rights are entrenched, then they cannot be redefined by ordinary law-making. Priority concerns the operation of human rights in the legal system. If human rights enjoy legal priority, then they somehow prevail over other legal categories that may conflict with them. Such conflict is considered an anomaly to be corrected through appropriate legal mechanisms, and the correction entails not the modification or repeal of human rights, but of the legal dispositions that conflict with them. This is so regardless of whether the norm giving legal recognition to human rights can be repealed or modified by ordinary legislation or not.

Together with priority, and as a consequence of it, legal human rights possess a second characteristic feature, which I call 'extensive reach'. Legal human rights prescribe something about the content of all law, even law that was adopted before a bill of rights or a human rights treatise or not even created by state institutions. In this sense, the law of human rights is not thought of merely as a specific area of law among others – a specific part of the law concerned with a specific domain.[7] Human rights law is unlike, say, corporate law, which rules some specific affairs regarding corporations; or criminal law, which regulates some aspects related to the community's reaction to certain wrongs; or contract law, which regulates contracts. The legal categories of corporate law have little or no application in the criminal

---

[5] See Aileen Kavanagh, *Constitutional Review Under the UK Human Rights Act* (Cambridge University Press 2009) 1–2, 11. Thus, for example, 'Parliament has never sought to defy the courts following a declaration of incompatibility.' Murray Hunt, 'Introduction' in Murray Hunt, Haley Hooper, and Paul Yowell (eds), *Parliaments and Human Rights: Redressing the Democratic Deficit* (Hart 2015) 20. For a thorough study of Parliament's response to declarations of incompatibility, see Jeff King, 'Parliament's Role Following Declarations of Incompatibility under the Human Rights Act' in Murray Hunt, Haley Hooper, and Paul Yowell (eds), *Parliaments and Human Rights: Redressing the Democratic Deficit* (Hart 2015) 165.

[6] On entrenchment in general, see Nicholas W Barber, 'Why Entrench?' (2016) 14 2 Int'l J Const L 325 (though the distinction I draw here between priority and entrenchment is not followed by Barber. See ibid 331, regarding the operation of the Canadian Bill of Rights 1960).

[7] As one thinks of the parts of constitutional law that are related to the functioning of government; see below note 10.

domain, and those of criminal law little or no application in contract law. Human rights law extends to all these areas: human rights legal categories apply to the whole legal system – all other legal categories are expected to be compatible with them. They permeate all branches of law.

These two features of legal human rights – their special legal priority and their extensive reach – set them apart from the rest of the law. These are uncommon features, which few other legal categories possess, and probably no other legal category possesses both features at the same time. Is there a reason for this? What is the point of granting such legal priority and extensive reach to this specific type of legal category?

9.5 Justifying the Characteristic Features of Human Rights

Legal priority and extensive reach are technical–legal devices that allow the legal system to express the extraordinary moral force of some rights and their being binding in all or nearly all situations in a particular community. This is their point, and thus the primary justification for the characteristic features of legal human rights. These features allow the legal system to reflect more accurately some particularly stringent moral requirements, thus providing sophisticated legal guidance to all those who operate with and under the law. This connects the legal features of legal priority and extensive reach with the specific moral requirements that call for such legal recognition. Awareness of this is crucial for the interpretation and practice of human rights law. I will expand on this in the following sections.

Legal priority and extensive reach are justified as means for giving expression in the law to some especially stringent requirements of political morality regarding what is due to each person in a given community. Suppose we are members of a community that strongly believes that no one should be tortured, or held in slavery, or coerced into adopting, abandoning, or changing his or her religious beliefs, or punished or censored in expressing political information and opinion, etc. Suppose we also believe that these are requirements that should always be respected in our society. Because of how grave their subject matter is, and how stringent are the demands of political morality that justify these requirements, we think that it is not the case that in some circumstances there are stronger reasons to disregard them (at least in the normal situation, and sometimes even in the state of exception).[8] As a consequence, these requirements are

---

[8] The especially stringent requirements I refer to here can be binding as requirements of the highest priority in a given community *insofar as that community and its characteristic*

understood to apply always with full force across different circumstances. It is not that we think that torture cannot be allowed as a way of obtaining information from terrorists, but it can be allowed as punishment for a grave crime or as a way of securing someone's cooperation in implementing government policy; or that political speech can be censored in matters concerning health and education, but not on matters concerning housing policy. It is always due to every person to be respected in what regards these requirements, and it is always a grave injustice not to fulfil them.[9]

One can think of such requirements in terms of priority. These are high-priority requirements for moral and political reasoning. They ought to be respected always, and therefore in sound practical reasoning they are understood to defeat opposing considerations. Thus, in a given political community it may be that allowing the police to torture terrorist subjects would be beneficial for national security, or for apprehending and judging those that have committed terrorist activities. Yet we still think of the

---

way of life are in existence. It could be the case that there are reasons for that community to radically change (say, for a democratic republic to change into a monarchy; or for a plurinational political community to become uninational), and these may impact what is owed to everyone in that society as his or her due as a fundamental matter of political morality. Though such radical changes are infrequent, a more common type of change is constituted by the 'state of exception'. In such circumstances the characteristic way of life of a community is altered. It is not simply that some rights are limited – the change at the level of rights is the consequence of a change in the life of the community, which is not as it is normally. Think of the life of citizens in a country that has been just subject to a terrorist attack, or that is in war. Thus, for example, in a community of some wealth some positive requirement that the state secures a certain level of housing for every person in that community may be considered a high-priority requirement. But if the community faces a great war the community changes to the point that such a requirement ceases to possess high priority (perhaps because the community is not wealthy enough any more). Here, it is no exaggeration to say that the community has changed, and thus again what is due to each member of that community can reasonably change as well. Though the community does not change completely, and it may still hold fast to its most cherished informing values, and therefore some requirements even in this situation will continue to be honoured as always binding. One would expect the community to assume as high-priority requirements a set of demands that ought to always be respected with regard to everybody, in every circumstance, as, for example, the requirement not to subject anyone to torture. But it is unnecessary to restrict human rights only to such absolute requirements. As with all law, they should be thought to operate primarily in the normal situation. Good specification and categorisation of human rights should determine as far as possible which requirements apply to the state of exception, and which do not, or do so in a qualified way.

9   Verdirame notes how the preambles of some of the main human rights documents entail a view of human rights as 'rights so fundamental that respect for them is what separates us from barbarism and war'. Guglielmo Verdirame, 'Rescuing Human Rights from Proportionality' in Rowan Cruft, S Matthew Liao, and Massimo Renzo (eds), *Philosophical Foundations of Human Rights* (Oxford University Press 2015) 352.

requirement not to torture anyone as having moral priority over such considerations. Or it could be convenient at some point to censor the political views of those promoting an irresponsible or immoral policy. Yet we
choose not to censor political speech because it likewise has moral priority. These are high-priority requirements.

High-priority requirements of the kind I have described deserve the
protection of the law. Because of their crucial importance and because they
apply across different areas of social life, it is desirable that all law conforms
to them. By conformity here it is meant that no legal norm opposes these
requirements, and also that the law itself promotes the fulfilment of these
requirements and is not merely agnostic about them. For these requirements to be operative in the law, they need to be part of the law, and for
this they need to be expressed in legal categories. Legal categories should
express the content of these requirements, but also the specific way in
which we want the legal system to relate to them – by conforming all legal
categories to said requirements. The legal categories that express these
high-priority requirements must possess specific legal qualities that allow
them to express not only the content of the relevant high-priority requirements, but also the way in which the legal system should relate to them.

These legal qualities are the two legal qualities characteristic of legal
human rights reviewed at the beginning of this section: special legal priority, and extensive reach. Now we see that these two legal qualities are
not arbitrary. Legal human rights give legal expression to a set of rights
that deserve a special kind of respect from the community and all its law.
The specific legal qualities of human rights are justified as a legal technique for ensuring that these rights are granted the respect they deserve
from all the legal system. So, the special legal priority of human rights is a
means for ensuring the conformity of the legal system to the high-priority
requirements protected by legal human rights. Legal priority is not arbitrary, because, as we said, these requirements are taken to deserve such a
high priority among all other opposing considerations, and thus the legal
tool that ensures that such priority is respected is justified.[10] Similarly

---

[10] This explanation for the priority of human rights does not extend to other prescriptions
that may enjoy legal priority as well, typically as parts of a written constitution, as for
example those that establish the competence and powers of the legislature, the executive, and the judiciary. These are appropriate matters for a norm of higher hierarchy. The
point is to achieve an adequate order between different state powers, so as to (among
other things) avoid abuse of power by carefully limiting their competences and allowing
for their reciprocal control, along with other such measures. Since these are limitations
and controls imposed, among select others, on the ordinary law-maker (the legislature,
but often in some respects the executive and the judiciary), it is an apt means to preserve

with respect to the extensive reach of legal human rights. They are not seen as applying to a single area, but rather need to be understood as bearing on all law. This again, is justified, precisely because the high-priority requirements given expression in human rights law, and their special moral force, apply across all the different areas of social life.

This normative account of the specific legal qualities of human rights ought to shape the process of specification and categorisation of human rights. It demands careful delimitation of such rights. As said above, legal human rights are often formulated in broad terms. If legal human rights possess special legal priority, and this priority is justified, then it cannot be the case that everything that can be included within the semantic reach of the subject matter of some human rights is protected with this special priority. This is especially true for those rights formulated as 'the right to/ freedom of . . .'. The subject matter of such rights is usually expressed using broad, vague terms, such as 'expression' or 'thought and religion'. But not every form of expression deserves the extraordinary protection granted by a legal right endowed with special legal priority. Publishing the names of police officials working undercover in a drug cartel is a form of expression, but it does not deserve any priority.

This calls for specifying these broad rights into more precise requirements or relations for which the special protection granted by human rights is indeed justified, and to express these requirements into more precise legal categories that grant such protection. Legal human rights are endowed with the two exceptional qualities of special legal priority and extensive reach; these qualities are justified on account of the special respect that ought to be paid to some requirements in our community. Thus, the specification and categorisation of legal human rights needs first and foremost to single out and give legal delimitation to these specific requirements that do ultimately deserve the special priority and extensive reach of human rights. There must be as close as possible a concordance

---

this order to enshrine it in a law of higher hierarchy than that produced by the ordinary law-maker. Otherwise, these limits and controls could be overridden by those who are supposed to be disciplined by them. But this explanation only reaches the form in which government organs operate. It does not justify a particular content of their decisions, even less a particular content for all law. Human rights are precisely about the content of the law in this sense, and not the form in which government institutions operate – despite the fact that institutional means to enforce human rights can affect the balance of powers. Thus their special normative hierarchy is not justified by the reasons for the special normative hierarchy of the provisions that establish the basics of the competence and powers of government institutions, and a different justification (as the one offered in this section) is needed.

between the delimitation of a human right requirement, the privileged treatment it is given in the legal system, and the moral and political priority that such requirement deserves. Good human rights specification singles out as requirements granted this privileged treatment those that truly deserve it. Good human rights categorisation expresses these requirements into precise legal categories, with the least possible over- and under-inclusion,[11] attributing to *these* requirements the legal qualities of special legal priority and extensive reach – as it is for these requirements, and not others, for which this legal treatment is justified.

This is reinforced by the need for preserving the significance of a relation of priority. Legal priority is pointless unless it is *significant*. By 'significant' I mean that it makes a substantial difference whether a requirement or a claim enjoys that priority or not. For any priority to be significant, the set of things that enjoy priority must be carefully delimited. The narrower the set of things that enjoy priority and the wider the set of things against which they enjoy priority, the more significant is the priority granted. And such is with human rights as well. This counsels against overextending the realm of requirements that enjoy special legal priority. The specific legal qualities of legal human rights are a valuable technical device. Through their operation, the whole legal system can be disciplined to conform to certain specific requirements of great moral force. If there are such requirements that as a community we would want the whole legal system to conform to, and if respect for these requirements is a matter of great importance, then the technical devices that allow us to discipline the legal system to conform to said requirements are a valuable tool for us. But for this tool to perform its function well, it needs to be used properly. To use it too generously will impact its capacity to serve its function.

The main point here is not about substance. The basic point is that whatever the moral foundations of legal human rights, the specific legal qualities of human rights need to be justified. Legal human rights should be specified in a way that the scope within which they possess such qualities matches the scope for which these legal qualities are justified. The specific legal qualities of human rights that grant them a place of prominence in our law should be attributed to requirements that truly deserve it.

It must be borne in mind that bills of rights and human rights treatises have a life outside any legal system. They also perform a political role in, for example, expressing valuable objectives for political action,

---

[11] A perfect match is not possible, since it would require total legal direction, and such legal direction is not possible or desirable. See Section 7.6.

or in symbolising some aspect of the community that adopts them. Some human rights or aspects of human rights are not intended to operate in the legal system, and as such there is no question as to their legal qualities, even if formally they are part of a legal norm of a high hierarchy. Human rights that are to operate in the legal system, and be attributed special legal priority and extensive reach, need to be carefully tailored to include only those specific requirements that deserve such treatment. But for the aspect of human rights that will not operate in the legal system, such concordance is unnecessary. Thus, in drafting a human rights document, and in interpreting it outside the legal system, there may be reasons to include in it things that from the perspective of political morality go beyond the high-priority requirements that deserve the special legal treatment granted to human rights. At the same time, those drafting such documents should be aware of the possibility for confusion, and for the legal system to reach into areas that were not intended for it, and thus attempt to draw the relevant distinctions in the text so as to minimise the risk of confusion.[12]

9.6   Expressing Human Rights through Law

Legal human rights need to be specified into relatively precise requirements. But it is not enough if each authoritative body deciding on the domain of legal human rights deliberates for itself and freely on the specification of the relevant human rights. It is not enough if, say, each individual judge or group of judges deciding human rights cases concerning freedom of expression deliberates as to the precise requirements in which the broadly formulated right of freedom of expression consists. It is also necessary that the specification of rights leaves the private mind or deliberations of judges and other officials and enters into the public realm of the law. The specification of legal human rights needs to be expressed in legal categories able to guide adequately the action and deliberation of all those concerned with the protection, promotion, fulfilment, and enforcement of legal human rights requirements. This is because of the need for legal direction in all areas of law (see Chapter 7). Human rights law is not immune to this need. Legal direction can never be total, but it must be enough for allowing officials and private persons to order their actions according to what law requires, and for the benefits of legal direction in adjudication to be achieved. This demands that the law guides primarily as

---

[12] For a *political* critique of proportionality and the understanding of human rights that it entails, see Verdirame (n 9) 354–6.

to what specific conduct it requires, from whom it requires it, and under what conditions. In human rights law, this level of guidance is not offered by the canonical formulations of legal human rights in bills of rights ('everyone has the right to . . .'; 'no one shall . . .'), but by more precise legal categories that give legal expression to specific human rights requirements.

By categorisation one can mean two things: the crafting of legal categories, and a way of deciding legal cases through the application of legal categories. In this section I focus on the former (the latter will be addressed below in Section 9.10). As said above, the object of categorisation in this sense is to fashion a body of legal categories the primary role of which is to give precise legal expression to the different requirements entailed by human rights once they are properly specified.[13]

To give precise legal expression to specified human rights requirements entails mainly two things. First, as to their content, it entails formulating them in legal language, and providing the tests, definitions, and other such legal tools that best convey how these requirements are to be understood in the law. Second, as to their operation, it entails categorising human rights as legal requirements endowed with the legal qualities of special legal priority and extensive reach. This is often expressed in the law by enshrining human rights in a norm of the highest hierarchy.

Take, for example, the right generally referred to as freedom of religion. This right is typically formulated broadly, as a two-term right: a 'right to freedom of religion' (as in the Canadian Charter) or a right to 'freedom of thought, conscience, and religion' (as in the Universal Declaration of Human Rights).[14] This right calls for specification. It must be determined what specifically does the right require. In doing this, it must be borne in mind that the requirements entailed by this human right must be of the high-priority kind that deserves the special legal treatment afforded to human rights. The right could be (and human rights often are) composed of more than one such requirement. The right to freedom of thought and

---

[13] Other relevant aims of a body of human rights legal categories are to give legal expression to the conditions under which human rights requirements apply or cease to apply (e.g. if their special priority extends to the state of exception or is temporarily suspended in these cases) as well as to the principles according to which it is determined which institutions are to decide on human rights (prominent in this last category are standards for judicial deference and restraint).

[14] See UDHR article 18. The article continues: '. . . this right includes freedom to change his religion or belief, and freedom, either alone or in community with others and in public or private, to manifest his religion or belief in teaching, practice, worship and observance'. For the purposes of my point here, it is unnecessary to address this brief elaboration on the content of the right.

religion can be specified at least into three high-priority requirements: that no one coerces anyone to accept, change, or continue to hold a religious belief; a requirement that the government does not ban or impose limitations on acts of worship or on manifestations of religious beliefs *as such*;[15] and, in some places (like in the United States), a requirement that the state adopts no official religion. These three requirements need to be expressed in the law. It is not enough if legal officials apply implicitly this specification of the broadly formulated right to freedom of religion. This specification must be made explicit in the law, by any of the bodies that participate in crafting human rights legal categories. The three specific requirements in which freedom of religion is specified could be formulated as legal rules with the same content as the requirements just mentioned. Furthermore, these requirements could be further determined in their content by subsequent legal categories. For example, by legal definitions on what constitutes 'coercion' or 'worship', or by further specification on what it means for the state to 'adopt an official religion'. The different requirements and the different tests, definitions, rules, etc., that determine how and when the requirements apply are all to be expressed in the law – they are to become legal categories. How does this happen?

Categorisation is typically a collective task, involving legislatures, courts, commentators, and others. This is so in all law, and human rights law is no exception. But unlike other areas of law, those crafting the law of human rights are commonly satisfied with broad and vague formulations of human rights. Instead, they should aim to produce a body of relatively precise legal categories of human rights. This applies in different ways to the different bodies involved in human rights categorisation. Whoever enacts a bill of rights or a human rights treatise creates typically broad and unspecified legal categories, which call for the elaboration of further legal categories able to provide the necessary guidance as to the content of human rights. Some human rights documents provide more guidance than others,[16] and there is no conceptual need for them to give broad and

---

[15] As opposed to, say, as murder. Thus, governments generally do not forbid ritualistic human sacrifices as such, but they forbid them and punish them as murder. They are not forbidden as a form of worship (as a 'wrong', 'false', 'heretical', etc. form of worship) or as a form of manifestation of ('wrong', 'false', 'heretical', etc.) religious beliefs, but as a grave violation of the right to life.

[16] The Inter-American Convention on Human Rights is considerably more specific than, say, the European Convention on Human Rights, and both are more specific than the Canadian Charter.

unspecified canonical formulations to human rights, as they usually do.[17] Courts applying bills of rights often elaborate further legal categories through their case-law. This is done in articulating explicitly the reasons for a decision; for example, by articulating the precise requirements that a court sees itself as applying in a concrete case, as well as the definitions, tests, etc. that the court uses for determining whether the requirement applies in that case. All these must be given precise but still general formulation in the court's reasoning. Depending on the institutional place of the court, and/or whether these reasons or similar ones are more or less consistently and generally adopted by courts deciding similar cases, a set of legal categories will arise from judicial decisions (I return to this below in Section 9.10). The legislature can also participate in specifying rights and expressing this specification in legal categories by giving them explicit formulation in legislation (though in fleshing out the way the legislature does this, the distinction underscored in the next section must be preserved). Legal scholarship commonly performs a crucial role in the elaboration of legal categories, both through proposing alternatives for interpretation of legal human rights, and by clarifying the reasons grounding human rights legal decisions and the principles given articulation in human rights legislation and executive action, and systematising them into a consistent body of legal categories.

9.7 Preserving Distinctions

Up to this point I have argued that human rights need to be specified and categorised into a body of precise and differentiated legal categories. This does not entail that legal human rights lose their characteristic qualities. I understand these qualities to be two: special legal priority and extensive reach. Human rights legal categories possess these qualities. On account of their specific legal qualities, legal human rights discipline the rest of

---

[17] This may obey sound practical reasons, as, for example, the need to achieve consensus. See Cass R Sunstein, *Legal Reasoning and Political Conflict* (Oxford University Press 1996) 35–6, and Cass R Sunstein, 'Incompletely Theorized Agreements in Constitutional Law' (2007) 74 Soc Res 1, 12. Vague terminology can be an obstacle for consensus as well, once it is understood that the fact that a right is vaguely formulated in law does not mean that it will be interpreted in terms of the minimum consensus on the content of that right, but rather that its interpretation will be settled in the future, typically by some other body. Depending on the circumstances in which a bill of rights is being drafted, this possibility may deter parties from settling on a bill of rights (because it leaves them uncertain as to what exactly will be required on account of the right), and they may prefer to settle on a more concrete and developed formulation.

the legal system. Other legal norms, such as ordinary legislation, need to conform to them. This requires that those norms not only do not oppose legal human rights, but also that they promote them. Legislation, case-law, and other legal sources are not best understood as curbing people's human rights, but, in the central case, as concerned with their promotion and protection. These other norms can rightly be said to further develop and determine human rights.

This in no way undermines the special (often constitutional) status of legal human rights.[18] In thinking about how ordinary norms can be concerned with human rights, an important distinction needs to be held in mind. Phrases such as 'what human right X requires' or 'what is included in the human right to X' are ambiguous. They can mean one of two things. First, they can mean what the right itself requires, taken in isolation. This is its most natural meaning. But they can also mean 'what the legal system requires by way of protecting right X'. There is a difference between the two. Legal human rights, on account of their architectonic place within the legal system, can impose requirements of different force not only on the conduct of persons but also on the whole legal system. This is what a 'human right requires'. The legal system, in fulfilling these requirements, imposes further, new requirements. What the legal system requires by way of protecting a human right is what that human right requires, plus what other norms of the legal system require as a form of protecting that human right.

Take the human right to life. This right can be specified into different requirements. Suppose that it includes a requirement not to intentionally murder – a right of all persons not to be intentionally murdered. Similarly, for most countries, it requires that the state protects this right through the criminal law. Once the criminal law provisions against murder are established, there is a set of new requirements in the legal system regarding the protection of life.

This distinction between what a human right requires, and what the legal system requires by way of protecting a human right, is important. It leads one to acknowledge that many ordinary laws have an important connection to human rights, such that human rights are protected in ordinary life precisely by the provisions of those laws, which further determine the obligations arising from human rights (e.g. the duties of officials in prosecuting and punishing murder according to the law); and thus to acknowledge as well that these laws are often premised on a certain view as to what human rights require, and thus they presuppose a specification of human rights.

---

[18] Barak raises a concern along these lines in *Proportionality* 494–6.

But, at the same time, the distinction between what a human right requires, and what the legal system requires by way of protecting a human right, leaves room for the distinction between legal human rights and their special hierarchy and ordinary legal categories; and more generally between higher law and the rest of law. To continue with the same example: it is the right to life and its requirements that possess a special legal priority in the legal system, not a Penal Code or an Offences Against the Persons Act. This legal priority commands the conformity of the whole legal system to the requirements of the right to life. The specific legal provisions that protect the right to life by criminalising murder are a manifestation of the legal system's conforming to the requirements of the right to life. If these provisions are derogated without being replaced this may entail that now the legal system is not fully conforming to the demands of the right to life. But it may not entail this if, for example, a more effective and just way of securing respect for life has been found. The legal provisions that criminalise murder as such enjoy no special legal priority and no part of the legal system needs to conform to them other than as a matter of satisfying the rule of law *desideratum* of coherence and respecting the ordinary hierarchy of norms.

The distinction between what a human right requires, and what the legal system requires by way of protecting a human right is not undermined when legislation is premised on or expresses a particular specification of legal human rights. The legislature is tasked with promoting and protecting human rights through legislation. In doing so, the legislature must deliberate as to what human rights require. This demands that the legislature comes to a conclusion as to the best specification of the relevant human rights.[19] Legislative specification of human rights (whether only in the deliberation of the legislature as a ground for a particular legislation, or explicitly expressed in the legislation through legal categories) does not conflate the distinction, but rather it is premised in that even legislation needs to conform to human rights, and therefore legislatures need to deliberate about what human rights demand of them and of others. Neither is the distinction subverted when a court is tasked with reviewing this legislative specification of human rights. Both legislative and judicial specifications of human rights are in principle compatible with the distinction presented here.

---

[19] Because the legislature does not need to decide 'in accordance with the law', it is not bound by a body of legal categories of human rights. But in deliberating about human rights, it needs to come to a conclusion as to the specification of rights, and this deliberation may be aided (not constrained) by the guidance offered by legal thinking and practice on human rights, expressed in legal categories.

9.8 Methodology

It may seem that the account of legal human rights that I have offered in the previous sections disregards the methodological principle I offered at the start of this chapter: that in thinking about legal human rights (as with all other areas of law) one must acknowledge that there is a priority of the moral level. Thinking about the moral considerations associated with human rights should inform thinking about the kind of human rights legal categories that we should have. But it may seem that in the previous sections, in providing a general account of legal human rights, I started backwards: I started from the specific legal qualities of human rights legal categories, and from there I went to the moral requirements those legal qualities serve.

Nothing of the sort. There is a priority of the moral level, in that legal categories need to conform to moral and prudential considerations, lest they be unjustified or even perverse. The moral level rules the legal–technical level, and not the other way around.

What thinking about good legal categories requires is to assess the conformity of legal categories with the moral and prudential considerations that they serve. One should certainly think about this conformity in thinking about creating a new body of legal categories. One should also think about this conformity in evaluating existing legal categories, and in making proposals as to how a body of legal categories in some area would be best understood, applied, and developed – as I do here.

But nothing in this entails that as a matter of inquiry and exposition one must necessarily start by analysing the relevant moral and prudential considerations, and only then address the legal categories that serve them. One can as well start with a set of legal categories that are the object of one's inquiry, and in respect of them assess whether they conform to (and to which) moral and prudential considerations, and how they should be understood, applied, and developed so that such a conformity is brought about and sustained. Both alternatives are equally legitimate from the point of view of the methodological commitments I have adopted here. What is recommended by said methodological commitments is to hold in view the need for conformity of legal categories with the moral and prudential considerations that they serve. This conformity is what I have attempted to highlight for human rights legal categories in the previous sections.

Thus, my account starts from some features characteristic of legal human rights, but the main aim is not faithful reconstruction, but critical analysis. I believe these characteristics are fundamentally valuable legal–technical devices, and that the reasons that account for them play a pivotal role in understanding the interplay between the content of human rights law and the operation of these technical devices. Attention to the characteristic features of legal human rights is crucial in understanding how the artificial legal order of human rights law can express the content and special moral force of certain important requirements of justice. It is in this sense that the legal qualities of human rights have a prominent role in my account. This does not subvert the priority of the moral level over the legal–technical level, but, rather, it follows from it.

9.9   An Alternative: Rights Inflation

On account of their canonical formulations, legal human rights can seem to have a virtually unlimited scope. Almost any act or choice can be seen as involving expression, thought, privacy, life, etc., and, as such, seen as protected by the right to freedom of expression, freedom of thought, privacy, life, etc. But human rights cannot grant a uniform protection as broad as their canonical formulations suggest, while at the same time enjoy the kind of high legal priority they are taken to possess. This would be senseless, as aspects not deserving such high legal priority would be granted it. It would involve a worrying lack of differentiation in the legal system, which would treat in the same manner a requirement that ought to be respected by all law and all government and private action, with other considerations that do not deserve the same level of protection. It would also be highly detrimental to the legal system, and to all the goods secured through it. This is because almost all laws establish some burden or limitation on someone's actions and choices, and, as such, they can be seen as constituting infringements of someone's legal human rights. If non-conformity with human rights can affect the validity of a norm (as in many jurisdictions) or at least its social legitimacy (as in many societies), then the validity and legitimacy of most law is compromised – a severe handicap for any legal system. This is how Jeremy Bentham saw the legal human rights embodied in such seminal documents as the French[20] and American[21] bills of rights of the late eighteenth century. Bentham noted how the unlimited scope of these rights conjoined with their particular force as commanding conformity

---

[20] See Jeremy Bentham, 'Nonsense Upon Stilts' in Stephen G Engelmann (ed), *Selected Writings* (Yale University Press 2011) 318.
[21] See HLA Hart, 'Bentham and the United States of America' (1976) 19 The Journal of Law & Economics 547, 555.

with all law and government action on pain of justifying civil disobedience and rebellion subverted all law and government[22] – thus he refers to the doctrine of human rights as a 'terrorist' or 'anarchical' doctrine.[23] On this interpretation, the doctrine of legal human rights has the two vices of being senseless – in that it grants special protection to that which does not deserve it – and of compromising the validity and legitimacy, and thus the function, of all legal system.

There are two alternatives to this understanding of human rights. On one view, they are not understood as having as wide a scope as their canonical formulations suggest; rather, they are seen as composed of a set of more narrow and specific requirements which possess the special normative force characteristic of these rights. This is the alternative favoured here. On the other, human rights are indeed as far reaching as their canonical formulations suggest, but they do not possess the special moral and legal priority commonly attributed to them.

The phenomenon referred to as 'rights inflation' constitutes a paradigmatic embodiment of this second alternative. It has been observed that in many jurisdictions courts are interpreting the domain of human rights as extending not only to basic requirements of justice, or even to the protection of important interests, but also to the protection of every interest that could be understood to fall within the semantic reach of a human right, including seemingly trivial interests.[24] The threshold for an interest

---

[22]   See Bentham (n 20) 321–3, 327–8, 332–4.

[23]   See ibid 323, 328.

[24]   See *Global Model* 3–5; George Letsas, *A Theory of Interpretation of the European Convention on Human Rights* (Oxford University Press 2007) 125. Perhaps the most commonly cited examples in this regard are cases from the German Federal Constitutional Court concerning the right to free development of the personality, where the court has found that such a right protects seemingly trivial interests such as feeding pigeons (54 BVerfGE 143) and horseback riding in the woods (80 BVerfGE 137). The *Elves* case (6 BVerfGE 32) established the broad interpretation of the right to the free development of personality in German case-law, though the interests of the complainant in that case were far from trivial. The right to privacy has been given a wide scope in ECtHR case-law, as Möller notes. *Global Model* 3–4. Webber exemplifies this trend in Canada with *R v Malmo Levine* [2003] 3 SCR 571, concerning a protected liberty interest to smoke marihuana. See Grégoire Webber, 'On the Loss of Rights' in Grant Huscroft, Bradley Miller, and Grégoire Webber (eds), *Proportionality and the Rule of Law: Rights, Justification, Reasoning* (Cambridge University Press 2014) 141 n 77. Theorists such as Barak and Möller argue for an expansive reading of human rights to include even clearly unjust actions, such as theft or murder. See *Proportionality* 42 and Kai Möller, 'Proportionality and Rights Inflation' in Grant Huscroft, Bradley Miller, and Grégoire Webber (eds), *Proportionality and the Rule of Law: Rights, Justification, Reasoning* (Cambridge University Press 2014) 163–5.

to become protected by human rights is low, or even non-existent.[25] Here, human rights are understood as having a scope as broad as their canonical formulations allow, and as a result the domain of what can be included under the protection of human rights is practically unlimited.[26]

There are two accompanying ideas to rights inflation. The first is that when human rights are understood to protect even trivial interests, there is a general weakening in the normative force attributed to human rights. This is natural, as the domain of rights is extended to include interests that do not deserve any exceptional priority, or at least not the strong priority often attributed to human rights in moral and political discourse. If rights are seen as monolithic, as they often are (Section 9.2), then this loss of priority must affect each right as a whole. Furthermore, the significance of the legal priority of human rights is substantially diminished when so many claims and interests are granted priority (Section 9.5).

The second accompanying idea, less often perceived, is that when a set of human rights is understood as having the extensive scope they have under 'rights inflation', the rights in that set tend to become less differentiated. And if the scope of the rights is extensive enough, then those rights become completely undifferentiated. Thus, for example, take the following set of rights: (1) a right to freedom of expression understood as a right to do or say whatever expresses something; (2) a right to freedom of thought and religion understood as a right to do and say whatever is in accordance with what one thinks best or reflects one's position on something; (3) a right to privacy understood as a right to autonomous behaviour in general. On such generous understandings, these three rights, though they all express it differently, entail a similar protection: a right to say and do what one wills.

Rights inflation and its accompanying ideas receive an explicit defence and articulation in Kai Möller's work. For Möller, rights inflation is a welcome phenomenon.[27] Human rights ought to be understood broadly as protecting any autonomy interests of a person, including seemingly trivial or wicked interests.[28] Möller makes a point of advocating the abandonment

---

[25] Möller, 'Proportionality and Rights Inflation', 159–63.

[26] The term 'inflation' in this sense is not completely precise. It conveys that new rights are somehow brought into circulation, thus reducing the value of existing rights. This is true in the sense that the more interests are protected as human rights, the lower the protection granted by human rights, as explained below. But the term is not fully accurate insofar as it suggests that 'new' rights are brought into circulation, rather than that the canonical formulations of human rights documents establishing existing legal human rights are given a generous (but supported by the text itself) interpretation as to the scope of those rights.

[27] *Global Model* Chapter 4; Möller (n 24).

[28] *Global Model* 77–8; Möller (n 24) 163–5.

of any threshold requirement for the protection of every autonomy interest as a human right.[29] For Möller, though rights have a generous scope, they possess little normative force. Legal human rights would not possess the special normative force that philosophers often attribute to rights.[30] Rather, they merely require that the government justify an action that engages human rights.[31] Also, for Möller human rights are highly undifferentiated. They are ultimately about protecting autonomy, such that 'nothing would be lost in theory by simply acknowledging one comprehensive prima facie right to personal autonomy', instead of 'a set of distinct constitutional rights'.[32] All human rights basically grant the same protection consisting in a power to demand justification from the government for affecting some persons' autonomy.

The details of Möller's theory are, of course, debatable, and they will naturally seem radical to not a few. But they have an important merit. Their radical character is a consequence of Möller's insight into the legal phenomena connected to rights inflation, and his willingness to pursue the trends entailed by these phenomena to their natural culmination. Rights on this account possess no special priority or pre-eminence whatsoever. And they are utterly undifferentiated. In so doing, Möller gives us a particularly explicit version of the ideas associated with inflation of legal human rights.

My proposal runs in the contrary direction. Human rights need to be carefully limited to those precise requirements that deserve legal priority. To delimit human rights more generously would entail attributing legal priority to demands for which such priority is not warranted. By matching the legal priority of human rights with the specific human rights requirements that deserve such priority, the specific force of human rights is preserved and given due expression in the legal system as legal priority.

When human rights are understood in more restrained terms, they become differentiated. Take the high-priority requirements I mentioned above, which I argued are the requirements that fully deserve the legal priority characteristic of legal human rights. These are different requirements: not to torture, not to compel someone to abandon his or her religion or adopt one not freely chosen, not to ban political debate and criticism of government, etc. To respect the requirement not to torture does not entail

---

[29] Möller (n 24) 159–63.
[30] Ibid 166.
[31] Ibid 166–7.
[32] *Global Model* 89.

respecting the freedom to engage in political discussion or to convert, and vice versa. These requirements cannot be reduced to one another. Even if they could be thought of as ultimately grounded on a single abstract principle, this would be irrelevant for our purposes, since we are concerned with specific requirements fit for operation in the legal system, not with ultimate foundations of morality. The diversity of such requirements is relevant for the purposes of the law. It demands a corresponding diversity of legal categories, precisely because legal categories are needed to capture the specificity of each requirement, and, since the requirements are different, legal categories will be different as well.

As a reconstruction of current human rights law and practice, my account and Möller's have different strengths and weaknesses. My account captures better the higher law quality typical of human rights instruments, and the special strength often associated with them; Möller better captures current practice of weakening the protection granted by rights. Mine better captures the diversity of human rights – that there is not a single human right, but many, as well as different more specific requirements sometimes given expression in canonical formulations.[33] Möller's better captures the expansive reach rights are given, both (commonly) in their canonical formulations as well as in much human rights practice. My aim, though, is not description, but to provide an outline of an alternative to the current proportionality model and its implied view of human rights. I provide a brief account of what I believe should be the general form of human rights law as a differentiated body of human rights legal categories. This account is primarily concerned with how a legal–artificial order (human rights legal categories) can most aptly reflect relevant moral and prudential requirements (see Section 9.8).

It is as a more attractive proposal for human rights law, not as a more accurate reconstruction of current practice, that my account is superior to the rights inflation model. If law is a technical–artificial order at the service of moral values and requirements, then the single most important criterion to evaluate a part of the law is how well it serves the moral considerations relevant for that part of the law. Because the law is concerned with guiding human action, law serves moral considerations by providing guidance as to how to choose and act. Legal direction thus is crucial. The better the law expresses the relevant moral and prudential considerations

---

[33] See, for example, the formulation of freedom of thought and religion in article 9 of the ECHR, which gives a differentiated treatment to freedom of conscience and to freedom of manifestation and exercise.

at stake, the better it will guide action in conformity with them, and the better it will realise its ultimate purpose of serving moral values and requirements. This demands, as seen above (Section 7.8), that the law gives expression to moral and prudential considerations with relative precision, so as to be able to effectively guide legal adjudication and, more generally, the behaviour of all those subject to the law. This requirement for precision leads to differentiation, since only at the most abstract level we find general principles that apply equally to different areas and problems. At the more concrete level necessary for providing effective guidance, the relevant moral considerations are diverse. Since law needs to express this diversity, legal categories must be diverse as well (see Sections 7.4.1.4, 7.5, and 7.8).

It is in capturing this diversity that my account is superior. It is aimed at articulating the features of a body of human rights legal categories that will allow it to give legal expression to the different content and specific moral force of human rights requirements. In doing this, the law of human rights is better able to provide legal guidance in conformity with the moral requirements it serves. This legal guidance directs not only the actions of particular persons or state officials in respecting human rights, but also the legal system as a whole through the specific way in which human rights discipline the rest of the law. On the rights inflation model, on the other hand, human rights law has a very limited capacity to provide legal guidance. Because human rights have no pre-eminent force, and are seen as unspecified and undifferentiated general requirements – as a general requirement for justification to interfere with someone's autonomy, for example – they give little guidance to those tasked with adjudicating these rights and to those concerned with acting in accordance with them. This is presented sometimes as a strength of this model (see Section 6.3), as it allows it to avoid some objections raised against proportionality reasoning. But as a proposal for shaping the law (including the understanding of the law of those that change and apply it) it is inferior to the one defended here, on account of its limited ability to provide legal guidance.

9.10 A Body of Human Rights Legal Categories in Adjudication

Courts, instead of using proportionality to decide human rights cases, should use a differentiated body of legal categories to frame and decide the different conflicts involving human rights. My contention in this chapter is that it would be best for human rights adjudication if a body of legal categories with the characteristics described in the previous sections were available for courts to address human rights cases. If such a body of legal categories is available for courts deciding human rights cases, they should decide in accordance with these legal categories. When they do this, as they so often do in other areas of the law, their decisions partake of the benefits of legally directed adjudication and thus better realise substantive human rights values and other relevant values at stake in legal adjudication (Section 7.4). By deciding in accordance with a previously established body of legal categories, courts give vigour to these legal categories – they validate the expectation of these legal categories being binding on those subject to human rights law. This is necessary for human rights legal categories to serve those subject to them as a reliable guide for action.

Those with authority and capacity to fashion human rights legal categories have good reasons to do so. As said above, in developed legal systems the production of legal categories is a collective task, in which many participate. Legislatures, courts, and legal commentators are commonly the main producers of legal categories. Courts bear the main responsibility in applying them in legal adjudication. When legal categories are not available for addressing the case, courts should develop them through legal interpretation and judicial specification of the legal sources at stake in the case. In the field of human rights, the relevant legal sources will commonly be quite vague and abstract. There is nothing odd in courts specifying an abstract set of legal sources so as to render them precise and sophisticated enough for legal practice, particularly by articulating the *ratio* of actual or potential decisions as a more precise legal category (or categories) that mediates between an abstract provision in the relevant legal source, and the specific decision in a relatively specific type of case.

In crafting legal categories there are two extremes to be avoided: first, excessive abstraction that is unable to provide enough guidance. Second, excessive concretion, which also fails to provide guidance, as the legal category developed is tailored to only one case, and not to a *type* of case. In the judicial developing of legal categories, the *ratio* of the decision must be couched in the form of a precise but still general principle, which applies to a specific *type* of case. Legislatures and legal doctrine should craft and systematise legal categories in the same general-yet-precise fashion. Thus the law develops into a body of legal categories precise and differentiated enough to provide legal guidance for different types of cases. Suitable examples of such precise-yet-general legal categories are those I mention above in relation to the right to freedom of thought and religion. A specific requirement that the government does not ban or impose limitations on acts of worship as such, for example, is precise yet it is also general.

It is precise in that it determines a particular behaviour that is required, the person from whom it is required, and also, implicitly, those in relation to whom it is required: everybody. It is general in that it applies to a type of situation, and not only to one situation. Even if further determined by legal definitions of what constitutes 'worship', tests to determine what constitutes a limitation, criteria as to who counts as the government for the purposes of this requirement, etc., it could still be general if those legal definitions, tests, and criteria are formulated to apply to types of situations and not simply to a particular case.

Besides applying human rights legal categories, and crafting them when appropriate, there are two other conducts required of courts in relation to human rights legal categories on the account presented here. The first is to participate in the continuous refinement of legal categories within their constitutional powers. Second, courts need to decide in a way that preserves a body of human rights legal categories of the kind proposed here when available. Courts have the potential to develop it, refine it, but they also have the power to decide in such a way that the advantages of having precise and differentiated legal categories are lost. This can happen when courts interpret precise legal categories in an overly generous way, such that the precise guidance offered by the legal category is traded for vague or ambiguous direction. Or when they subordinate the application of precise categories to vague or ambiguous ones. Or when a complex body of precise legal categories is seen as ultimately giving expression to some open-ended value or principle, which is then applied directly to the case, rather than mediated by the more precise legal categories (see Section 7.5), etc. When a body of legal categories is available for deciding a case, courts should decide in a way that leaves such body of legal categories in better or equal shape than the one it had before the decision: more or equally apt at guiding behaviour and decision, and more or equally tightly related to the moral and prudential considerations that legal categories attempt to reflect.

When courts decide cases in this way, applying a body of legal categories with the characteristics I have explained in this chapter, they decide cases based on a specification of human rights expressed in legal categories. Thus, on this proposal, human rights are not taken to grant an extensive, *prima facie* protection to everything that falls within the semantic reach of their subject matter (life, privacy, speech, etc.). Instead, they grant a stronger and legally conclusive protection for a narrower set of specific requirements. When a given government measure is challenged in a court on the grounds that it violates a particular human right, the court decides the case based on an understanding of what specific requirements the right consists on – an understanding that should be largely controlled by legal categories. These requirements are high-priority requirements that deserve to possess the specific legal qualities of special legal priority and extensive reach. As such, they are narrowly formulated (they do not over-reach beyond what deserves this special legal treatment), and conclusive in legal force.

On the now orthodox approach to human rights adjudication, courts resolve human rights cases through a two-step approach. First, they ask whether a measure infringes a human right. Second, they ask whether this infringement is justified. On a specified rights approach, only one step is necessary. Courts ask whether a given measure infringes a human right. If so, that measure is in violation of human rights and subject to the full reaction that the legal system reserves for actions and norms that contradict human rights. In order to establish whether a measure infringes a human right, the court will operate with an understanding of what that human right really requires: what are the specific requirements in which that human right consist. These requirements are expressed in carefully tailored legal categories, and courts apply those legal categories to determine whether the measure truly violates someone's human rights. When, for example, a law forbids a conduct that is mandated by a religious precept, the question is not whether the religious freedom interests of religious believers (or some general value of religious freedom broadly conceived) outweigh the public interest in banning the conduct, but whether religious freedom requires that no such legal prohibition is adopted. This, in turn, may depend, for example, on whether the conduct is banned as a form of religious worship or manifestation of religious beliefs, or under a different general description. If the former, the measure in question would violate the requirement that the government does not ban or impose limitations on acts of worship or manifestations of religious beliefs as such[34] – a specific requirement given expression in the law as a specification of the right to freedom of thought and religion.

Some might characterise this as the American model, as opposed to a European model based on proportionality. The American model is said to privilege more categorical forms of legal reasoning in the form of clause-bound interpretation.[35] To the extent that what is referred to as the

---

[34] See above n 15.

[35] See Frederick Schauer, 'Freedom of Expression Adjudication in Europe and America: A Case Study in Comparative Constitutional Architecture' in Georg Nolte (ed), *European and US Constitutionalism* (Cambridge University Press 2005) 50, and sources cited in n 2.

American model is a view of human or constitutional rights that is centred on a body of precise legal categories, the role of adjudication consisting primarily in the faithful interpretation and application (and also develop-ment within the constitutional powers of courts) of said legal categories, then I have no objection to my approach being understood as a form of, or structurally similar to, the American model. I offer two caveats, though. First, sometimes the difference between the American and the European models is presented as a difference between a model of rules and a model of standards.[36] As explained above (Section 7.4.1.3), my proposal does not rely on that distinction, since both rules and standards can be used to provide enough legal direction in some type of case. Second, and more important, it has been argued that the American model of constitutional rights adjudication is not in fact centred on legal categories in the way I propose here. Thus, Paul Yowell argues that the tiered scrutiny approach to adjudicating constitutional rights in American constitutional law leads to balancing rights and state interests in a manner that is fundamentally similar to the European model.[37] Be that as it may, the proposal for law-making and law-applying that I sketch here is far from novel. It can rightly be labelled 'traditional', since it is used in most jurisdictions in almost all areas of law other than the law of human (or constitutional) rights. What has been missing, and which I attempt to provide here, is an account of how traditional forms of law-making and law-applying are indispensa-ble for the legal system to best express the content and force of the moral requirements associated with human rights. This view is to a large degree the opposite of what is now prevalent in human rights law.

What happens when specified human right requirements conflict with other relevant public goods such as national security and public order? And when human rights requirements conflict with each other? On the received approach, human rights are broadly construed. Their protec-tion extends at least as far as the semantic reach of the subject matter of the right. Because their scope is extraordinarily broad, they are expected to routinely clash among themselves and with public goods. These con-flicts are resolved through proportionality and balancing, or some other

See also Jacco Bomhoff, *Balancing Constitutional Rights: The Origins and Meanings of Postwar Legal Discourse* (Cambridge University Press 2013) 14–15.

[36] See Moshe Cohen-Eliya and Iddo Porat, 'American Balancing and German Proportionality: The Historical Origins' (2010) 8 Int'l J Const L 263, 264.

[37] See Paul Yowell, 'Proportionality in United States Constitutional Law' in Liora Lazarus, Christopher McCrudden, and Nigel Bowles (eds), *Reasoning Rights: Comparative Engagements* (Hart 2013).

such legal test. This is not the case with the account of legal human rights proposed here. On this account legal human rights are narrowly tailored to those high-priority requirements that deserve the special legal treatment afforded to human rights. Understood in this way, human rights do not systematically clash among each other and with other relevant public goods. Given that their scope is substantially reduced, the potential for conflict is considerably diminished. But it is not completely eliminated. Conflicts are a legal possibility. This can take two forms.

First, a specific human rights requirement can conflict with a public good such as national security and public order. Human rights documents commonly contain limitation clauses explicitly allowing for the limitation of (at least a set of) human rights for the sake of some public goods. These limitation clauses are often read as requiring the two-step assessment so pervasive now in human rights adjudication, as well as the application of the proportionality test at the justification stage. On the account of legal human rights outlined here, these limitation clauses are unnecessary. Legal human rights contain only those high-priority requirements that already reasonably should prevail over other public goods. In cases of conflict, human rights prevail, though they must have been carefully specified first. Human rights need to be adequately tailored to those requirements that actually deserve to possess the specific legal qualities of human rights, so as not to extend their protection without justification, and not to unduly affect other relevant requirements of the common good. It is based on the latter consideration that limitation clauses, where they exist, could be read as requiring the proper specification of human rights[38] so as not to impose without justification obstacles on the community's pursuit of relevant public goods such as those referred to in limitation clauses. This is how existing limitation clauses would be understood on the general account of legal human rights I defend here.

Second, legal human rights requirements can conflict among themselves. If legal human rights have been specified carefully, this should be extremely infrequent. Nevertheless, it is not impossible. If the high-priority requirements expressed in human rights requirements were only negative requirements, then it would always be possible to satisfy all of them in every circumstance. But high-priority requirements in a given community can be positive as well. And even if these requirements were perfectly compatible in an ideal world, in the real world they are formulated as legal categories, and given that legal categories are a human construct, they are imperfect. They can over-extend, or be ambiguous or vague in some respects.

---

[38] As suggested by Webber in *Negotiable Constitution* 133–4.

It is possible that in a given case the judge encounters a genuine conflict of human rights requirements as formulated in received legal categories. This is a deficiency in the body of legal categories, as it constitutes an incoherence in the legal system, and thus it entails a failure to provide legal guidance in an important matter for the type of cases where the conflict arises.

In addressing this problem judges need to engage in moral and political reasoning of their own. This can take different forms. At its most modest, where the deficiency is least severe, the problem will be one of formulation of the legal categories that apply to the case. The legal categories will be taken to express certain specified human rights requirements which are compatible and which thus could ground a consistent answer to the case at hand, just that in formulating one or both of these requirements as a legal category, there has been some imprecision or vagueness that allows for some human rights legal category to give too generous expression to some human rights requirement. Addressing this situation requires some open-ended moral and political reasoning on behalf of judges, since they need to come up with their own understanding of the specification of the relevant human rights. But in doing this, they are guided by the legal categories in place. They are following that guide up to the point where it seems that legal categories present some flaw: they are holding in mind some specific legal human rights requirements, the exact scope of which needs to be revised. Here, the diagnosis will be that the problem took place at the level of categorisation. The specification of the relevant human right requirements is left unchallenged. The problem has occurred in giving precise formulation to those requirements through legal categories. Of course, for judges to understand the problem in this way, and to remain guided by the specification entailed by the received legal categories, they need to be convinced that the problem is one of precise formulation, of detail, and not one that calls into question the very essence or existence of a particular requirement.

But the deficiency can have deeper roots. It can be at the level of specification rather than that of categorisation. It could be that there is some incompatibility in the high-priority requirements that a community gives protection to in the law of human rights. This incompatibility may not be so severe so as to be immediately noticed in the specification of human rights. But it could occur that in some cases there is a genuine conflict between specific human rights requirements, and this conflict is not owed to some lack of precision in the formulation of human rights legal categories. Here from the perspective of human rights what is the parties' due is X and not X at the same time. In resolving this contradiction, it will be necessary to further specify the relevant human rights requirements, so that the contradiction is eliminated and the commitments of the community as to what is each party's due can be understood as harmonious and responding to coherent principles. This requires considerably more open-ended moral and political reasoning from the judge. Yet this is different from the idea of proportionality as unconstrained moral reasoning. Here the moral and political open-ended reasoning is undertaken when legal categories are exhausted in their guidance; it is not the default way of addressing cases. The tension is seen as an anomaly to be resolved, not as the normal situation. Here the task of courts (and other lawmakers) is not only to resolve the contradiction in deciding one particular case, but to articulate a more general legal ground for their decision that gives expression to a better non-contradictory specification of the relevant rights. The expectation is that once the issue is resolved in one case, or in a line of cases, legal categories have been improved or complemented so that now the contradiction in the specific human rights requirements at stake has been overcome, and the body of human rights legal categories can be applied unproblematically to subsequent cases.

9.11 Conclusion

In previous chapters I criticised the proportionality test. I argued that there are two main accounts of the test, and thus a successful critique of proportionality needs to be a critique of both these accounts. Each of these accounts speaks of an underlying conception of human rights, under which they are seen as monolithic, defeasible, and broad in their scope, and as requiring maximisation (on one account), or as triggering an assessment of the justification of a measure through the unconstrained moral reasoning of judges (on the other). I contend that the best alternative to proportionality is not a single method for deciding about human rights limitations, but a complex and differentiated body of legal categories. This alternative also relies on a conception of legal human rights, and its implications are better understood once this conception has been explained.

Here I have only provided a general picture of this conception, and substantial more work would have to be done to give a full justification of it, and to flesh out many aspects of it that are barely mentioned or suggested here.[39] But a fully detailed account would not be desirable at this

---

[39] Because here I am concerned with a general way of understanding human rights law, my account is relatively abstract. It remains to be determined how it would apply to particular legal systems, addressing specifically institutional concerns: who undertakes the set

point, at least not before the kind of outline I provide here is presented. There is a danger as well in the trees not allowing us to see the forest. The main features of such an account of human rights, centred on the characteristic legal qualities of human rights, can easily go unnoticed, and their implications for determining the content and force of rights are easily missed. This account stands in sharp contrast with the current human rights orthodoxy that understands rights as broad in scope and defeasible in force, and attributes to proportionality the central role in human rights adjudication.

The main objective of this book is to provide a critique of the proportionality test, and particularly of its most characteristic, balancing, subtest. Its basic argumentative strategy is to distinguish between different accounts of proportionality and provide separate critiques for each account. Engaging with each of these accounts required substantial elaboration to assess faithfully their nuances, strengths, and weakness. The critique of proportionality offered here attests to the insight, originality, and sustained work of many authors who have defended it through decades. A full alternative to proportionality, equal in detail and doctrinal elaboration, cannot be provided in the last chapter of a book. Such an alternative, I have explained in this chapter, entails a different understanding of legal human rights. What one can realistically aim for at this stage, is to make a case for the idea that we do need an alternative to proportionality and the idea of human rights entailed by it, and convey a sense of how this alternative departs from prevalent understandings of human rights law.

---

of tasks entailed by my conception of human rights law? What are the roles of judges for that conception? And of legislatures and the executive? How should they interact? What impact do these institutions have in specifying and enforcing human rights, and what impact do human rights have on these institutions? My account here only raises some of these questions and frames their answers within a general conception of what human rights law *qua* law should be.

BIBLIOGRAPHY

Aleinikoff TA, 'Constitutional Law in the Age of Balancing' (1986) 96 Yale LJ 943

Alexander L and Schauer F, 'Law's Limited Domain Confronts Morality's Universal Empire' (2006) 48 Wm & Mary L Rev 1579

Alexander L and Sherwin E, *The Rule of Rules: Morality, Rules, and the Dilemmas of Law* (Duke University Press 2001)

Alexy R, *A Theory of Legal Argumentation: The Theory of Rational Discourse as Theory of Legal Justification* (Ruth Adler and Neil MacCormick trs, Oxford University Press 1989)

  A Theory of Constitutional Rights (Julian Rivers tr, Oxford University Press 2002)

  'Constitutional Rights, Balancing, and Rationality' (2003) 16 2 Ratio Juris 131

  'On Balancing and Subsumption. A Structural Comparison' (2003) 16 4 Ratio Juris 433

  'Balancing, Constitutional Review, and Representation' (2005) 3 4 International Journal of Constitutional Law 572

  'Thirteen Replies' in Pavlakos G (ed), *Law, Rights and Discourse: The Legal Philosophy of Robert Alexy* (Hart 2007)

  'The Construction of Constitutional Rights' (2010) 4 1 Law & Ethics of Human Rights 1

  'The Weight Formula' in Stelmach J and Załuski W, *Game Theory and the Law* (Copernicus Center Press 2011)

Allan TRS, 'Democracy, Legality, and Proportionality' in Grant Huscroft, Bradley Miller, and Grégoire Webber (eds), *Proportionality and the Rule of Law* (Cambridge University Press 2014)

Alon-Shenker P and Davidov G, 'Applying the Principle of Proportionality in Employment and Labour Law Contexts' (2013) 59 McGill LJ 375

Anscombe, GEM, 'Who Is Wronged? Philippa Foot on Double Effect: One Point' in Geach M and Gormally L (eds), *Human Life, Action, and Ethics: Essays by GEM Anscombe* (Imprint Academic 2005)

Aristotle, *Rhetoric* (W. Rhys Roberts tr, Dover 2004)

Barak A, *Proportionality: Constitutional Rights and Their Limitations* (Cambridge University Press 2012)

Barber NW, 'Why Entrench?' (2016) 14 2 Int'l J Const L 325

Beatty D, *The Ultimate Rule of Law* (Oxford University Press 2004)

Bentham J, 'Nonsense Upon Stilts' in Engelmann SG (ed), *Selected Writings* (Yale University Press 2011)

Berlin I, *Liberty* (Henry Hardy ed, Oxford University Press 2002)

Berman HJ and Spindler JW, 'Soviet Comrades' Courts' (1963) 38 Wash L Rev 842

Bernstein P, 'Cuba: Last Look at an Alternative Legal System' (1993) 7 Temp Int'l & Comp LJ 191

Bomhoff J, *Balancing Constitutional Rights: The Origins and Meanings of Postwar Legal Discourse* (Cambridge University Press 2013)

Bücheler G, *Proportionality in Investor-State Arbitration* (Oxford University Press 2015)

Chang R, 'Introduction' in Chang R (ed), *Incommensurability, Incomparability, and Practical Reason* (Harvard University Press 1997)

Choudhry S, 'So What Is the Real Legacy of Oakes? Two Decades of Proportionality Analysis under the Canadian Charter's Section 1' 34 Sup Ct LR 501

Christoffersen J, *Fair Balance: A Study of Proportionality, Subsidiarity and Primarity in the European Convention on Human Rights* (Martinus Nijhof 2009)

Cohen-Eliya M and Porat I, 'American Balancing and German Proportionality: The Historical Origins' (2010) 8 Int'l J Const L 263

'Proportionality and the Culture of Justification' (2011) 59 2 American Journal of Comparative Law 463

Proportionality and Constitutional Culture (Cambridge University Press 2013)

Da Silva VA, 'Comparing the Incommensurable: Constitutional Principles, Balancing and Rational Decision' (2011) 31 2 OJLS 273

Dixon SO, 'Concerning Judicial Method' (1956) 29 ALJ 468

Dworkin R, *Taking Rights Seriously* (Harvard University Press 1978)

Law's Empire (Harvard University Press 1986)

'On Gaps in the Law' in Amselek P and MacCormick N (eds), *Controversies About Law's Ontology* (Edinburgh University Press 1991)

Ekins R, 'Legislating Proportionately' in Grant Huscroft, Bradley Miller, and Grégoire Webber (eds), *Proportionality and the Rule of Law: Rights, Justification, Reasoning* (Cambridge University Press 2014)

Endicott T, *Vagueness in Law* (Oxford University Press 2000)

'Proportionality and Incommensurability' (2012) 40 Oxford Legal Research Paper 1

'Legal Interpretation' in Marmor A (ed), *The Routledge Companion to Philosophy of Law* (Routledge 2012)

Administrative Law (3rd edn, Oxford University Press 2015)

Finnis J, *Aquinas: Moral, Political, and Legal Theory* (Oxford University Press 1998)

'Endorsing Discrimination Between Faiths: A Case Extreme Speech?', in Hare I and Weinstein J (eds), *Extreme Speech and Democracy* (Oxford University Press 2009)

Natural Law and Natural Rights (2nd edn, Oxford University Press 2011)

Human Rights and Common Good, Collected Essays: Volume III (Oxford University Press 2011)

Intention and Identity, Collected Essays: Volume II (Oxford University Press 2011)

Philosophy of Law, Collected Essays: Volume IV (Oxford University Press 2011)

Reason in Action, Collected Essays: Volume I (Oxford University Press 2011)

'Judicial Power: Past, Present, and Future' (a lecture in Gray's Inn Hall, 20 October 2015)

Finnis J, Boyle J, and Grisez G, *Nuclear Deterrence, Morality and Realism* (Oxford University Press 1987)

Fish MJ, 'An Eye for an Eye: Proportionality as a Moral Principle of Punishment' (2008) 28 OJLS 57

Frantz LB, 'The First Amendment in the Balance' (1962) 71 8 The Yale LJ 1424

Fried C, 'Artificial Reason of the Law or: What Lawyers Know' (1981) 60 Tex LR 35

Friedmann W, *Legal Theory* (5th edn, Stevens & Sons 1967)

Fuller L, *The Morality of Law* (Yale University Press 1969)

Gardbaum S, 'A Democratic Defense of Constitutional Balancing' (2010) 4 1 Law & Ethics of Human Rights 1

'Proportionality and Democratic Constitutionalism' in Grant Huscroft, Bradley Miller, and Grégoire Webber (eds), *Proportionality and the Rule of Law: Rights, Justification, Reasoning* (Cambridge University Press 2014)

Gardner J, 'Rationality and the Rule of Law in Offences Against the Person' (1994) 53 03 Cambridge LJ 502

Gelbach JB and Kobayashi BH, 'The Law and Economics of Proportionality in Discovery' Georgia LR

Greer S, '"Balancing" and the European Court of Human Rights: A Contribution to the Habermas–Alexy Debate' (2004) 63 Cambridge LJ, 412

Grey TC, 'Langdell's Orthodoxy', (1983) 45 U Pitt LR 1

Grimm D, 'Proportionality in Canadian and German Constitutional Jurisprudence' (2007) 57 2 The University of Toronto LJ 383

Guzmán Brito A, *Andrés Bello Codificador. Historia De La Fijación Y Codificación Del Derecho Civil En Chile* (Ediciones Universidad de Chile 1982)

Habermas J, *Between Facts and Norms* (William Rehg tr, MIT Press 1996)

Hart HLA. 'Rawls on Liberty and Its Priority' (1973) 40 3 The University of Chicago LR 534

'Bentham and the United States of America' (1976) 19 The Journal of Law & Economics 547

The Concept of Law (2nd edn, Oxford University Press 1994)

Henckels C, *Proportionality and Deference in Investor-State Arbitration: Balancing Investment Protection and Regulatory Autonomy* (Cambridge University Press 2015)

Heydon JD, 'Are Bills of Rights Necessary in Common Law Systems?' (2014) 130 LQR 392

Hogg PW, *Constitutional Law of Canada* (5th edn, Thomson Carswell 2007)

Honoré AM, 'Legal Reasoning in Rome and Today' (1973) 4 Cambrian LR 58

Hunt M, 'Introduction' in Murray Hunt, Haley Hooper, and Paul Yowell (eds) *Parliaments and Human Rights: Redressing the Democratic Deficit* (Hart 2015)

Jackson VC, 'Being Proportional About Proportionality' (2004) 21 Const Commentary 803

'Constitutional Law in an Age of Proportionality' (2015) 124 Yale LJ 3094

Jestaedt M, 'The Doctrine of Balancing – Its Strengths and Weaknesses' in Klatt M (ed), *Institutionalized Reason: The Jurisprudence of Robert Alexy* (Oxford University Press 2012)

Kavanagh A, *Constitutional Review under the UK Human Rights Act* (Cambridge University Press 2009)

Kelsen H, *General Theory of Law and State* (Anders Wedberg tr, Transaction Publishers 2005)

Kennedy IM, 'Cuba's Ley Contra La Vagancia – The Law on Loafing' (1972) 20 UCLA L. Rev. 1177

Khosla M, 'Proportionality: An Assault on Human Rights?: A Reply' (2010) 8 2 Int'l J Const L 298

King J, 'Parliament's Role Following Declarations of Incompatibility under the Human Rights Act' in Murray Hunt, Haley Hooper, and Paul Yowell (eds) *Parliaments and Human Rights: Redressing the Democratic Deficit* (Hart 2015)

Klatt M and Meister M, 'Proportionality – A Benefit to Human Rights? Remarks on the ICON Controversy' (2012) 10 3 Int'l J Const L 687

The Constitutional Structure of Proportionality (Oxford University Press 2012)

Kommers D and Miller RA, *The Constitutional Jurisprudence of the Federal Republic of Germany* (3rd edn, Duke University Press 2012)

Kumm M, 'Constitutional Rights as Principles: On the Structure and Domain of Constitutional Justice' (2004) 2 Int'l J Const L 574

'Who Is Afraid of the Total Constitution?: Constitutional Rights as Principles and the Constitutionalization of Private Law' (2006) 7 4 German LJ 341

'The Idea of Socratic Contestation and the Right to Justification: The Point of Rights-Based Proportionality Review' (2010) 4 2 Law & Ethics of Human Rights 142

'Political Liberalism and the Structure of Rights: On the Place and Limits of the Proportionality Requirement' in Pavlakos G (ed), *Law, Rights and Discourse: The Legal Philosophy of Robert Alexy* (Hart 2007)

Kumm M and Walen AD, 'Human Dignity and Proportionality: Deontic Pluralism in Balancing' in Grant Huscroft, Bradley Miller, and Grégoire Webber (eds), *Proportionality and the Rule of Law: Rights, Justification, Reasoning* (Cambridge University Press 2014)

Letsas G, *A Theory of Interpretation of the European Convention on Human Rights* (Oxford University Press 2007)

'Rescuing Proportionality' in Rowan Cruft, S Matthew Liao, and Massimo Renzo (eds), *Philosophical Foundations of Human Rights* (Oxford University Press 2015)

Locke J, *Two Treatises of Government* (first published 1689, Peter Laslett ed, Cambridge University Press 1988)

Luban D, 'Incommensurable Values, Rational Choice, and Moral Absolutes' (1990) 38 Clev St LR 65

Lyons D, 'Justification and Judicial Responsibility' (1984) 72 Cal LR 178

MacCormick N, *Rhetoric and the Rule of Law* (Oxford University Press 2009)

Manning J, 'What Divides Textualists from Purposivists?' (2006) 106 Colum LR 70

McHarg A, 'Reconciling Human Rights and the Public Interest: Conceptual Problems and Doctrinal Uncertainty in the Jurisprudence of the European Court of Human Rights' (1999) 62 5 The Modern LR 671

Merges RP, *Justifying Intellectual Property* (Harvard University Press 2011)

Miller B, 'Justification and Rights Limitations' in Huscroft G (ed) *Expounding the Constitution* (Cambridge University Press 2008)

Möller K, 'Balancing and the Structure of Constitutional Rights' (2007) 5 3 Int'l J Const L 453

  'Proportionality: Challenging the Critics' (2012) 10 3 *Int'l J Const L* 709

  The Global Model of Constitutional Rights (Oxford University Press 2012)

  'Proportionality and Rights Inflation' in Grant Huscroft, Bradley Miller, and Grégoire Webber (eds) *Proportionality and the Rule of Law: Rights, Justification, Reasoning* (Cambridge University Press 2014)

  '"Balancing as Reasoning" and the Problems of Legally Unaided Adjudication: A Rejoinder to Francisco Urbina' (2014) 12 Int'l J Const L 222

Mureinik E, 'A Bridge to Where: Introducing the Interim Bill of Rights' (1994) 10 S Afr J Hum Rts 31

Nozick R, *Anarchy, State, and Utopia* (Basic Books 1974)

Ohlin JD, 'The Doctrine of Legitimate Defense' (2015) 91 Int'l L Stud 119

Panaccio CM, 'In Defence of Two-Step Balancing and Proportionality in Rights Adjudication' (2011) 24 1 Can J L & Jur 109

Pila J, 'Pluralism, Principles and Proportionality in Intellectual Property' (2014) 34 OJLS 181

Rawls J, 'Two Concepts of Rules' (1955) 64 1 The Philosophical Review 3

  A Theory of Justice (rev edn, Harvard University Press 1999)

  Justice as Fairness: A Restatement (Harvard University Press illustrated, reprint 2001)

  Political Liberalism (Columbia University Press 2005)

Raz J, *The Morality of Freedom* (Oxford University Press 1986)

  Ethics in the Public Domain (Oxford University Press 1996)

  Between Authority and Interpretation: On the Theory of Law and Practical Reason (Oxford University Press 2009)

Réaume D, 'Limitations on Constitutional Rights: The Logic of Proportionality' (2009) 2009 26 Oxford Legal Research Paper Series 1

Rivers J, 'Proportionality and Variable Intensity of Review' (2006) 65 1 Cambridge LJ 174

'A Theory of Constitutional Rights and the British Constitution' (translator's foreword to Alexy R, A Theory of Constitutional Rights (Oxford University Press 2002)

Rolim JD, 'Proportionality and Fair Taxation' (2015) 43 Intertax 405

Salas L, 'The Emergence and Decline of the Cuban Popular Tribunals' (1983) Law and Society Review 587

Sandel M, Public Philosophy: Essays on Morality in Politics (Harvard University Press 2005)

Schauer F, 'Easy Cases' (1985) 58 S Cal LR 399

'Formalism' (1988) 97 4 Yale LJ 509

Playing by the Rules: A Philosophical Examination of Rule-Based Decision-Making in Law and in Life (Oxford University Press 1991)

'A Comment on the Structure of Rights' (1992) 27 Ga LR 415

'Freedom of Expression Adjudication in Europe and America: A Case Study in Comparative Constitutional Architecture' in Nolte G (ed) European and US Constitutionalism (Cambridge University Press 2005)

'Balancing, Subsumption, and the Constraining Role of Legal Text' in Klatt M (ed), Institutionalized Reason: The Jurisprudence of Robert Alexy (Oxford University Press 2012)

Schlink B, 'Open Justice in a Closed Legal System' (1991) 13 Cardozo LR 1713

'Proportionality in Constitutional Law: Why Everywhere but Here' (2012) 22 Duke J Comp & Int'l L 291

'Proportionality (1)', in Rosenfeld M and Sajó A (eds), The Oxford Handbook of Comparative Constitutional Law (Oxford University Press 2012)

Schneiderman D, 'Proportionality and Constitutional Culture (book review)' (2015) 13 Int'l J Const L 769

Shapiro S, Legality (Harvard University Press 2011)

Simmonds NE, 'Review of Institutionalized Reason: The Jurisprudence of Robert Alexy' (2013) 129 LQR 292

Sloane RD, 'Puzzles of Proportion and the "Reasonable Military Commander": Reflections on the Law, Ethics, and Geopolitics of Proportionality' (2015) 6 Harvard National Security Journal 299

Solum LB, 'The Supreme Court in Bondage: Constitutional Stare Decisis, Legal Formalism, and the Future of Unenumerated Rights' (2006) 9 U Pa J Const L 155

St Jeanos CJ, 'Dolan v. Tigard and the Rough Proportionality Test: Roughly Speaking, Why Isn't a Nexus Enough?' (1995) 63 Fordham LR 1883

Stone Sweet A and Mathews J, 'Proportionality Balancing and Global Constitutionalism' (2008) 47 72 Colum J Transnat'l L 72

'All Things in Proportion? American Rights Review and the Problem of Balancing' (2011) 60 Emory LJ 797

Sunstein C, *Legal Reasoning and Political Conflict* (Oxford University Press 1998)

'Incompletely Theorized Agreements in Constitutional Law' (2007) 74 Social Research 1

Sunstein C and Vermeule A, 'Interpretation and Institutions' (2003) 101 4 Michigan LR 885

Tsakyrakis S, 'Proportionality: An Assault on Human Rights?' (2009) 7 3 Int'l J Const L 468

'Proportionality: An Assault on Human Rights?: A Rejoinder to Madhav Khosla' (2010) 8 2 Int'l J Const L 307

Urbina F, '"Balancing as Reasoning" and the Problems of Legally Unaided Adjudication: A Reply to Kai Möller' (2014) 12 Int'l J Const L

Veel PEN, 'Incommensurability, Proportionality, and Rational Legal Decision-Making' (2010) 4 2 Law & Ethics of Human Rights 177

Verdirame G, 'Rescuing Human Rights from Proportionality' in Rowan Cruft, S Matthew Liao, and Massimo Renzo (eds), *Philosophical Foundations of Human Rights* (Oxford University Press 2015)

Vermeule A, *Law and the Limits of Reason* (Oxford University Press 2008)

Waldron J, 'Introduction' in Waldron J (ed), *Theories of Rights* (Oxford University Press 1984)

'Fake Incommensurability: A Response to Professor Schauer' (1993) 45 Hastings LJ 813

'The Primacy of Justice' (2003) 9 4 Legal Theory 269

'The Core of the Case Against Judicial Review' (2005) 115 Yale LJ 1346

'Lucky in Your Judge' (2008) 9 Theoretical Inq L 185

Torture, Terror, and Trade-Offs: Philosophy for the White House (Oxford University Press 2010)

The Harm in Hate Speech (Harvard University Press 2012)

Walen A, 'Doing, Allowing, and Disabling: Some Principles Governing Deontological Restrictions' (1995) 80 2 Philosophical Studies 183

Webber G, *The Negotiable Constitution: On the Limitation of Rights* (Cambridge University Press 2009)

'Proportionality, Balancing, and the Cult of Constitutional Rights Scholarship' (2010) 23 1 Can JL & Juris 179

'Rights and the Rule of Law in the Balance' (2013) 129 (Jul) LQR 399

'Proportionality: Constitutional Rights and Their Limitation' (2013) 2 Public Law 433

'On the Loss of Rights' in Grant Huscroft, Bradley Miller, and Grégoire Webber (eds) *Proportionality and the Rule of Law: Rights, Justification, Reasoning* (Cambridge University Press 2014)

Weber M, *Economy and Society* (University of California Press 1978)

'Politics as Vocation' in Gerth HH and Wright Mills C (eds) *From Max Weber: Essays in Sociology* (Routledge 2009)

Young AL, 'Proportionality Is Dead: Long Live Proportionality!' in Grant Huscroft, Bradley Miller, and Grégoire Webber (eds), *Proportionality and the Rule of Law: Rights, Justification, Reasoning* (Cambridge University Press 2014)

Yowell, P, 'Legislation, Common Law, and the Virtue of Clarity' in Ekins R (ed), *Modern Challenges to the Rule of Law* (LexisNexis NZ 2011)

'Empirical Research in Judicial Review' in Huber H and Ziegler K, *Current Problems in the Protection of Human Rights: Perspectives from Germany and the UK* (Hart 2013)

'Proportionality in United States Constitutional Law' in Liora Lazarus, Christopher McCrudden, and Nigel Bowles (eds) *Reasoning Rights: Comparative Engagements* (Hart 2013)

INDEX

CPSIA information can be obtained
at www.ICGtesting.com
Printed in the USA
LVOW13*1700010518

575566LV00010B/226/P